**"ESSENTIAL READING FOR
PROFESSIONAL WOMEN EVERYWHERE."**
—Library Journal

"Our position in the corporate world has improved in the ten years since I first wrote this book. We have seen some giant gains in women's advancement. Most companies now count at least one woman among their highest echelons as senior vice president or chief financial officer. But nuanced differences still exist in the rules regulating how men and women behave at work. You can bet that most of the senior executive women now enjoying their success also played hardball at one time or another during their ascent in order to reach their lofty positions. And I believe that once you understand these rules of business, it will reduce your frustration and even allow you to make choices that can help your career."

—From the Introduction

Pat Heim, Ph.D., is an internationally known speaker and consultant. Her Los Angeles firm, The Heim Group, has been providing services in the areas of leadership, communication, team building, and gender differences to hundreds of organizations, including Procter & Gamble, General Electric, Johnson & Johnson, New York Life, and BP. She has a Ph.D. in communication from the University of Colorado.

Susan K. Golant, M.A., writes books on biopsychosocial and women's issues. She has coauthored more than twenty-five books, including *Helping Someone with Mental Illness* (with former First Lady Rosalynn Carter), *Going to the Top* (with Carol Gallagher, Ph.D.), and *In the Company of Women* (with Pat Heim, Ph.D., and Susan Murphy, Ph.D.).

Hardball for Women

Winning at the Game of Business

Pat Heim, Ph.D.

with

Susan K. Golant

A PLUME BOOK

PLUME
Published by the Penguin Group
Penguin Group (USA) Inc., 375 Hudson Street, New York, New York 10014, U.S.A.
Penguin Group (Canada), 10 Alcorn Avenue,
Toronto, Ontario, Canada M4V 3B2 (a division of Pearson Penguin Canada Inc.)
Penguin Books Ltd, 80 Strand, London WC2R 0RL, England
Penguin Ireland, 25 St Stephen's Green, Dublin 2, Ireland
(a division of Penguin Books Ltd)
Penguin Group (Australia), 250 Camberwell Road, Camberwell, Victoria 3124, Australia (a
division of Pearson Australia Group Pty Ltd)
Penguin Books India Pvt Ltd, 11 Community Centre,
Panchsheel Park, New Delhi – 110 017, India
Penguin Books (NZ), Cnr Airborne and Rosedale Roads,
Albany, Auckland, New Zealand (a division of Pearson New Zealand Ltd)
Penguin Books (South Africa) (Pty) Ltd, 24 Sturdee Avenue,
Rosebank, Johannesburg 2196, South Africa

Penguin Books Ltd, Registered Offices: 80 Strand, London WC2R 0RL, England

Published by Plume, a member of Penguin Group (USA) Inc. This is an authorized reprint of a
hardcover edition published by Lowell House. For information address Lowell House, 2029
Century Park East, Suite 3290, Los Angeles, California 90067.

First Plume Printing, September 1993
First Plume Printing (Revised Edition), February 2005
10   9   8   7   6

Copyright © RGA Publishing Group, Inc., 1992, 2005
All rights reserved

Ⓟ REGISTERED TRADEMARK-MARCA REGISTRADA

LIBRARY OF CONGRESS CATALOGING-IN-PUBLICATION DATA

Heim, Pat.
    Hardball for women : winning at the game of business / Pat Heim with Susan K. Golant.—
Rev. ed.
        p.   cm.
    Originally published: New York : Plume, 1993.
    Includes bibliographical references and index.
    ISBN 0-452-28641-7
        1. Businesswomen. 2. Career development. 3. Corporate culture. 4. Interpersonal
communication. I. Golant, Susan K. II. Title.

HD6053.H39 2005
650.14'082—dc22   2004053462

Printed in the United States of America

To the women who told me their stories,
and
to the generations to come

CONTENTS

ACKNOWLEDGMENTS

This book reflects the support I received from many individuals. The women who told me their stories are the heart and soul of the book. Many of them have kept in touch, telling me of their success and sending me articles and research for which I have been extremely grateful.

The book came about because of the vision of Janice Gallagher, editor in chief at Lowell House. Her unflinching support kept me going through the rough times.

The insight, inspiration, and just plain hard work of my coauthor, Susan Golant, created a book I could not have hoped to have written on my own. Lynette Padwa's comments as editor were probing and always encouraging.

Also critical in their unique contributions were my dear friend Pat Palleschi, who always forces me to see the world in a wider scope, and my literary mentor, Elwood Chapman, who kept me believing in myself and in the book.

And throughout the past twenty-five years, during which ideas for this book have been forming, my husband, Serge Lashutka, has been my emissary from the male culture, helping me to understand that different world.

PAT HEIM, PH.D.
Pacific Palisades, California
May 2004

For my part, I am indebted to matchmakers Janice Gallagher and Betsy Amster for having had the foresight to wed me to this wonderful project. Without their support, I would have never entered into the mind and experience of Pat Heim, for whom I feel the greatest respect, and thus would have been deprived of a marvelous opportunity to learn and grow and laugh. For that I am grateful. I also wish to thank Lowell House publisher Jack Artenstein for his continuing faith in me, and editor Lynette Padwa for her incisive comments and attention to detail. Finally, I am forever grateful to my husband and dearest friend, Mitch Golant, whose financial, emotional, and spiritual support allow me the freedom to do my work.

SUSAN K. GOLANT
Los Angeles California
May 2004

INTRODUCTION

In the ten years since we first wrote *Hardball for Women,* I have witnessed many behavioral shifts among men and women in the workplace. A sea change occurred in 1991 after President George Bush nominated Clarence Thomas for a seat on the U.S. Supreme Court. During the Senate confirmation hearings, Thomas's employee, attorney Anita Hill, accused him of sexual harassment, creating an enormous stir. Suddenly, the discussion of relationships among men and women at work was on the front page of every newspaper and on the lips of every working person in the United States.

Prior to that time, when I had conducted workshops on gender differences in the work setting, 95 percent of the participants were women. But afterward, men started showing up. Even though I don't deal with sexual harassment, they thought they might be at risk legally if they didn't understand the dynamics of the female world.

These days, the population in my workshops breaks down to 60 percent women and 40 percent men. In fact, when I present two workshops in one day, men flock to the later offering. I believe this occurs because those few brave souls who attend the morning session return to their departments charged up. "Wow," they say, "now I really understand my wife!" or "That was interesting, and I had a lot of fun." It's clear to me that some men fear they will be berated for their behavior and stay away. However, when they realize that the seminar is safe, they happily participate.

The workshop is called "She Said/He Said: Gender Differences in the Work Setting," and it's about the different cultures that men and women inhabit, and as a result, how we have divergent rules about "appropriate" adult behavior. Of course, most of the time we're unaware of these cultural differences or that we have these contradictory rules—and therein lies the rub. When people of the opposite gender behave in ways we find irritating, we think they're doing it to drive us nuts rather than simply seeing that their behavior makes sense to them based on their culture. I always take care to discuss the flip side—that is, I'll expose some female behavior that drives men up the wall and then talk about the parallel male behavior that pushes women's buttons. None of us are immune.

What has been the impact on the workplace of this kind of mixed gender education? Before, it was women's responsibility to determine how to function effectively in a man's world and therefore change our behavior to fit in. Now, when I speak to both men and women in an intact department team, they all learn what I call "non-loaded language" with which to discuss the differences in how they behave. After participating in the workshop, they're able to talk about these disparities openly during work, and they will even laugh about them as they pop up. This is all for the good. I see that progress has been made.

▶ DO WE AIM TO HURT?

Often at the break during the mixed gender workshops, male participants approach me and with a sheepish grin admit, "You know my wife. You've been under my bed. This happens to me every night when I go home." On the other hand, the women will sidle up to me and whisper conspiratorially, "You know my boss. You're under my desk. This happens to me every day at work."

After a while, I was struck by the odd symmetry of these confessions. They indicated to me that home is an area of conflict for men while the workplace is an area of conflict for women. Indeed, men truly have no idea what it is that women are so upset about at the office because men simply go there and hang out—they're completely and unconsciously themselves. I have come to see that they do not intentionally try to make the workplace uncomfortable for women. So when women grouse, their male colleagues are often bewildered about what they're supposed to change. And that can render them defensive. Look at it this way: If someone complains about your behavior and you don't recognize what's problematic about it and therefore can't determine how to improve it, it's a natural human reaction to become defensive.

Yes, it's true: In my many years conducting these workshops, I've come to the conclusion that there is no organized, concerted conspiracy on the part of men to undermine women. But that doesn't mean that we're out of the woods. Not by a long shot. We still have issues. Men may not intentionally try to make the work-place uncomfortable for us, but they still perceive our behavior as problematic. Why? The answer is surprisingly simple: It is different from what is appropriate and accepted in the male culture. Male coworkers may therefore react to their female colleagues as irri-tants because they don't understand that we are acting out of our own set of rules. The behaviors we exhibit are perfectly appropri-ate in the female culture. The unfortunate result of this disparity is that we can be perceived as less competent and can consequently lose out on opportunities for advancement.

As a corollary, if we want to get promoted and accepted, we are still aggravated that we often have to do things in a "male" way even though that's not our strength. Despite the inroads we have made into the corporate world, we may still find ourselves stymied, confused, and frustrated if we don't understand the rules of the male culture, which are synonymous with the rules of business.

That's why I've undertaken a revision of *Hardball for Women.* Our position in the corporate world has improved in the ten years since I first wrote this book. We have seen some gains in women's advancement. Most companies now count at least one woman among their highest echelons as senior vice president or chief fi-nancial officer. But nuanced differences still exist in the rules reg-ulating how men and women behave at work. You can bet that most of the senior executive women now enjoying their success also played hardball at one time or another during their ascent in order to reach their lofty positions. And I believe that once you un-derstand these rules of business, it will reduce your frustration and even allow you to make choices that can help your career.

This book offers you the keys to unlocking the secret culture of business so that you can, at minimum, not be as irritated with what your male colleagues do and at best understand how sometimes the way men behave might be more effective than what would nat-urally occur to you as a woman.

▶ WHICH WOULD YOU RATHER BE?

Society has shifted. The first edition of *Hardball for Women* was angrier and more polarized than this one. In this newly revised edition, I will be addressing some of those changes and we'll also look at how gender issues are no longer a one-way street. In the past, organizations have said, "Okay, you women, if you want to succeed in this business, you need to figure out how to fit in because our culture is what it is." Today, organizations are realizing that they can no longer afford to steadily lose women, particularly those who are successful and experienced in middle management, not just because of recruitment and relocation costs but because we have more knowledge workers. Take for instance a woman working in pharmaceuticals who has been studying a particular compound for three years. If she quits in frustration, even though her notes are available to her successor, she takes away the thinking machine that had been studying and mulling that compound. Simply replacing her with another Ph.D. is not equivalent.

When I initially started studying gender differences and wrote the first edition of *Hardball for Women,* I was often irritated at men's behavior, which I saw as just so much chest-beating. Over the last decade, I have come to appreciate the male and female cultures as simply different, both having their strengths when applied at the appropriate time. The issue is to understand what these differences are and how to use them to your advantage. I find this does two things: By understanding the male culture, you need not be as annoyed at what can seem like arrogant, aggressive behavior. Secondly, as a woman you can make a choice about whether to behave in a "male" way because that would be to your advantage or to continue in your own way because that will work best.

In the last chapter, we will talk about creating some rules of your own, your three options when dealing with gender related problems, and how to choose among them.

One of the changes in my perception over the last ten years is that it's not easy being a guy. You live every moment of your life in a hierarchy; every interaction is an opportunity to lose position and status. Therefore you must be constantly on guard and be ready to push back. What used to look to me like mindless chest-beating now I understand is often necessary to a man living in a very male culture. As women, we live in a world of relationships and don't experience this kind of constant tension. If I were to choose which gender I would come back as now, it would be as a woman. It's just a more comfortable place to live.

1

THE GAME OF BUSINESS

▼ ▼ ▼ ▼ ▼ **I**t was past 7:30 PM but the computer screen at Barbara's desk still flashed numbers, and her mind raced to complete her project—on time and within budget, as always. A crackerjack systems analyst and supervisor, Barbara prided herself on her top-notch technical skills. She worked harder and longer than any of her peers. She got along well with colleagues, made constructive suggestions, and supervised the most productive employees in her division, by far. In fact, as a manager, her output was flawless.

Yet despite her consistently superior performance, Barbara got passed over time and again for promotions. Finally, she sought my help. Her voice tight with anger, she explained her predicament: "I'm ignored for promotions in favor of men who are not nearly as productive or hardworking as I am. Why? When I ask my boss for feedback, he tells me I'm doing 'just fine'—whatever that means. Besides, I don't feel 'just fine.' I'm miserable and frustrated in a dead-end position, and I'm truly mystified about why I can't seem to move forward."

In leading hundreds of workshops with businesswomen ranging from supervisors to managers to senior executives throughout the United States, I have heard Barbara's lament over and over again: "I'm a technical ace. I work harder than anyone else. I'm highly respected by my peers. Why have I been passed over . . . laid off . . . overlooked? Why can't I be as successful as the men in my company?"

These questions have been asked repeatedly for the past thirty years—ever since the women's movement of the 1970s began to encourage female students, housewives, and workers to pursue careers that would challenge their intellect and reward their efforts on a par with men. In record numbers, women traded their dresses for power suits, doubled their overtime, and delayed having children. The phrase *glass ceiling* didn't exist back then, and they figured by the 1990s they'd be set. Meanwhile, young women entering the workforce in the new millennium assumed that the playing field is level, that their contributions would be justly rewarded, their achievements gratefully acknowledged. Clearly they are mistaken.

What went wrong? Why, after more than four decades of raised consciousness and affirmative action, are women still struggling to achieve parity with their male coworkers? Consider Allison, the regional sales manager for a national furniture manufacturing company. Like Barbara, she is a master at management. Her region has the highest sales in the corporation. As the most senior and productive member of the sales team, she is in a position to move up in the company. Instead, she finds herself cut out of memos and meetings.

In talking with her supervisor about her performance, she was told, "Allison, you do your job well but you're too scattered."

"What does that mean?" she demanded.

"Well," her boss continued, "you do too many things at once. You're just not focused enough."

Although Allison perceived her ability to juggle many projects as an asset—especially since she was successful at it—her boss didn't concur. In fact, he gave a plum promotion to a less efficient man who was, by the way, his friend, but was less productive.

Jennifer's progress was also impeded. A brilliant aerospace engineer, she headed a team of five men at a prestigious southern space exploration laboratory. Her group was put in charge of testing a newly launched satellite system. Jennifer's approach to management was highly collaborative. Rather than simply barking out orders, she would ask her employees for input and feedback in order to make decisions. Her male colleagues perceived this as weak. Before long, she discovered her staff went behind her back to her supervisor, Tom, to ask questions. Consequently, he lost faith in Jennifer's leadership abilities and slowly diminished her responsibilities until she was shut out of the position entirely.

Marjorie also found herself at an impasse. As the chief nursing officer for a large midwestern hospital, she was responsible for 60 percent of the institution's employees and budget. She was proud of her performance: She had managed to cut costs and increase patient satisfaction, as documented on patient surveys. Because of her fine record, Marjorie applied for the position of operations officer. In fact, she sought the position on three separate occasions, and each time she was passed over in favor of a younger, less-experienced man, When Marjorie asked why she hadn't won the position, she was told, "You're not ready yet." This, despite the fact that she already ran virtually half the hospital.

Why were these women stymied in their efforts to move ahead? Most likely because the majority of women in the business world today are oblivious to the fact that they are standing on a playing field while a game is being played around them. The men we work with are using their own set of rules. Their sport is rough-and-tumble and aggressive. Players are expected to be bloodied when they take risks and put themselves on the line.

Unfortunately, without understanding the culture of men, you will remain sidelined like Barbara, Allison, Jennifer, and Marjorie. Until you realize that business is conducted as a sport—and a game of hardball, at that—you'll never move ahead and you'll never win.

▶ WARMING THE BENCH

Ironically, women who entered the workforce en masse in the mid 1970s were perhaps more aware than we are today of the extent to which male coworkers operate in a rarefied business culture. Then, women were up against huge and obvious hurdles such as discriminatory laws, exclusive clubs, and other culturally sanctioned trappings of the old-boy network.

But since these larger issues consumed women, they never mastered the subtleties of communicating with men—even while they recognized the dilemma. Indeed, attempts were made to break into the private club and to understand male language, but many of these early efforts fell short. Too many women tried to copy men without understanding the basic differences in male and female culture—differences that will be revealed in this book. Sometimes the approach women used was too rigid, even hostile, rather than sportsmanlike. Other women felt they could legislate their way into the workforce and then succeed on merit alone, ignoring the politics and gamesmanship inherent in the business world.

Betty Lehan Harragan's groundbreaking *Games Mother Never Taught You,* written in 1978, clued women in to the fact that there was a different game going on, one that they were unaware of. But most of Harragan's suggestions smacked of "do it like the men do."

During the 1980s, with more women in the workplace, a false sense of progress set in. But soon, however, the "glass ceiling" became apparent, and women began to realize that they still weren't playing in the big leagues.

In the 1990s, women were making some advancements, but many were still frustrated that they didn't have parity with men; they were warming the benches but not getting to bat. Today, women often do advance but then they realize that their potential success is hinged on an unconscious requirement that they behave like a man, which takes a lot of energy. This is essentially saying, "Use your nondominant hand." Yes, you can do it, but it's going to take a lot of effort, and you won't do the work as well. I want you to understand the system first, then you can make the choices as to whether you should "behave like a man" because there are times that it will be critical for your success to do so.

The real issue lies in women's misperceptions about the rules governing business. When individuals enter the workforce, initially they are rewarded for technical skill. Often, women move up with good performance appraisals at this early stage. But many hit a period during their late twenties and early thirties when feedback suddenly turns negative. Ceasing to do well in their boss's eyes, they get such vague feedback as, "You're not being a team player." Most women fail to realize that employees are judged on interpersonal and not technical skills as they progress in their careers. And interpersonal skills often rise and fall on the nuances of male and female cultural differences.

Today, if you're a woman in any type of career, from high tech to high finance, from manufacturing to medicine, from aerospace to automotive engineering, there's a good chance you'll find yourself in one of these baffling and infuriating situations:

- You're more productive and successful than your male peer, but suddenly you find yourself reporting to him.
- Your boss becomes irritated when you make helpful suggestions.
- Your female colleagues are first to attack when you win a big promotion.
- You've sought the input of your employees in order to make a decision, only to be criticized for not being a leader.

- You feel angry with yourself for having given in to a bully.
- Your valuable input goes unacknowledged during important meetings, yet when a male colleague makes the same point, he receives accolades.
- You don't know how to work with people you dislike and can't understand how your male associates are at one another's throats by day but drinking buddies by night.
- You try to cooperate, only to discover the most underhanded staff member gets the recognition you deserve.
- You've been caught off guard by a colleague who brutally attacks your ideas at a meeting, only to have him tell you, "You shouldn't take it so hard," as the two of you walk out.
- You wonder what men really mean when they tell you to be a "team player."

Hardball for Women will help you resolve these dilemmas and get you off the bench so you can play with the big boys.

▶ HOW I SLIPPED INTO THE LOCKER ROOM

For more than two decades I've watched women struggle with gender-related business crises, from minor misunderstandings to career-threatening lapses in communication. In that time, I've developed a strategy that enables women to flourish in the workplace *while remaining true to their inner selves*. Time and again, I have seen that once women understand the male culture of business, they can thrive in it, enjoy it, and achieve great success.

In 1977, I received my Ph.D. in communication from the University of Colorado and became a professor of communication at Loyola-Marymount University in Los Angeles. Two years later, I became a communication consultant for corporations. My interest in the gender component of business began while I was working as a management development specialist at the headquarters of a national health-care organization. I found myself one day at a high-level meeting. I can't remember why I was there, because I certainly wasn't high level, but I'd been invited nonetheless. During this meeting, two male executives began to viciously attack each other. My stomach began to churn. I remember wanting to stand up and shout, "You both have a point," or to duck under the table because it was just so upsetting to witness. Eventually the meeting adjourned. Those two combatants walked out of the room in front of me. One turned to the other and said in a friendly voice, "Wanna get a beer?"

I was shocked. I couldn't imagine how they could switch gears so quickly or would ever speak to each other in a civil tone again. I realized that there was something about their world that differed from mine, and I worked in their world. To survive, I had to understand their rules. So I started reading all the research I could find about gender differences in the workplace. And one day, maybe six months later, I began putting that information to good use. A woman director at that company asked me to conduct a communication workshop for her managers; she was having problems in her unit.

"What seems to be the trouble?" I asked.

"My boss, Ron, says my managers are poor communicators. He's critical because they want to involve everyone in decisions they make," Carrie explained. "He says they never seem to get to the point and they're so darned sensitive about negative feedback."

Based on the research I'd been doing, I knew that the employees she referred to were all women, and I voiced that perception.

"How did you figure that out?" Carrie responded, dumbfounded.

I had read enough about gender differences to recognize that men and women face different problems in the workplace. At that moment, I decided to create a workshop to help women in their business communications. The next time the opportunity arose to work with a group of female managers, I focused solely on the rules of hardball and cultural gender differences. The ideas I presented clicked with the participants, and many went on to become highly successful in their fields.

In 1985, I left my corporate position to become a private management development and communication consultant. I have worked with CEOs, boards of directors, managers, and supervisors in many fields, including manufacturing, health care, pharmaceuticals, finance, the energy industry, engineering, and government, in companies such as Procter & Gamble, General Electric, British Petroleum, Johnson & Johnson, Microsoft, IBM, Xerox, and Sony. I've spoken to more than one hundred groups a year for the last twenty years.

As an outside consultant—a hired gun, so to speak—I have been privy to information I would never hear were I an employee of a company. When a corporate vice president is paying dearly for my services, he is unlikely to play political games or lie. And so I have become a "fly on the wall" in countless business meetings. As a result, I have experienced firsthand how frequently gender-based communication issues can stop a woman from the success she so richly deserves.

In this book, I've condensed the knowledge and techniques that have helped tens of thousands of women walk confidently into any business environment. But underscoring everything you read in these pages is a simple concept: *Become "one of the guys" is not necessarily an adequate, comfortable, or feasible way to win the game of business.* Understanding *the guys is what it takes to triumph in their world.*

▶ WHY CAN'T A WOMAN BE MORE LIKE A MAN?

Women in business today walk an interesting tightrope. If we become the aggressive, no-nonsense, win-at-all-costs players that our male counterparts pride themselves in being, then we are labeled "bossy," "obnoxious," "overbearing," "ambitious," or "strident bitches" who are "just mouthing off," and our input or achievements are summarily dismissed. If, on the other hand, we adhere to our feminine ways and continue to be passive, nurturant, and cooperative in the business setting, then we're labeled "weak," "overly sensitive," and "unambitious," and again, what we perceive as important contributions and successes are diminished. What a double bind!

How to get rid of this bind? The solution lies in gaining a fuller understanding of the male culture in order to work well *within* it. I'm not advocating that women become more like men, but rather that by understanding the culture of men they can better navigate to the top.

Think of it this way: If you were suddenly plunked down in the middle of Japan, you would find certain customs familiar, but others quite foreign. In order to fit in and do well in Japanese society, you might try to behave, in part, as the Japanese do. You might feel willing to adapt to or at least earnestly try to understand that culture. On the other hand, some customs would likely feel unacceptable, and so you would sidestep them, and further refuse to surrender certain habits that are fundamental to your sense of self.

The same is true in the world of business. Since, for the moment, you work in the culture of men, you may have to make some accommodations in order to fit in. Your motivation? Once you learn the rules of hardball, you can eventually work your way to the top. And having acquired enough power and success, you may be able to call the shots and shape the future direction of your corporation so that it capitalizes on your own strengths.

It's important to note that gender differences, and human behavior in general, are best depicted as a bell curve. The hitch is there are two tails to that bell curve. That is, there are always exceptions to how we humans behave. We've all met women who have more masculine qualities than other females and men who have more feminine traits than other males. Some argue that we shouldn't talk about gender differences at all because it will only make it more difficult for us to work together. But I believe that pretending men and women are the same only damages women's chances of succeeding and requires that we continue to adapt to the male culture of business. By pointing to the different ways men and women approach issues, as we do here, we legitimize alternative strategies. The message is that men and women often bring different approaches to looking at problems, opportunities, and decisions. The more approaches available, the better the outcome for both individuals and business.

Besides, we all have a hidden masculine side to us (just as men have more feminine aspects that they rarely reveal). Reevaluating your behavior may be a question of connecting to parts of yourself you haven't fully used in the workplace. Old cultural messages you've assimilated, like "good girls don't brag," or "be nice and get along," may have held you back. But you can observe how men succeed and adopt their best strategies without losing your values.

Success is more than a pipe dream. When you learn the game of hardball, it can become a reality. I frequently get calls like the following from Stacy Miller, a participant in one of my workshops. Stacy is the president of a small textile manufacturing company. Shortly after attending my seminar, she became involved in a negotiation with the president and vice president of an international clothing corporation for the purchase of products her company manufactured. She suddenly found herself in the big leagues.

In a phone call to me following this negotiation, Stacy gushed with enthusiasm. "I did the things you talked about," she explained excitedly. "When they began to attack me, I didn't flinch or fidget. I kept my body open and didn't smile to show my vulnerability. In fact, my face was stony during the negotiation. The president of the corporation tried to interrupt me, but I just continued talking as if he weren't there. It was great!"

It really was great. For not only did Stacy clinch the deal, but the president of the international corporation called her boss, the chairman of the board, and said with respect and admiration, "That Ms. Miller, she's something else. What a tough negotiator!" Stacy had learned to play hardball.

When men don't understand the culture of women and, perhaps more important for our discussion, when women don't understand the culture of men, they both place negative value judgments on behaviors they consider alien. What we must all appreciate is that our disparate approaches are not conscious choices but ways of perceiving reality instilled since childhood that might even have some basis in our biology. The goal of *Hardball for Women* is not necessarily to make you behave like a man, but rather to give you an opportunity to understand the "foreign" male culture so that you can make conscious choices that will open the door to greater successes in the future.

Before we go any further, let's take a look at one of the most obvious elements of male business culture: the language.

▶ THE SPORTSMANLIKE LANGUAGE OF BUSINESS

An article in the entertainment section of the *New York Times* reminded me again of just how pervasively sports lingo permeates business perceptions and communications. In the article, Peter Tortorici, CBS executive vice president for programming—the person in charge of prime-time scheduling—referred to Wednesday night as "a jump ball: not dominated by one network." According to reporter Bill Carter, Mr. Tortorici is "one of the players looking to grab the ball and run with it." Now there's a sports idiom if I ever heard one.

If you have any doubt that business is conducted like a team sport, simply pay attention to words people use in describing business behavior. If your *team* gets to *carry the ball*, you'll need a *game strategy* to *score points* with the *coach* or at least to make an *end run* around the *opposition*. You may *position yourself as a player* and hope that you're not abandoned *out in left field*. When the *ball is in your court*, it's time to *step up to bat* and *compete to win*. If they're *playing hardball*, you'll need a *game plan* just to *get the ball rolling* so you can get on *first base*. You may have to *punt, pass the ball, touch base* with other *team players*, or *tackle* the problem yourself. Your *goal* may be the *whole nine yards*, but be careful not to *step out of bounds*. If you're a *pro* you'll know when to *take the offensive*, but if you're a *rookie* you may have to *go to the mat*, and if you *lose* or *strike out* you may have to *throw in the towel*; but if you *win* you can make it into the *big leagues*.

I could go on, but I think you get the idea. When I present the list of over fifty sports expressions applicable to business transactions (there are more, such as *par for the course, slam dunk, batting average, ball-park figure, sportsmanship, pinch hitter*, and the most offensive, *playing like a girl*) during my "She Said/He Said" workshops, the response is universal. After the first ten or fifteen of such expressions, eyebrows raise in surprise. After about twenty, some participants begin clapping in recognition. By the end of my experiment, the assembled crowd applauds in unison. They have had a moment of insight. Business is conducted by the rules of sports (the way boys play) and not by the rules of house and dolls (the way girls play).

In Chapter 2, we'll take a closer look at the divergent acculturation of men and women that contribute to these differences.

▶ BUT GIRLS PLAY SPORTS NOW!

While large groups of little boys roam up and down the field, playing freewheeling games of cops and robbers, cowboys and Indians, dodge ball, superheroes, soccer, and war—the aggressive game of hardball—we girls play intensely with one or two best friends, thoroughly engaged in make-believe: dolls or house or school, safe in our homes and backyards.

"Now wait a darn minute," you might be thinking. "I was a

tomboy growing up. I competed with my older brother and his friends. I was on a soccer team and played varsity softball in high school. Didn't I learn the rules of hardball too?"

Indeed, the most common question posed to me lately when I talk about the different cultures of men and women is, "Now that girls play sports, doesn't that change the dynamics?" To answer this important question, I went to Anson Dorrance, the coach of the University of North Carolina women's soccer team since 1983. His are some of the most successful teams in the history of the sport: Within a twenty-four-year period, the women on his teams have won the national championship eighteen times. Many of the greatest players in women's soccer, including Mia Hamm and Kristine Lilly, came out of UNC. I asked Anson during an interview if he found differences in coaching women as compared to men.

"There are so many differences, I don't know where to begin," he replied. "The core is the kind of relationship you establish with your athletes. One of the critical aspects in motivating, training, and leading men is that you have to be strong. Men respond to strength and a part of your capacity to ultimately lead in men's athletics is a capacity for you to demonstrate this strength. Some male coaches do this by being physically, psychologically, or verbally intimidating.

"Women aren't led by that. In fact, if you try to lead that way athletically you actually end up intimidating them. It causes a loss of confidence and separation. Women respond to your humanity, so you lead women with your capacity to care and your capacity to relate. Connection with them is critical. They didn't want me to use speeches with words like 'fury,' and they didn't want me to raise my voice and get in their face. They want me to care about them. They want me to relate to them personally."

Remember, these are not women who are out to have a good time on a Saturday afternoon. They are driven to win and they do. But they do it in a very female way. While you may well have played with boys and participated in team sports, to my mind experiences such as these are dwarfed by the influence of social norms. That is, despite your contact with males and masculine forms of play, other factors such as parental attitudes, television commercials, movies, teachers, peers, and even biology may have shaped your attitudes minute by minute. Even former tomboys show up in my workshops because they are not enjoying business as usual. Whether at home, at school, or on the playground, women have been socialized to value relationships and equality.

And in the final analysis, when boys and girls grow up, they play business in much the same way they play as children: Men continue to see business as a team sport—aggressive hardball— while women perceive business as a series of separate personal encounters; they seek out cooperation and intimacy. To understand why so many women are frustrated in their attempts to advance in their careers today, let's take a closer look at the lessons we learned during our differing play activities.

▶ HOW TO BE A GIRL

In our culture, girls learn:

How to play one-on-one. For the most part, girls play with only one person, usually a best friend. As a result, girls learn exceptional interpersonal skills, including how to "read" and respond to others' emotions.

How to get along. Good little girls are sweet, calm, gentle, charming, mild, and helpful. Conflict, assertiveness, and direct confrontation are not only absent from play but are to be avoided at all costs. Instead, girls learn more indirect methods of dealing with dissention, such as involving a third party, dropping hints, or practicing avoidance in order to preserve relationships, their main focus.

How to be fair to everyone. Little girls try to resolve conflicts by compromising and being fair so that everyone wins.

How to engage in play as a process. Girls' games often don't have a goal. I've never heard of a little girl winning a game of dolls, for instance. If there is a purpose at all, it's to get along with one's playmates, create intimacy, and share imaginative ideas. I'll explain the significance of this issue more fully in Chapter 2.

How to negotiate differences. Decisions among girls are reached by group consensus. When several friends have different views about the best way to set up a dollhouse or at whose home to play dress up, they learn to talk out their differences, take turns, and compromise. This format of negotiation has as its goal a win/win (as opposed to a win/lose) outcome.

How to keep the power dead even. Girls grow up in flat organizations rather than hierarchies. They learn to cooperate within this structure. Rather than having a coach or a top banana tell them what to do, girls cooperate in a web of relationships for the sake of preserving the friendship. It doesn't take long for a little girl to discover that if she wants to be the leader and she starts pushing her playmates around, relationships will suffer; friends will call her bossy and avoid her. As a result, she tries to keep the power dead even.

Because of these lessons, we learned how to be competent interpersonally and how to develop and sustain relationships with others. Boys, on the other hand, learn to subordinate relationships to aggressiveness, competition, and winning.

▶ HOW TO BE A BOY

The lessons boys absorb help them succeed in the business setting. In *Hardball for Women,* you are going to learn what these lessons are. Some you may wish to adopt or adapt to your own style; others may seem repugnant to you. In terms of personal behavior, each of us has a basic comfort level that we must acknowledge and respect. Yet even if you don't want to emulate your male counterparts—and you don't always have to—becoming conscious of masculine culture will help you understand how men reach judgments and decisions that may affect your life and your potential success. The key is to know which choices you have, rather than operating on automatic pilot. With awareness come power and the possibility to exercise new options.

Among the lessons boys learn are the following:

Always do what the coach says. Boys learn early that in order to win a competition, there must be a leader or coach who is at the top of the heap. This creates a structural hierarchy in which there is always someone above and someone below in status, rather than the flat organization so common among girls, in which the power is dead even. In order to move up within the hierarchy, boys learn to do what the coach says—period. See Chapter 3 for a discussion of how this applies to your position within your corporation.

Competition is the name of the game. All games that boys play involve adversarial relationships: us versus them. Boys learn that competition and conflict are stimulating and fun, to be embraced and not avoided. Boys also know that when the game is over, it's over. A boy's agenda during a game may be to cream the opposition, but after the ninth inning, both teams can enjoy a pizza and ice cream. The fact that they tried to pulverize each other only an hour earlier has little impact on their relationship.

Business is also competitive between companies, within companies, among department, and among peers. Chapter 4 will explore in more detail how you can develop a competitive edge.

How to be a good team player. Boys learn right off the bat that they won't always get to be team captain or the coach and be able to tell others what to do. Rather, most often they will be in the position of receiving instructions. Good team members, therefore, give up their individuality and independence for the sake of the team. They recognize the importance of supporting the other players—it's critical not to be a star when the situation requires one to take a supportive role. The reward comes when their loyalty allows the team to win. Then they can refer to the success as "their" win. Whereas girls cooperate to preserve relationships, boys may sacrifice themselves to the hierarchy for the sake of winning.

In being a team player, it's also vital to know how to play with people you don't like. Boys insist on having the meanest, roughest, toughest kid on their team because they realize that despite his personal shortcomings, this bully will help them achieve their goal of winning at all costs. Chapter 5 covers what it takes to be a good team member.

How to be a leader. Despite the team nature of play, from time to time boys do get to be team captain. That gives them the opportunity to take on authority. In practicing leadership, boys learn how to give orders and make them stick. In Chapter 6, you'll learn those lessons too.

How to be aggressive or to posture aggressiveness. Boys learn that if you're going to do well for your team and save your own hide, it's important to look like a mean, aggressive player— even if you're not feeling all that tough. In order to act aggressively, boys learn power plays: posture, facial expressions, verbal bantering, and other trappings of power. In truth, how you speak, present yourself, and are introduced all contribute to the illusion of power. In the game of business, if you don't know how to do something, often the best idea is to fake it! Chapters 7 and 8 show you how.

How to take criticism and praise. Criticism and praise go hand in hand with losing and winning. While engaged in sports, boys receive constant criticism, primarily from the coach, but also from team members. As a result, they learn the connection between getting feedback and improving their performance. They also learn how to take criticism so it doesn't damage their self-esteem and destroy their feelings of self-worth. In Chapter 9, you'll learn ways to receive, respond to, and give criticism and praise that will help further your career.

How to stay focused on the goal. Rather than focusing on perfecting the details (as girls and women might), in team play boys set their sights on the goal line. If they make a mess in getting there or knock some people over, that's part of the game. Boys learn early on that they can't do everything perfectly, but perfection really doesn't matter anyway, since winning is all that counts. Chapter 10 will help you find and stay focused on your own goals, be they within your current career or for future professional advancement.

Winning is all that matters. Boys have heard since time immemorial that "it's not whether you win or lose, it's how you play the game." I have yet to find a man who actually believes this. Boys play games to win. So do men in business. From their perspective, there is no point in becoming involved in the game if you aren't out to win. And to win, you must take risks. Playing it safe will never make your team number one.

In this regard, boys also learn that it pays to cheat. Whether it's pitching a spitball, "facemasking" a football opponent, or fouling an opposing player in basketball, it's never a question of whether to cheat but how to do it without getting caught.

Boys learn how to talk about a big win or a faked play so that it keeps on working for them. But even though winning is all, statistically about half the time boys lose. Rather than feeling devastated by the failure, however, the repeated experience of losing teaches boys how to take a loss, learn from it, and move on. Chapter 11 explores hardball strategies for winning and losing.

How to have a game plan. Little boys play in crowds, not in dyads or triads as girls do. And so they need a strategy to organize such an unwieldy group of people. They follow the coach's game plan. Anyone who plays soccer or football knows that when each player does what he alone thinks is best, independently of the others, the team will never move the ball to the other end of the field to score that coveted goal or touchdown. The same is true for business. Whether your purpose is to increase your department's production, get a big promotion, or become an independent entrepreneur, you must have a strategy in place before you start making your moves. Chapter 12 gives you some pointers.

▶ SCORING THAT GOAL

The truth is, since business has been run overwhelmingly by men until only recently, male culture permeates corporate life today. And men have simply transposed the rules of their childhood games onto their jobs as CEOs, managers, salesmen, supervisors, and entrepreneurs.

Female culture must be addressed, because our coping skills are functional and suit our own reality. It's the aim of this book to render these mostly invisible cultural imperatives more opaque, so that professional and managerial women who find that their skills have little to do with opportunities for advancement can choose the action most appropriate to their circumstances.

Research has shown that behaving like a man will backfire;

women are judged on women's rules, not men's. And while women do have more options than mere stereotypical behavior, their choices are more limited than men's. As Ann M. Morrison, Randall P. White, and Ellen Van Velsor explain in *Breaking the Glass Ceiling,* women must operate within a "narrow band of acceptable behavior." *Hardball for Women* will ease the process of figuring out how far to go without overstepping the bounds.

This book will teach you the rules. Exercises, journal work, and questionnaires will help you focus on your current attitudes and the goals you wish to achieve. When you read this book, you will learn:

- how to display confidence and power, even if you feel frightened and powerless
- how to offer help so you're not seen as obstructionist
- how to be on either end of an attack during a business meeting and still remain cordial later
- how to work with people you don't like
- how to lead men, how to lead women, and how to recognize the differences between the two
- how to take risks
- how to hide your vulnerability
- how to be a team player, in the masculine sense of the word

My aim is to teach you to be more successful, so you can attain the goals you have set for yourself.

2

WE LIVE IN TWO
DIFFERENT WORLDS

▼ ▼ ▼ ▼ ▼ **A**lthough we grew up together in the same homes, eating the same foods, watching the same television shows, and sitting in the same classrooms, men and women in our society come from disparate cultures. We may be blinded to the differences in male and female culture by our assumption that since we've been raised in the same country, we all must share similar values. After all, the differences are not as great as if our male counterparts had come from Pakistan, Bali, or Nigeria. Or are they?

The truth is, they just may be. Social psychologists studying sex role development have found that American girls and boys are acculturated quite differently: Girls have been taught to be fragile, dependent, compliant, cooperative, and nurturing, while boys learn to be sturdy, independent, active, assertive, aggressive, and unemotional. As Dr. Sandra L. Bem, an expert on sex roles, wrote, "Adults in the child's world rarely notice or remark upon how strong a little girl is or how nurturant a little boy is becoming, despite their readiness to note precisely these attributes in the 'appropriate' sex."

When does this teaching take place? You're probably aware that gender-specific behavior begins at birth, the moment we wrap our infants in color-coded blankets. Though we may do it unconsciously, the subtle messages we send shape our children's future behavior.

For example, Drs. R. Stewart and R. Marvin reported that the needs of infant girls are responded to more consistently than are those of infant boys. Another group of researchers headed by Dr. Alyson Burns at the University of California, Davis, observed hundreds of families in the Sacramento zoo and found that girl toddlers are more likely to be carried or pushed in a stroller while boy toddlers are more apt to walk, especially with their fathers. In these and countless other small ways, girls learn dependence while boys learn independence.

We can validate these research findings in our everyday lives.

When mothers play dolls with their girls, they tend to hold onto the toy so that their female children come to them. When they play with boys, however, they roll a ball away so their sons will fetch it on their own.

Have you ever noticed that babies swaddled in blue blankets are held less gently than those wrapped in pink? Putting a baby girl into a carrier becomes a group project. "Watch her head," we cry. But a baby boy, a tough little guy who can take a bit of rough handling—or should, for his own good—tends to get plopped into the carrier without a second thought.

Children learn gender-appropriate cultural lessons well, and they learn them early. Dr. Carol Nagy Jacklin, a professor of psychology at the University of Southern California, explains that youngsters practice sex-appropriate behaviors at astonishingly young ages. Along with Dr. Eleanor Maccoby, a noted Stanford University developmental psychologist, Dr. Jacklin demonstrated that boys and girls as young as thirty-three months are aware of the differences in the sexes, prefer same-sex playmates, and are wary of one another. They found that by the time children reach the age of six and a half years, they spend eleven times as much time with children of the same gender as they do with those of the opposite gender. This gender segregation contributes to our growing up in different cultures; same-gender children reinforce one another's behavior.

▶ HARDBALL LESSONS IN THE CLASSROOM

Gender segregation continues into the classroom where, according to a major study by the American Association of University Women on gender differences and educational opportunities, teachers unwittingly but consistently shortchange girls. Research has shown, for example, that teachers force boys to work out problems they don't understand but tell girls what to do, particularly in subjects such as math or science for which girls are traditionally perceived to have little affinity. (This perception, by the way, has been proved false by many studies.) Teachers also go easier on girls when it comes to discipline. As a result, boys receive more criticism and become more adept at coping with it by the time they reach adulthood.

In addition, girls are rewarded with attention and praise for nonacademic achievements such as neat penmanship or getting along well with others and are given the erroneous impression that tidiness or congeniality will stand them in good stead in the world at large. An agreeable person makes few waves and avoids confrontation and disagreement.

This kind of gender training can begin as early as kindergarten. A recent *Wall Street Journal* article highlighted kindergarten awards for five-year-old boys and girls at a school in the midwest. The awards were given in the following categories:

BOYS' AWARDS	GIRLS' AWARDS
Very Best Thinker	All-Around Sweetheart
Most Eager Learner	Sweetest Personality
Most Imaginative	Cutest Personality
Most Enthusiastic	Best Sharer
Most Scientific	Best Artist
Best Friend	Biggest Heart
Mr. Personality	Best Manners
Hardest Worker	Best Helper
Best Sense of Humor	Most Creative

In the school environment, girls will learn lessons about their "proper place." They learn, for example, that if they speak up, if they are assertive—even aggressive—in pursuing information and achievement or in rejecting pat explanations, if they push to get their answers heard, they may be considered "bossy show-offs," "obnoxious," and "unfeminine." Sadly, this has the effect of encouraging girls to hide their abilities and interests and to shun competition.

Indeed, an intriguing study by Myra Sadker and David Sadker documents how girls are taught to be passive in the classroom. This team looked at more than one hundred fourth-, fifth-, and sixth-grade classrooms in four states and Washington, D.C. They found that "at all grade levels, in all communities, and in all subject areas, boys dominated classroom communication."

Upon observing how teachers responded to students calling out answers, the Sadkers found that when boys answered without being called on, their responses were accepted. When girls called out, they were admonished to raise their hands. The implicit message: Boys should be academically assertive and grab teacher attention; girls should act like ladies and keep quiet, or at the very least, wait their turn and be polite.

Lest you think this double standard ends with high school, a study reported by Edward Fiske in the *New York Times* documents how sex-role differences continue in college. The study showed that faculty members at Wheaton College took male contributions to class discussion more seriously than female, and allowed the men to dominate the classroom. This substantiates other findings that college professors are more likely to remember their male students' names, call on them in class, and value their answers. According to Fiske, these same professors "feel free to interrupt women and ask them 'lower-order' questions" such as the date of a particular event rather than its significance.

From the time we are tiny tykes, our society teaches us how to be successful men and women. These lessons are profound and stay with us for the rest of our lives. Boys learn to be competitors on the field of life, while girls learn to be warm, nurturing mothers. Our training is critical in helping women fulfill our biological roles, but it may work against us in the business world. Think of it this way: If you put a great basketball player into a baseball game, it's likely that his strengths won't be valued or even evident.

▶ THE BUSINESS OF PLAY

Although much learning occurs at our parents' knees and in school, gender-specific play activities are where we learn the most about how to function in the business setting. In every culture, children learn to be "appropriate" adults through the games they play. Games may look like lots of fun—and they are—but their underlying intent is serious. Almost all games teach children lessons of success. The famous Swiss psychologist, Jean Piaget, described play as the crucible of social development during the school years. As such, child's play becomes a laboratory for us to observe how children develop social skills and sex-role identities.

It's important to note the difference between "play" and "games." The former is an informal, cooperative interaction that has no particular goals, no rules, no score-keeping, no end point, no strategy for winning, and no winners or losers—say, creating a structure out of Tinker Toys or playing with dolls. Games, on the other hand, are competitive interactions with definite rules, a clear goal, and a predetermined end point (nine innings, four quarters, a particular score). There are always winners in games, and consequently there must be losers. Certain activities, such as bike riding, can be considered play or games depending on how they are organized. If you're just tooling along on a bike with your friends, you're playing, but if you decide to race to the corner and back, it's a game.

In a series of seminal studies in the 1970s, Janet Lever, a social psychologist at Northwestern University, documented exactly how boys' and girls' activities differ. Lever observed nearly two hundred fifth-grade children (between the ages of ten and eleven) for one year at Connecticut suburban and urban elementary schools during recess, physical education, and after school. She also collected children's diaries, documenting how they used their leisure time when not in school (what they did, for how long, and with whom), and she interviewed them. She concluded that the children spent 52 percent of their free time playing—but as you might guess, there were distinct differences along gender lines in how the boys and girls organized their activities.

Boys, Lever found, play outdoors far more than girls. Their favorite games—basketball, baseball, football, cowboys and Indians, cops and robbers, and war—must occur outside because they require larger spaces. Ultimately, this allows boys to venture farther from home, encouraging independence. Girls prefer to play with Barbies or board games, which are best played one-on-one indoors. Because of the kinds of games boys engage in, they often play in larger groups. Even when girls play outside, their groups are smaller than boys'. The kinds of games girls play (hopscotch, jump rope, tag) do not require a large number of participants, but even more significantly, the girls seem to strongly prefer playing in pairs—with a best friend whom they get to know intimately. Lever considered girls' indoor activities "private affairs," whereas boys' games were "public" and open to surveillance.

Although the boys Lever studied may have preferred to play with children their own age, they were more likely to include younger players in their groups, using the rationale, "You're better off with a little kid in the outfield than no one at all." The younger boys tried to keep up with the older ones and learned to "accept their bruises, stifle their frustrations, or not be invited to play again." The few times that Lever observed the ten-year-old girls playing with younger girls (aged five or six) they treated them as "live dolls," practicing maternal behaviors.

Finally, the girls Lever studied were more likely to play in boys' games than the reverse, probably because there is less social disapproval for this arrangement. When boys did join the girls' activities, it was usually to interrupt and annoy the girls in the role of a "tease" or "buffoon."

▶ COMPETITION AND TAKING TURNS

Of great interest to us is that the boys Lever observed played far more competitive sports than the girls did. Sixty-five percent of the boys' activities were formal games, compared to only 35 percent of girls' activities. "Girls *played* more than boys and boys *gamed* more than girls," Lever explains. Competitive games are all organized by hierarchies: there are coaches, team captains (often chosen by the children themselves because of their merit), star players, average players, and bench warmers, and it is clear that the primary way boys interact in such sports is through conflict, striving with their team to come out on top.

Some boys are more powerful and/or skillful than others—this is a given—and boys learn to accept their status in the hierarchy. An executive at AT&T once told me, "As a boy, I always knew my place in the pecking order." He says that gave him the mental space to stop jockeying for position and start playing the game.

What goes on during these games? Mostly, boys rehearse being "strong" competitors—perhaps as preparation for their adult lives. In *Staying the Course,* social psychologist Robert Wiess describes how boys learn to maintain hierarchical status in their play environments:

> [P]eers are the most effective teachers of values. Boys slightly older than kindergartners . . . learn from one another, in playground games and in more or less organized sports, to condemn cheaters and showoffs, the clumsy and the incompetent, the cowardly, the egocentric. They learn in con-

frontations with other small boys to resist aggression, to conquer fear or at least to mask it, to stand up for themselves. In the world of small boys they learn hardihood. They learn not to cry when their feelings are hurt. . . .They learn not to offer alibis for poor performance, not to ask for help. . . . They learn not to talk about their uncertainties and fears except, perhaps, as a means of overcoming them.

There are no such lessons for girls—quite the contrary. When playing Barbie, there's no star player or coach. In their one-on-one play with a best friend, girls are, in fact, playing "relationship." They prefer intimacy and reciprocity in their play activities: Far from hiding their feelings, the sharing of secrets creates a close bond and is a sign of friendship. Girls collaborate on making up games and fantasy play and enjoy deep emotional ties. The divulging of a secret to others can precipitate a break-up, but if a girl gets hurt and cries during a game, she quickly becomes the center of a concerned and supportive group of female playmates. In girls' games, power is shared equally—no one is trying to get the better of the other.

Conflict, an inherent element of competition, means we disagree about something. Friendship, on the other hand, means we're in harmony. Since the game of "relationship" is central in the female culture, conflict is to be avoided. It damages friendships. Consequently, when they get into a squabble, girls are repeatedly admonished to "Get along and be nice." These are code words for "avoid conflict at all cost." One woman told me that when her daughter orders her friends around, she calls her, "Miss Bossy Cow." When asked what she would call her son if he were to display the same behaviors, she blanched and then replied, "A natural-born leader, of course." It suddenly dawned on this woman that she had imposed a double standard on her daughter, and it stunned her.

Girls grow up with different rules: The power is always kept dead even. Even when girls play spontaneous competitive games like hopscotch or jump rope, they actually do not compete directly with one another. These are "turn-taking" games in which there's no expressed goal, no strategy for winning, and no defined end to the game. In jump rope, for instance, each girl patiently waits her turn, and when the players are tired or must stop the game, the children compare their achievements. One person's success does not necessarily signify another's failure, as it would in direct competition where there is always a winner and a loser.

Women gravitate toward win/win situations so they can keep relationships intact. Among girls, it is more important to be popular than to win. In fact, boasting about prowess almost guarantees that the gloater will become friendless, isolated from others. Since girls place a high value on intimacy with other girls, being ostracized is excruciatingly painful. In the female culture, popularity and intimacy are signs of status—they are more important than success or achievement. In the male culture, having a high position in the hierarchy is what counts most.

▶ CONFLICT AS CHILD'S PLAY

Going back to Lever's study, perhaps her most interesting finding is that boys' games last so much longer than girls' do. Seventy-two percent of all the boys' activities that Lever documented spanned an hour or more while only 43 percent of girls' did. She did not watch a single girls' activity, even at recess, that exceeded fifteen minutes. It was common for boys' games to fill the whole twenty-five-minute recess period.

Why should this be so? Lever proposed several answers to this question, some of which are germane to our understanding of hardball. To begin with, competitive boys' games are rule-bound, which makes them far more complex than girls' games. Due to the existence of so many rules, boys often become involved in procedural or other disputes with the children on the opposing teams. The boys, Lever found, were able to resolve those disagreements effectively. Although she observed the boys arguing all the time, no game ended because of a fight—the chief goal was to keep the ball in play. In the worst of disputes, the boys would simply agree to repeat the play. A physical education teacher at one of the schools in Lever's study noted that the boys seemed to enjoy these debates as much as they did the actual game, and that older boys would model how to resolve the arguments for the younger ones.

The social learning that occurs during competitive games teaches boys many valuable lessons about resolving conflicts. It encourages the development of the organizational skills necessary to coordinate the activities of several people at once. It provides experience in successfully settling disputes. It may even improve boys' abilities to deal forthrightly with interpersonal competition and conflict. As Lever explains:

A boy and his best friend often find themselves on op- posing teams. They must learn ways to resolve disputes so that the quarrels do not become so heated that they rupture friendships. Boys must learn to "depersonalize the attack." Not only do they learn to compete against friends, they also learn to cooperate with teammates whom they may or may not like personally. Such interpersonal skills have obvious value in organizational milieu.

In the turn-taking games that Lever saw the girls play, however, the children had little experience in settling disputes. When a squabble broke out among them, the game promptly ended, with- out an attempt at resolution. For most girls, the object of a game like hopscotch is not winning so much as interacting with each other; it's an excuse for talking and sharing feelings. If a game stops, there may be tears, threats such as "I won't be your friend anymore," counterthreats, and pouting. Some girls in Lever's study even complained that their friends "couldn't resolve the basic is- sues of choosing up sides, deciding who is to be captain, which team will start, and sometimes not even what game to play!"

We can surmise from these observations that having far less ex- perience with competition in their play experiences, the girls did not acquire the hardball skills that boys did in childhood. Lever ob- served in later research on the complexity of play that "The style of [girls'] competition is indirect, rather than face to face, individ- ual rather than team affiliated. Leadership roles are either missing or randomly filled."

Though girls think less in terms of winning and losing than do boys, they have their own unique way of coping with defeat. Ac- cording to psychologist and marriage expert John Gottman, rather than masking and suppressing their emotions like boys do, girls "encourage each other to express their anxieties directly and then take a parental, comforting role, soothing it away with words of love, loyalty and affection." But boys learn that when the game is over, it's over. Because they know how to "depersonalize the attack," after attempting to destroy each other on the playing field, they happily go out to the video arcade together after the game.

For little girls, the game is never over. If they have a conflict, it is not readily forgiven and forgotten. In a study of preteens and teenagers at play, anthropologist Marjorie Harness Goodwin found that when girls strongly disapproved of one of their friend's behaviors, they exercised the utmost social control by ostracizing her for up to six weeks.

In adulthood, the dynamics change little. Two women condemning each other's ideas in a meeting rarely go to lunch afterward arm in arm; the enmity is retained. But among men accustomed to living in a competitive world, such clashes are soon dismissed as "part of the game." It's just business, they tell themselves.

This difference in behavior may, in fact, be based on differences in the way men and women process conflict. According to Colin Camerer, an economist at Caltech University in Pasadena, California, MRI images have shown that after a negotiation, male and female brains follow different patterns. "Men seem to shut down once the decision is made," Camerer explained in "How We Think," an article by Michael D'Antonio published in the *Los Angeles Times Magazine.* "In women, the process continues, and the caudate, which is a sort of error-checking center, continues to work as if it's considering whether the right choice was made." So, perhaps for women, it is true that the conflict is never over!

▶ POWER PLAYS

Many research studies have shown that children have definite ideas about how powerful males and females "should" be and also who "should" control interactions between them. In one study, children as young as two or three already understood that "girls don't hit but boys like to fight," and that "boys will be the boss when they grow up." In another investigation, five-year-olds were aware that "women are supposed to be gentle and affectionate and that men are supposed to be strong, aggressive, and dominant."

Competitive behavior and imposing your power on another are not typical social expectations for females. In a study of fifth graders, social psychologist Dorothea Braginsky asked groups of girls and boys to get a peer to eat several crackers that had been soaked in quinine—a bitter taste. If they were successful, they would be rewarded with a nickel for each cracker their classmate consumed. The successful boys manipulated their peers using lies in a direct and aggressive approach. They were, according to Braginsky, "less concerned with future encounters than with their immediate success," and their methods were "crude." But the successful girls behaved in a more indirect manner, using "a subtle, evasive method of impression management."

Many of the successful girls used a technique Braginsky called a "money-splitting bribe"—they revealed to their classmate what the experimenter had requested of them and offered to share the money if the other girl ate the crackers. Although Braginsky viewed this as a negative manipulation (after all, these successful girls never offered to share in the eating of the noxious crackers and didn't stress that they would keep half the money), I am inclined to believe that the girls had found a nonconfrontational, nonaggressive way to create a win/win situation and preserve their relationships. According to Braginsky, these girls "emerged from the situation having won the confidence and friendship of the TP [the Target Person, i.e., her classmate]." Interestingly, the girls who attempted to convince their classmates to eat the crackers using the boys' more aggressive methods were unsuccessful.

This research implies that females who play hardball in the guise of coercive power strategies—who order other females around, for instance, or who lie outright—tend to meet with resistance. With women and girls, indirect methods generally prove to garner greater success.

Researcher Diane Carlson Jones has found that "The key difference between boys and girls is the perception of power holders. Boys readily accept the occupants of top-ranking positions while girls reject the powerful." In searching for what might account for these differences, Jones surmised that when boys act aggressively, this corresponds to our sex-role expectations of them. But the same cannot be said of girls. Their aggression runs counter to our norms. "For females, . . . only the indirect power style is socially sanctioned; the aggressive style is increasingly closed off as an option. Aggression is never reinforced for females, regardless of age, and in fact is punished with affective rejection," one of the least desired consequences for the relationship-oriented female. No wonder women tend to be afraid of power.

▶ "IT'S A PROCESS!" "WHERE'S THE GOAL LINE?"

Many of the lessons we learn in childhood are called into play when we're adults—especially in the way we might view solving a problem. Imagine a couple on a Saturday morning. Samantha tells Jonathan she needs to buy a black skirt and asks him to accompany her to the mall. Jon moans, he groans . . . but eventually he reluctantly agrees. Upon entering the mall, he makes a beeline for the first women's apparel store he sees. He flings open the door, goes directly to the skirt section, sorts for black, finds Samantha's size, holds up the prize, and says, "Here, honey. I found it for you!" He has killed the black skirt and is ready to drag it back to the cave.

But Samantha is not sure she wants *that* black skirt. She'd like to browse in several stores, maybe look for shoes and a sweater to go with it, and since this is going to take a while, she suggests, "Let's have lunch."

Jonathan feels tricked. Samantha said she wanted a black skirt. To him, this was a goal-focused activity: find black skirt—kill black skirt—go home, and watch game. He felt he'd accomplished the task for her, but now she has moved the goal line. Sweaters, shoes, and lunch have been thrown in to complicate matters. But to Samantha, this was a process activity. Yes, she needed the black skirt, but she also wanted to spend some time with her sweetheart. As he sees it, she fools him every time they go shopping. From her point of view, you ask this guy to spend more than five minutes with you, and he starts whining.

Most of the time, men engage in Jon's kind of goal-oriented behavior. If you reflect back on the games boys play, it's clear that all of them are goal focused. Boys establish the finish line, end zone, or objective in the game (the most runs, the lowest golf score, the highest pole vault), and then methodically go about achieving it. You'd never hear a bunch of boys saying, "Let's get started and figure out where the goal line is later." The whole purpose of playing is to achieve the agreed-upon objective and win.

Women, on the other hand, may be more involved in the *process* of reaching that goal line than actually achieving the goal itself. Like Samantha, they may see goals as the means to various other ends—opportunities to spend time together enjoying one another's company. There are no "goal lines" in games of house and school. We have process instead. The game simply elaborates in many directions as we play at developing and nurturing relationships. We play, play, play, play, and play until we get into a fight, it gets dark, or your mother sends me home.

I have come to believe that this goal focus versus process focus underlies many of our problem-solving interactions and the difficulties we can encounter when dealing with the opposite sex in the workplace. Take the critique Allison's boss hurled at her as noted in Chapter 1. "You do your job well but you're too scattered. . . . You do too many things at once. You're just not focused enough."

This is a bad thing? To a woman, most likely not! Allison's behavior was comfortable and effective for her. However, for a male who values the ability to be singularly focused on a goal, having the capacity to juggle many activities at once looks like distraction and disorganization. Goal versus process focus is so basic to gender differences I believe it is probably hardwired in us. I like to think of it in evolutionary terms: 99 percent of all human beings who have ever lived have been hunters and gatherers. If you're a man out hunting, you must remain exceptionally focused on your prey and not get distracted by other activities around you or you might go hungry (or worse yet, get eaten). But as a gatherer, a woman must be able to divide her attention among multiple stimuli simultaneously: the fruit in the trees, the grubs, the tubers growing underground, even as she minds her many children.

These differences in the ability to focus have been borne out in laboratory situations. In one classic experiment, men and women are given a sheet of paper covered with twenty symbols such as a star, a horse, a crescent, and a cross, and allowed one minute to study it. This paper is removed and a different one is substituted with some of the symbols missing and others in new positions. The subjects are asked to identify how the new page differs from the old one. Women are much more adept at this activity than men, In part, I believe this skill underlies the female's ability to process:

Women can do many more things at one time than men can, and as foragers are required to form mental patterns for discrete, seemingly disconnected bits of information.

In another study, Sally and Bennet Shaywitz of Yale University, using an MRI scanner, gave men and women a rhyming task. In men, a small center of the brain lit up on only the left side. When women performed the same activity, the brain looked more like a pinball machine, with sites lighting up simultaneously on both sides of the brain. Perhaps this is what drives a typically male comment about a female colleague, "I went to talk to her about it, but she was all over the map." This may, in fact, be literally true.

The goal focus versus process focus plays itself out in many different ways among men and women. By having one part of the brain focused on the activity, men tend to look directly to the bottom line while women take a circuitous route getting there. ("Get to the point!" may be a man's frustrated way of sharing his discomfort with these differences.) On the other hand, women are much more facile at processing multiple issues at once than are typical males.

That we're different isn't a problem. But how we assess the other can become a problem. For instance, a female executive at a biomedical company approached me with, "I have a problem employee. I'd like your advice about what to do about him. Peter can't multitask. I give him five things to do, but he has to do them one at a time."

"Do you get the outcome that you need?" I asked.

"Yes, but he can't do more than one task at time."

Peter's performance was fine. But his boss was judging it negatively because it wasn't the way she would have done things. This is parallel to Allison's problem in which her male boss saw her as scattered even though she perceived her ability to multitask as an asset. It's important to honor the other gender for the way that works for them, rather than making them bad or wrong because they're not "like me." And that goes for men as well as woman. In fact, when this is accomplished great strides can be made.

Consider what happened when I was working with the executive team at an international toy manufacturer. The CEO had made a commitment to the board of directors that he would have three women on the executive team in the next four years. The company was more than one hundred years old and had never had a woman at such a high level. The CEO was out gunning for women to promote.

Mitchell, the VP of operations, counted among his responsibilities the oversight of all the manufacturing plants. He came up to me after one of our meetings and said, "Pat, I'm really confused. A woman runs one of my plants. I know from the numbers that Marci's plant has the highest productivity and the highest morale. I'd love to recommend her to the executive team, but she can't solve any of her own problems, so I feel uncomfortable with the situation."

I probed further. "When Marci brings you a problem, do you give her a solution?"

"Of course."

"Does she usually do what you say?"

"No, not usually."

Immediately, I knew that Marci was perfectly capable of solving problems. This was a conflict between process and content orientation as well as a classic example of what keeps the glass ceiling in place. Mitchell wasn't holding Marci down intentionally, but when we judge the other gender by our own rules, we often misinterpret what's going on with them. "Well, Mitchell," I continued, "when Marci approaches you with a problem, she's not bringing it to you to 'kill.' She wants to process through options with you so she can come up with her own solution."

Mitchell, having participated in my gender workshops, immediately recognized the issue. From that point on, whenever Marci approached him with a problem, rather than jumping in with a solution, he asked, "What do you think you ought to do about that?" Or "Do you think that's the best solution?" Or "Do you see any other alternatives?" As a result, the productivity in Marci's plant shot up even higher, and she even won that much-coveted spot on the executive committee.

▶ SOCIAL LESSONS AND HARDBALL

In this chapter, you've seen how as girls we have been raised to develop and preserve intimate relationships with close friends. We've been taught to be gentle, loving, and interdependent. We've been encouraged to be empathic and humble. We've learned to share secrets with our best friends and to expect that they will comfort us when we're upset. We've learned to wait and take turns, whether we're playing or answering a question in the classroom. We've learned not to fight, not to compete, not to speak up, not to draw attention to ourselves, and most definitely not to act too powerful or other girls won't like us and may even reject us.

Boys have learned different lessons—the lessons of how to survive in a hierarchy. They have become accustomed to experiencing conflict and differing degrees of interpersonal power. They're used to rough-and-tumble aggression, and they're accustomed to, if not exerting power over others, at least to jockeying for position among them. Boys have had much practice settling disputes and conflicts, and they are able to distance themselves personally when attacked.

As products of these two different worlds, it is not surprising then that men and women behave differently at work. Men tend to experience friendliness with other men whereas women develop friendships that are deep and lasting. If women are friends, they're friends everywhere—in their personal and professional lives. The friendliness of men, on the other hand, can come and go as needed. At the beginning of a workshop I once asked the men in the room to tell me what they had learned from the team games they'd played as boys. One man exclaimed, "Loyalty! Loyalty to the team." When queried how he would react if he were traded to another team, he responded without missing a beat, "Loyalty to the new team."

Whatever team a man is on, he has already learned how to function within the confines of its hierarchy—a valuable experience most girls have missed. And, as we'll see in the next chapter, one of the first lessons a boy learns while finding his place in that hierarchy is to always do what the coach says—period!

3

DO WHAT THE COACH SAYS—PERIOD!

▼
HARDBALL LESSONS BOYS LEARN

- Don't challenge the coach.
- There's always someone above me and below me.
- The guy on top gets all the privileges.
- The only way to get to the top is to do what you're told.
- If you've got power, you need to use it or lose it.
- Demonstrate your loyalty to the coach.
- Never say never.

▼
HOUSE AND DOLL LESSONS GIRLS LEARN

- We're all equal, so the power is dead even.
- Decisions are discussed and negotiated.
- Everybody is equal.
- Power is always shared.

▼ ▼ ▼ ▼ ▼ **L**iz was a manager in the communications department of a large Fortune 500 company. When I stopped by to see her, she was putting the finishing touches on a film about the company's history, a project that had taken her six months to complete.

Liz was proud of her efforts and excited about the visibility this film would give her at a forthcoming companywide meeting. As Liz and I spoke, the chairman of the board, looking every inch the CEO, entered her office. He drew himself up and told Liz in a deep, resonant voice that he'd just seen the final cut of the film and didn't like the 1950s television footage of the company's founder. "The quality is poor, and I want you to take it out," he said. Liz explained that it was the only usable film she could find and that television footage from the 1950s always looked grainy. He repeated, "I don't like it, take it out."

"Gee, I wish I had known your objections ahead of time," Liz countered. "It's going to take a lot of work to change the film at this point. I won't have enough time to get it ready for the upcoming meeting."

The CEO's reply: "I don't like it, take it out."

"But it will cost forty thousand dollars to redo it," Liz said desperately.

His response: "I don't care, take it out."

Inside of six months, Liz had lost her job. In her CEO's eyes, she had committed a cardinal sin: She had talked back to her coach.

Liz, of course, saw it differently. She felt her CEO should have paid attention to the project at the outset, taken time to review it carefully, and made his wishes known then. "Now I've got to go through all this hassle and redo the work," she complained. "It wastes my time, a lot of company money, and I won't be able to show the film at the big meeting." But her CEO runs a $5 billion corporation. When he tells a manager to change something, he's baffled when she has the audacity to resist his directive and to whine on top of it. To him, Liz didn't understand who was in charge.

How could Liz have handled her situation more effectively? Above all, she needed to recognize her CEO's authority: She had to do whatever he asked. If that meant spending as much time and money as necessary to finish the film by the big meeting, then so be it. After all, the CEO had clearly signaled that money was no object. Liz could have created a win/win situation for herself and her company. Unfortunately, she came out the big loser because she was blinded by her perception of her CEO as unreasonable. As a result, her film was shelved and she was kicked off the CEO's team.

Liz and the CEO saw each other across a broad chasm of cultural differences. Unfortunately, neither was aware of the chasm. They believed they operated by the same rules about "appropriate" behavior. But men and women follow different guidelines about authority. As Liz and her CEO dealt with this issue, all they saw was each other's unreasonableness, and not the underlying issue that they were operating from different frames of reference.

▶ HIERARCHY AND THE MALE REPRODUCTIVE IMPERATIVE

When it comes to gender, whether you are a man or beast, the name of the game for both males and females is progeny: that is, getting our genes into the gene pool. We feel driven to procreate. If you're a male, this may take just a few minutes, and if you're lucky, you can do it many times a day. Unfortunately, your fellow males all have the same agenda, and they're vying for access to the females too. This creates conflict. Males of many species fight with other males for the opportunity to continue their line—some (from animals as tiny as mice to those as mighty as lions) will even eat the young of their rivals in an attempt to insure their own genetic dominance.

When I was a student in Boulder, Colorado, I had firsthand experience with the male reproductive imperative—and it wasn't because of the proximity of hundreds of frat boys. My university was perched against the Rockies, and every fall the canyons would echo with the terrifying din of male elk up in the mountains running at each other, butting heads, and tangling antlers. Some even died in these violent clashes. I was mystified as to why these majestic animals would behave this way to each other. But as time went on, I learned that elk use their annual bloody battles to establish the dominant males—the ones who would mate with the females.

This innate need to compete for position seems brutal, yet it may have a purpose beyond that of reproduction. Many social scientists believe it has led to the creation of hierarchical social structures (an alpha male on top with the other lesser males finding their positions below him in a sort of pyramidal arrangement). Such an order prevents constant bloodshed and anarchy among males. Indeed, one of the advantages of this type of dominance hierarchy is that it eventually engenders security and peacefulness. Every male knows his place and keeps to it until and unless he feels ready to challenge the leader.

▶ SOME LESSONS FROM OUR MALE PRIMATE COUSINS

Although it might be unwise draw direct links between primates and humans—after all, we have a level of intelligence that they do not—according to psychology professor Shelley E. Taylor and her research associates at the University of California, Los Angeles, "it would be foolish to claim that there is nothing to be learned from primate behavior." Chimpanzees are our nearest living kin, with 99 percent of their genes overlapping our own. (In contrast, only 50 percent of the mouse genome is identical to ours.) If we examine the differences in social order among male and female chimps, we can find some similarities as to how we humans function. We may even uncover there some of the roots of hardball strategies.

The bonds between male chimpanzees are ephemeral. Males form coalitions to achieve status: together they establish the alpha male; they join forces to hunt down dinner, to defend against intruders, or to attack the lowest monkey on the totem pole. Dutch-born zoologist and ethologist Frans de Waal, one of the world's leading researchers in primate behavior, working out of the Yerkes Regional Primate Research Center at Emory University, has found from his research that, "Adult male chimpanzees seem to live in a hierarchical world with [. . .] a single permanent goal: power." Once the goal is reached, a coalition will dissolve, only to reform with a different combination of players when a new challenge arises.

Males base their relationships on a tit-for-tat strategy: If you help me, I'll help you. If you hurt me, I'll get even. Such male chimp coalitions are difficult to predict, de Waal explains. "The unreliable, Machiavellian nature of male power games implies that every friend is a potential foe and vice versa," he writes in *Peacemaking Among the Primates*. Indeed, as Deborah Blum, author of *Sex on the Brain*, tells us, male chimps are "constantly plotting coups and negotiating for better allies." Sound familiar?

The male hierarchy among chimps is formal, and members communicate their status to one another frequently. The dominant male shows his superiority by literally making his hair stand on end—this gives the illusion of his being even larger than he actually is. Subordinates will demonstrate their lowliness by grunting and bowing in submission. When this status communication breaks down, fights erupt. According to de Waal, male chimps have twenty times as many aggressive incidents among them as females do. But they are also quick to make up; 47 percent are conciliatory after a conflict. "The formal hierarchy may be seen as a device to maintain cohesion in spite of rivalry," de Waal explains.

Among males, the display of status is helpful. When you don't have to fight constantly about the social order, you automatically understand the limits of your behavior, what you can and cannot do. This sort of solidarity can be important if the males in a troop must close ranks to defend against aggressive rivals in neighboring territories.

In case you think that such struggles for dominance occur only among lesser beasts, social psychologists have documented how human adolescent boys also jockey for position among themselves. In an interesting series of studies conducted over a period of eight years, researcher Ritch Savin-Williams at the University of Chicago investigated the behavior of children between the ages of eleven and seventeen at sleep-away summer camps in New England, Michigan, and New York. The adolescents were observed when they arose and went to bed, during meals and cabin cleanup, in the course of cabin discussions, and while participating in athletics.

Savin-Williams found that within the first few days (if not hours) of coming together, skirmishes broke out among the boys. The more dominant boys ordered around the less dominant ones; they ridiculed, bragged, shoved or pushed, verbally threatened, interrupted, or otherwise tried to control their bunkmates. Soon, the most physically mature boys took their positions as the leaders of the group.

But this hostile environment didn't last long. Over time, Savin-Williams explains, "the frequency of dominance acts within a group decreased as the hierarchy became more clearly linear; the expression of one's status also became more overt." That is, once each boy knew his place in the social order, the need to fight for position subsided. The boys settled down and went about the business of being happy campers.

▶ A LITTLE HELP FROM OUR FRIENDS

We females also have the reproductive imperative to move our genes into the gene pool, but of necessity we must proceed differently from males. Once a female has been impregnated, gestation will, depending on the species, physically tax her body for a period of several weeks to several months. During this time, she is vulnerable as she becomes less agile and less able to physically protect herself. And once the baby or litter is born, she must now care for her offspring until they are independent enough to fend for themselves.

For the most part, unlike males, females do not need or use conflict to establish a hierarchy to guarantee the continuation of their genes. Rather than competing with other females, they tend to rely on help from their same-gender friends to ensure their offspring's survival. Females don't fight over access to power. Their quarrels usually revolve around access to *resources*—food, protection of the young, males, promotions, coveted assignments.

Raising a baby, whether you are a human or a lower-order mammal, is a time- and energy-intensive activity. To make the best use of both, chimpanzees will often reciprocally care for and nurse each other's infants. But if a female chimp takes more than her fair share of food or otherwise imperils one of the group's babies, the other females will severely ostracize her. Says de Waal, "While it's uncommon, females do appear sometimes to completely lose their tempers, fighting to crippling injury or worse." The chimps even seem to hold a grudge. De Waal describes females hurt by the offense as "vindictive and irreconcilable. They're angry for days or even longer; they slap, they push, and won't come to the ex-friend's aid." Compared to male chimpanzees, says de Waal, "A trespass, a failure of a trusted friendship, is apparently much harder for females to forgive."

In contrast to male conciliatory behavior after conflict, de Waal has found that only 18 percent of female chimpanzees make peace following a fight. They have a good reason to take group offenses personally—a transgression of a female friendship can endanger the children, and biologically speaking, a threat to offspring is high stakes indeed, perhaps necessitating sustained anger until the threat has been thoroughly eliminated.

Surrounded by other females, there is significant connectedness among female primates, and their relationships tend to be more constant than are male relationships. Female chimps also have hierarchies, but their structure tends to be rather vague, with only rare status communication. Female chimpanzee hierarchies are far less oriented toward dominance and power than the protean male hierarchies. And while the male groups will continuously re-create themselves through conflict, matrilineal social contracts are unchanged over many years and often generations. De Waal explains that adult female chimps live in "a horizontal world of social connections," whose goal is *security,* not power. It is of paramount importance to keep good relationships within this small circle of family and friends.

Going back to Ritch Savin-Williams's research with adolescents at summer camp, his findings indicated that the social structure among girls (even "high-ranking" girls) was much more flexible than that of the boys. The girls in his studies seldom asserted their influence by physical means or by arguing, since they were not seeking power. There was no obvious leader—and sometimes an "alpha" girl would slip to "beta" position and then back to "alpha" during her stay at camp. In fact, often more than one leader would emerge from these groups: one girl who was adept at getting things done and another who was good at helping others with their feelings.

▶ WHO'S ABOVE ME, WHO'S BELOW ME?

Liz had so much trouble because she and her CEO understood the organizational structure differently. Liz perceived it as a flat playing field where everyone is equal, and when it comes to solving problems and mapping out the next play, flatness implies collaboration and equality. But Liz's CEO understood the structure to be a pyramid-shaped hierarchy. And he clearly saw himself at the top of the heap.

From childhood on, most men become accustomed to living their lives in such hierarchical organizations; everyone is either above or below someone else. The coach, team captain, star player, and average player all know their relative power and importance. The leader expects that when he gives an order, it will be followed. Without this chain of command, he believes all will be chaos. Each team member needs to know how much power he has in relation to the others for the system to run smoothly. A boy may hate being last in the batting order, but he recognizes that the only way to work up to a leadership position is to accept his present rank and, as men say, be a good soldier.

I was speaking on gender differences at a meeting of The Rotary Club when this very issue emerged. A man in the audience threw up his hands and shouted, "Help me understand. I'm an attorney with fifteen years of experience. I've hired an assistant who has been out of law school only six months. I give her an assignment and she starts asking me why we're doing this. I just want her to do what I tell her, but she wants to talk everything over. I don't have time!"

I explained to this gentleman that since his employee had grown up in a culture that had a relatively flat structure, she saw him as an equal, and as a result her agenda differed from his. He just wanted the work to get done, but she needed to understand the issues so she could get the bigger picture. She offered helpful suggestions because she perceived pitfalls and opportunities he had missed.

"Be careful," I warned. "If you tell her, 'Just do what I say and don't ask questions,' someday you'll misspeak and she *will* do just what you say." The lawyer simmered down appreciably.

But the issue didn't die there. Immediately following the meeting, a CPA, the only woman in her firm, corraled me. "I'm on the other side of the problem," she said. "My boss frequently gives me assignments that don't make sense. When I ask questions in order to better understand the job, he dismisses my concern and acts as if I've created a problem. He treats me like a peon."

"Now you know why," I replied. "You need to understand your position in the hierarchy and honor your boss in the way he expects to be honored given his position in the pecking order. It may be useful for you to figure out other ways to play the game, such as engaging in 'student and mentor' with him. You could say, for example, 'Oh, Bob, you know so much about this. Can you show me why . . .' so that he explains the assignment to you. Or you could educate yourself elsewhere by asking cohorts or your mentor for the rationale behind an assignment."

The lawyer had become frustrated because he felt the junior attorney was questioning his authority. The CPA was frustrated because she felt her intelligence was ignored. And yet the bottom line had nothing to do with these issues. The problem lay in the fact that men live in hierarchies and women don't. The senior CPA felt burdened with an uppity woman who didn't know her place, while the junior attorney was doing her best to help out by making sure she understood the big picture.

I believe the best way out of this miasma is to talk about the cultural differences. That's what I eventually suggested to the attorney. The issue is not whether a subordinate woman should ask questions—that would be arguing about whose culture is "right." The key is to talk about the underlying differences in expectations and to negotiate agreements about how to work together.

For example, the lawyer could have said to his employee, "You and I come from different worlds. When I give you an assignment, I see myself as the coach, and I expect you to run with the ball." He could also acknowledge her side by saying, "I know you see yourself as helpful when you ask all those questions, but today they're driving me nuts! I just want to get going on this."

Unfortunately, women may have a harder time discussing cultural differences with their male supervisors. From my experience, the latter don't cotton to being educated by their female employees. But even if the boss is set in his ways, understanding why he reacts the way he does can help smooth the road to working more harmoniously. On the other hand, it may be useful to discuss disparate expectations with male peers. As long as the cultural difference is invisible and unaddressed, the problem can never be fully rectified.

▶ IF YOU'VE GOT IT, YOU'VE GOT TO USE IT

Most men value the business hierarchy and feel comfortable in it. Rank and status tell them how to relate to each other: when one should expect deference and when one should defer. Because of this, when a leader refrains from displaying power, male subordinates can feel deeply unsettled. Growing uneasy, they come to believe he is a bad leader and soon resist his authority. He loses power.

A few years ago I heard an internationally known professor of management who had written dozens of books and hundred of articles on leadership speak to a group of male managers about Jimmy Carter. He pointed out that Carter had made the grave error of carrying his own luggage into the White House when the family moved in. All the men nodded in agreement over the inappropriateness of Carter's behavior. I, on the other hand, had been impressed with Carter for his egalitarianism. I was also stunned to hear such a different perception from the men.

A woman might also be uncomfortable with a leader who appears weak or indecisive. She needs a boss who will take charge and take care of business. In the male culture, however, power isn't simply the ability to get things done; men must display and strut their power by ordering others around to underscore their leadership position.

In the female culture, on the other hand, strutting power can cause one to lose it, especially among female employees. Displays of power can seem odd because they're not part of our own culture. After all, if we're all equal, what's the point of throwing one's weight around? But such displays, often taking the form of requests or demands, are part and parcel of the hierarchical system. The person on top gets to give the orders.

Take the coach of a baseball team. If a team member fouls up by going against orders and swinging and missing on the first pitch, his coach may demand 100 sit-ups during practice as a demonstration of his authority. The player hasn't followed the coach's game plan. A boy may comply more or less willingly, but a girl in the same situation would wonder, "What do sit-ups have to do with judging when to swing the bat?" She may miss the point that the punishment is meant to reinforce the coach's authority to call the plays, that it's simply a demonstration of power.

Nicole, a bank vice president, experienced her own boss's power play. Flying to a meeting in Canada, she sat in coach while the senior executive vice president flew first class. After landing, they collected their luggage. His included several large bags, skis, ski boots, and poles. After plucking his belongings from the carousel, he turned to Nicole, told her to take his bags and equipment to the hotel for him, and strode out with only his briefcase in hand. This woman was barely five feet tall, whereas her boss was well over six feet.

And what did Nicole do? She dutifully lugged everything to the hotel. She knew very well this was a display of power, so she refrained from whining or pointing out the absurdity of the situation. Nicole understood her place on her boss's hierarchy. She played the game.

Seeing the hierarchy at work can be difficult for women. Because leaders have to maintain status within the hierarchy, they often ask people beneath them to do work they could very well accomplish themselves. The following exercise will help you assess how well you have adjusted to the hierarchical structure of business.

POWER PLAYS

Read the situations listed below, and in each case carefully consider the questions at the end of the exercise.

- Your boss asks you to reschedule a major meeting just because his old college buddy is going to be in town that day.
- Your boss, who seems to be doing nothing at all, asks you to make restaurant reservations for her.
- After a business lunch, your boss asks you to stay and take care of the check while the rest of the team goes back to the office.
- While on a business trip, your boss asks you to pick up her laundry and bring it to her hotel room.

1. How would you feel?
2. How would you act?
3. Would your reaction be consonant with the female or male culture?
4. What impact would your reaction have on your career?
5. How might you respond otherwise?

In organizational life, privilege is part of rank, and such imperious behavior is not meant as a personal affront to the subordinate but as a necessary demonstration of power. In the game of business, either you use power or you lose it.

▶ LOYALTY TESTS

Most men in leadership positions constantly assess if those around them recognize their power to lead. To do so, they assert their authority by using loyalty tests. These can take the form of seemingly illogical, oddball requests or circumstances in which the follower is required to put herself out, as in the case of Nicole lugging the bags to the hotel. By nature, loyalty tests must be outlandish—if they made perfect sense, they wouldn't verify your loyalty.

What is a loyalty test? That depends on the situation. If your boss asks you to spend your weekend finishing a report being presented to a client on Monday morning, you may dislike giving up your free time, but you can understand why it needs to be done. That's not much of a test. But if your boss makes the same demand just because he feels like looking at the report Monday, that may be a test.

A man might respond to the request by thinking, "The boss doesn't *need* the report. But he *wants* it, so I will do it." A woman, on the other hand, may think, "This demand just doesn't make any sense! Can't it wait till Tuesday?"

Women don't perceive putting up with illogical demands as having anything to do with loyalty. We grew up in a flat organization in which all the girls had equal power. There was no boss doll player. At work we also expect equality from women. In Nicole's case, imagine the scenario with a woman as senior executive vice president. If she had asked Nicole to maneuver the luggage to the hotel, most likely Nicole would feel resentful and label her boss a calculating bitch. Women are judged by different rules.

Loyalty tests can take more subtle forms as well. Kathryn was a top sales executive in a national snack foods company and the only woman at the senior executive level. The company was growing by leaps and bounds. Then a new operations manger, Marilyn, was hired. Marilyn took an immediate dislike to Kathryn. Not too long after joining the firm, Marilyn was put in charge of a move to a new building. Kathryn was shocked when she saw that Marilyn had relegated her to an office in the "outfield," away from the rest of the executive staff. Marilyn's rationale was that such a location would allow Kathryn to be closer to her sales staff.

Infuriated at Marilyn's arrogance, Kathryn talked to her boss. He agreed to move her office, but she came away from the meeting with the unsettling feeling that Marilyn had far more power than she had imagined.

"I will never work for Marilyn," she said in a parting shot.

Her boss replied, "Kathryn, I'm very disappointed to hear you say that. If I ask you to work for someone, I expect you to."

It took Kathryn more than six months to repair the damage she had wrought in that one sentence. Her boss saw himself as the coach, and he expected that when he called the play, a loyal team member like Kathryn would follow. He was surprised to hear Kathryn say that she would be loyal to him only when it made sense to her. As far as he was concerned, Kathryn committed a grave error on the playing field, which called her loyalty into question and shook his trust.

As a member of an organization, you may be expected to prove your loyalty in ways that seem to have little to do with allegiance. I often find that work hours fall into this category. Kathryn told me that in her organization, getting to work as early as 7:00 AM is highly valued. But she's not a morning person, so she stays later than virtually anyone else. She recently made the significant career decision to come to work at 8:30 AM, and she was astute enough to know the costs. "My life with all the travel and transferring to the corporate offices had been extremely stressful," she explained. "I just can't start work that early on top of it all. I'm probably screwing myself politically, but I'm happier."

When I bring up these situations in workshops, women often ask me, "Why do they care if she's there early? Why don't they just care if she gets her work done well?" They don't understand that coming to work early has nothing to do with productivity; its sole purpose is to demonstrate loyalty to the boss.

Some years ago, I was teaching a class in a UCLA extension program. During the break, one of the participants approached me. Her difficulty: about a year and a half prior she had graduated with a Ph.D. in astrophysics from one of the best two science universities in the United States. As one of the top graduates in the country, she was immediately snapped up by a space research institution. Suddenly, she did everything wrong. She was faltering in her job, which is why she ended up taking the class. I took a real shine to Lisa and met with her numerous times to talk about her strategy for managing her difficulties at work.

I suggested that she flex her style and do what works in the male culture. Eventually I lost touch with her, and one day, I was sitting on a plane, reading my *USA Today,* and there she was on the front page because of her team's success in a major space exploration project. Purely by chance, I was going to be at this space institution two weeks hence, so I called her up and said, "Congratulations. We need to have lunch, and I want to find out what happened."

She told me that she had continued to do what worked in the male culture and that her boss had put her through a series of difficult loyalty tests, one of which was to fire a much-beloved employee who didn't produce, bringing upon her own head the wrath of her coworkers. Her boss continued with these tests for about two years, at the end of which he said, "Tell me what job you want." That's how she ended up on the front page of the newspaper.

I asked her how that two-year time span was for her. "It was terrible. I went through a major depression."

"Why did you put up with it?"

"I had dreamt about doing this kind of work since I was eight years old. This is one of the only places in the country, let alone in the world, where I could do it. For me it was worth it to go through this hell."

To women, this is not a pretty picture. The pressure to kowtow to an autocratic leader with a giant ego can make us want to dig in our heels and not budge. Unfortunately, much of business is run with this command and control approach, and your allegiance to the coach will be tested in ways that make no sense, given our female culture. I do not suggest that what Lisa did was right or wrong; we all must make judgments based on our personal values. But you can make a more informed decision if you understand how men play the game.

Let's face it. Most organizations don't have the kind of hold on an employee that Lisa's did. Women will go elsewhere, which is why I believe there is such a serious turnover of women in middle management. They put up with doing things in a male way but a toxic buildup occurs over time. Eventually, they can get fed up and leave.

▶ EXPECT THE ILLOGICAL

Loyalty tests can come in many forms, some of them quite odd. The president of a large corporation where I worked sent a memo decrying the service he had received at a particular car dealership. He was boycotting the place, and clearly his message indicated that we should too. Since the company paid for my car expenses, it would have been easy for accounting to find out if I had been loyal. In fact, I had no doubt someone would be monitoring the expense forms to see if anyone used this dealership. Yes, it was my right to have my car serviced anywhere I chose, but I was acutely aware that my independence could cost me my job.

Loyalty tests are often subtle. If you're unaware of their existence and if you're not actively looking for them, you can miss them. I once worked with an executive whose wife owned and ran one of the largest necktie companies in the country. Gradually, I realized that all the men working in *his* company wore ties from *her* company. (Of course, the women were exempted from this particular loyalty test.) You can easily overlook the signpost indicating this type of loyalty check.

Loyalty tests that either take away a woman's right to make an independent personal decision or that just seem illogical simply gall us. Angela had become a representative for a lumber company. She was pleased to be the first woman in such a position.

Not long after she started, she needed a new car. Her boss asked what kind of *American* car she was thinking of getting.

"I've never owned American cars because I don't like them," Angela explained to me. "They just don't hold their value." She related this as we were driving in her sleek new American car and the gear-shift knob came off in her hand. Despite her better judgment, Angela had capitulated without making waves. She understood the rules of the game.

A man is likely to see a loyalty test as just a game. He realizes that driving the required car, wearing the obligatory tie, shunning the offending dealership are part of the price he must pay to be a good team member and to position himself for a big win in the future. Angela, like other women, is likely to perceive such a loyalty test as an encroachment on her freedom to make personal decisions in the world. For some, it may also raise the specter of a domineering, overbearing father who demanded obedience.

When confronting a loyalty test, we women feel forced to abandon a basic human right in order to get a chance to win. And yet that is the price of living in a "foreign" culture. Sometimes in order to win at hardball you must abandon your own customs, which are familiar and comfortable, and submit to the practices of the "other." This requires effort, adaptation, and surrendering what you know well. If you find yourself overreacting to a loyalty test by becoming enraged or withdrawing, it might be worthwhile to explore the tenor of your father/daughter relationship as it impacts your career today.

▶ NEVER SAY NEVER

In the realm of loyalty tests, "no" or "never" are words to be avoided. As Kathryn felt the threat of reporting to her archrival Marilyn looming, she told her boss that she would *never* accept such a position. This did dramatic damage to her relationship with the boss. In the game of hardball, "never" can be a four-letter word.

Even if there is no way on earth that you will ever fetch the coffee, do his typing, or cancel a date with his girlfriend—don't say it. Chances are, the situation will never arise. And if it does, then you

can decline or elegantly weasel out. But until you're in that corner,
don't say "I won't."

I saw the president of a company quickly do an internal edit on
what she was about to say. We were meeting with her boss, the
chairman of the board, who was frustrated with the performance
of some of his senior executives. In the discussion about whether
they should be replaced, the CEO turned to the president and said,
"Do you think you could do about 15 percent more work?"

The look on her face told me she was thinking, "I'm so busy
now, how does he think I could do any more?" But she smiled
sweetly and said, "I'm sure I can do whatever you need me to."
When he turned his back, she winked at me. This woman was
savvy enough to know that her boss wanted to hear that she would
get the job done. He wasn't interested in how overworked she felt.
Her response was a demonstration of her loyalty.

Once I sat in on an interview my own boss was conducting. He
asked the woman applying if there was any aspect of the job she
had problems with. She replied, "I don't do typing." In the end he
chose not to hire her.

When I asked why, he said, "I didn't like her attitude." I probed
further and discovered that her comment about typing was her undoing. This perplexed me, because the job had never required typing. But simply saying no had foreshadowed future disloyalty, and
it did her in.

On another occasion, several of us were working late on a project. The support staff had gone home. When we had finished, this
same boss turned to the most senior woman and asked her to type
the report for a meeting the next morning. I was taken aback and
eager to hear how she was going to handle it. She said in a tone
half exasperated and half joking, "Oh, Andrew, you know I'm all
thumbs," and then snatched the report from his hands.

The next morning the report was finished and on his desk.
When I asked Maxine if she'd been up all night she laughed. "Oh,
heavens, I didn't type it! I took it to an all-night typing service, for
which the company will pay a pretty penny. It will go on my expense form and Andrew will approve it." Now that's an elegant
weasel. Although Maxine might have railed at the sexism inherent
in Andrew's request, in the real world elegant solutions go a lot
further than indignant proclamations.

Even being honest and forthright can work against you in ways you might not imagine. I was working at a pharmaceutical company where a team was being formed to take a new product to market. The three men and two women already on the team were interviewing for the sixth position. They all met with Wrenn individually and then came together as a group to make a final decision. The men unanimously disliked her, but the women loved her. The group was shocked at their polarized opinions and surprised that they divided along gender lines. They had all been through one of my workshops, though, and were able to sort out the cause of this disparity.

Wrenn had behaved in the same way with all of them. Essentially, she'd said: This is what I'm good at; this is what I don't do well. Here's the kind of work I want to do and this is the work I don't want to do.

The team realized it was her interview style that caused the rift among them. The men saw Wrenn as acting above them in the hierarchy and they focused on the weaknesses she'd shared with them. They feared she wouldn't be a team player. The women, on the other hand, enjoyed her candidness. They felt they knew who they were hiring and had no problem with Wrenn's confession. When the team members realized that their gender perception difference had caused their conflict and that Wrenn was doing what makes sense in a female culture, they decided to hire her. I'm happy to report that they were all pleased with this decision as time went by.

At the same time I must say we all have personal boundaries we just won't violate, no matter what the cost. If you are asked to do something immoral, illegal, or outside your value system, it makes sense to say no and pay the price. Knowing your boundaries is the bottom line. The following exercise will help you evaluate how you deal with loyalty tests.

THE LOYALTY GAME

Think of a time your boss or someone above you in the hierarchy gave you an assignment that made little sense or had significant flaws.

1. Did you point out the problems?
2. How did the senior person react?

3. If the reaction was negative, why was your handling of the problem unsuccessful?

4. How could you have approached the situation differently to indicate you were a team player?

▶ LOYALTY HAS ITS LIMITS

While the rules of hardball dictate that you should do what the coach says, period, there are times when you must stand up for yourself. Even if you like your boss, or don't want to jeopardize your or his job, loyalty has its limits when it comes to sexual harassment. Being a teammate doesn't mean being a playmate.

Sexual harassment on the job is defined as any unwelcome sexually oriented behavior, demand, comment, or physical contact initiated by an individual at the workplace that is a term or condition of employment, a basis for employment decisions, or that interferes with the employee's work or creates a hostile or offensive working environment.

According to Barbara Gutek, professor at the University of Arizona and a national expert on sexual harassment, this behavior is most likely to occur in professions that were traditionally male-only clubs, such as trucking and neurosurgery. Perhaps it's used as a tool of intimidation, to frighten women away. But harassment can also be a means to use women and their vulnerabilities, as in the case of the Hollywood casting couch.

If your boss asks you take off your clothes, clearly he is violating your right. But much of what can be construed as harassment may fall in a gray area. Your boss may tell an off-color joke. Or he may rub up against you as he leans over to tuck in a label at the nape of your neck.

One of my clients, a female neurosurgeon—a member of a very rare breed—was the only woman on a medical committee. The men on this committee chose a name for it whose acronym was C.U.N.T. They thought this was funny, but she was highly offended and told me that she had to decide whether to try to "fit in" and keep her mouth shut or confront the committee. She chose the latter approach and was able to get the name of the committee changed, but it emphasized her marginality in this group. In her mind, she had no choice.

What should you do if you find yourself the victim of subtle or not-so-subtle sexual innuendo? You may find the following approach helpful:

1. Determine your limits. You need to determine what sexually oriented behavior, demands, comments, or physical contact seem inappropriate to you or interfere with your work.

2. Indicate your disapproval. If your boss's activity falls into the gray area, signal that his behavior is unacceptable by

- remaining stonefaced at his jokes
- changing the subject
- asking him to step back

Your response or lack thereof can be a subtle way of indicating that his behavior is unacceptable to you.

3. Become more assertive. If the subtle approach brings no relief, speak up. Say:

- "I would prefer if you don't use that kind of language around me."
- "I would prefer that you not rub against me."
- "I would prefer that you not give me a hug."

4. Establish a consequence. Use the following three-part statement, filling in the blanks:

- I would prefer that you not _____.
- It makes me feel _____.
- If you continue, I will have to _____. (let someone in HR know, talk to your boss, file a complaint, and so on).

Now here's the bad news. Barbara Gutek has found that of the women who claim sexual harassment, 50 percent are fired and 25 percent quit in frustration. If you find yourself caught in this difficult situation, it's probably time to start looking for a new job. Do file a report, but be smart: Have an escape route planned in advance. The sad dilemma here is that if you simply quit without filing, the harasser will continue his behavior with others. You should know that only 1 to 7 percent of harassed women file legal claims, and that only 30 percent of those who do actually win. Is it any wonder that women fail to report these incidents? Most fear reprisals and lack confidence in the system.

Cases in which disciplinary action is taken are often extreme. The *Los Angles Times,* for example, reported on one instance in which a navy pilot explained to the disciplinary board that he was only trying to lighten up a situation with a female subordinate when he pulled down his fly, got up from his desk, pulled out his penis, turned toward the woman, and said, "So, what do you think of that?"

In such cases, you must report the individual to his superior. If no action is taken, go farther up the chain of command. If you must, send a registered (return receipt requested) letter to the president of the company. At that point, action should be taken. Let's just hope it's not against you.

▶ CREDIT WHERE IT'S <u>NOT</u> DUE

When I was employed at the corporate headquarters of a large medical enterprise, one of the hospital heads sent veritable tomes documenting her hospital's progress to the corporate offices each month. Other administrators wrote mere two- to five-page monthly reports. The executives at corporate headquarters were all impressed with Linda's prodigious output.

As luck would have it, one day I had the opportunity to find out how Linda achieved this feat. I hired one of her former employees. When I commented on the monthly compendia Linda continued to produce, Joel said, "Oh, yeah. Every month I would take the other managers' reports, put them all together, put her name on it, and send it to the corporate office."

Since Linda wasn't giving credit to her managers, was she overstepping ethical boundaries? As hard as it may be for women to swallow, the truth is Linda was merely acting in accordance with the rules of hardball. In the male culture, a boss can take responsibility for all the work of employees beneath him in the hierarchy. Since his employees report to him, he is, in fact, responsible for their output and so has the right to claim ownership. Linda's act wouldn't be considered credit stealing in the male culture. Indeed, you need to recognize that your product is the property of your department or corporation.

At the same time, however, a good manager is one who gives credit for employees' work; positive recognition "grows" employees and motivates them to excel the next time out.

What to do if you find your boss taking credit for your work? If you fight by saying, "You're sending my reports under the guise of their being yours," you'll distance yourself from the coach. Like it or not, from the hardball point of view, it would be better for your career to say, "Linda, I understand that you're taking our reports and collapsing them into one. Is there any way I can write mine that will make your job easier?" In the long run, you are likely to enhance your opportunities as a result of working with the coach rather than bucking her authority.

There is a hitch, however. You may sense that your boss is taking credit but you'll never gain any reward from it. This would be the time to think about getting strategic to win the recognition due you. You could drop comments to power brokers like, "I heard you liked the report. It was challenging doing the research for it." Or you could solicit feedback from the power brokers with statements such as, "What did you think about the information I put together for the restructuring plan?"

But be careful. If you proclaim your ownership too loudly, you'll undercut your boss's position in the hierarchy, and he'll most likely lean on you even harder. On the other hand, if you're already being oppressed and getting no credit, this is a what-have-I-got-to-lose strategy.

Although credit stealing cannot occur from the boss's perspective, you may run into it among peers. In that case, you would be wise to confront the culprit and assert firmly and clearly, "I know you took credit for my work. If you do it again, I'll tell the boss." And follow through, if you have to.

CREDIT STEALING, OR PROPER MANAGEMENT?

Identify when someone took credit for your work.

1. Was that person above, below, or equal to you in the hierarchy?
2. What did you do?
3. What would be the most appropriate response, given that individual's place in the hierarchy?

▶ WHEN THE COACH IS A WOMAN

As we have seen, little girls usually don't live in hierarchies as do boys; instead, their relationships can be relatively flat. When one girl tries to tell another what to do, the second child usually won't put up with it and will tell her friend how she thinks the task should be done.

Certainly girls, like boys, would prefer getting their way, but usually they aren't as direct in their approach. A girl may ask questions such as, "Wouldn't it be a good idea if we played school?" or make suggestions like, "How about if we played school?" but she is not likely to give a command, "We are going to play school," without damaging the relationship. Girls do play competitively in games such as Monopoly, hopscotch, Candyland, and cards, but they're still careful about relationships in the process. If one child is good at jacks and the other excels at hopscotch, they may alternate to be fair. The power must be kept dead even.

Because their groups simply don't have a formal authority figure, no one girl's ideas are accepted carte blanche. Girls know that negotiation is the key to getting things done their way. More often than not, their goal is to sway the other person, not direct her.

Boys, on the other hand, learn early to follow the coach's directions without question. A boy may have a better idea, but he knows he'll impress the coach more by following directions, not making suggestions. When the coach says, "Okay, kid, I want you to run down 10 yards and turn right," he does it. He's not about to suggest, "I don't really think that's the best plan. Let's go left. Come on, Coach, let's give it a try." Boys learn that they may not think the coach's idea is the best, but it's his role to call the shots and their role to carry them out.

If your female boss maintains the "flat structure," you may have few problems. I have been fortunate to have female bosses who have kept the power dead even. We've become friends and have shared details of our personal lives. Indeed, when I was ready to move on to a new job, one of my bosses even helped me find a better position elsewhere. By the same token, I was committed to my boss. Because she was my friend, I wanted her to succeed and look good. But I still understood and accepted the hierarchy. If she wanted me to carry out a task that I disliked, I knew I was obligated to see it through, despite my feelings.

Unfortunately, this mutual support system doesn't always exist in the business setting. Differences in culture can create problems when women are managed by other, more powerful women. The hierarchical female supervisor already functions under the rules of male culture. She looks upstairs and observes how the game of hardball is played among her male colleagues. She emulates that behavior with the women who report to her and runs right into their resistance.

Frequently, women who must serve hierarchical females feel resentful because they take as personal attacks the natural displays of power required of those in authority. The boss may understand it as her prerogative to make seemingly arbitrary changes, but her employees may wonder, "Who does she think she is, anyway, telling us what to do? After all, we're equal . . . aren't we?"

The tendency to keep the power even is an unconscious throwback to the childhood social structure that dictated we were all peers. In order to flatten the structure again, disgruntled female employees may use passive-aggressive behaviors such as slamming doors, avoiding confrontation or even eye contact, and "forgetting" to deliver important messages. Even direct confrontations may not settle the problem if the employees and boss don't recognize the cultural dissonance.

If you find yourself in this situation, you may discover that you have more difficulty serving your boss than you would if she were a man. You might disparage her accomplishments or refuse to follow her orders. If this is the case, you might find it interesting to imagine how you would respond if your supervisor were a man rather than a woman. Would you be more apt to fulfil requests and loyalty tests? If so, for the sake of your job and your sanity, you may find it beneficial to imagine that your boss is a man.

HOW DO YOU RESPOND TO WOMEN IN POWER?

Answer the following questions in your journal:

1. Do you find it easier to work for a man than a woman? If so, why?
2. Does the woman's position of being more powerful than you tie into this discomfort?
3. Think of a woman you didn't like working for. Identify what you didn't like about her and write it down. Now, look at the adjectives you used to describe her. Are they ones that apply more to women (such as bossy, bitchy, catty) than to men?
4. Think of a time a woman above you in the hierarchy gave you an order. Did you feel uncomfortable? Would you have felt more comfortable had it come from a man?
5. What is your reaction when a woman is promoted to a senior position? Are you more likely to snipe or congratulate? When you hear other women sniping, do you join in, remain silent, or defend?
6. Think of a time a woman told you she was unhappy with your performance. Did her comments feel more personal or nastier than if a man had told you the same?
7. Do you evaluate men and women differently? How might you change your attitude, recognizing the disparate cultural pressures placed on women and men in power?

▶ EVERYONE NEEDS A GUIDE

Valerie ran a sizable and highly visible strategic planning department in a large bank. In response to financial losses the previous year, the bank began to lay off employees and reorganize. As a result, senior management gave her department to a man from out of state who had very little background in strategic planning. Valerie was devastated. In a ten-year period she had built up her department from nothing and had received only accolades for her work. Now, all was lost in twenty-four hours. To make matters worse, management moved her from an exciting "big picture" position to a detail-oriented, low-level job in the compensation department that drew on neither her strengths nor her interests.

Prior to this change, Valerie had reported to Susan, who had acted as her mentor. Susan gave advice, explained the long-term strategy, warned who to watch out for, and served as a role model. When Valerie asked for guidance in her difficult situation, Susan strongly recommended that she take the compensation job and hang in there. "It will be good for you," she advised.

Personally, I couldn't see how the demotion was a positive step for Valerie. She hated going to work, her new boss was demeaning (he had her spend one weekend buying gag gifts for an off-site meeting), and her morale was in the cellar. But Valerie hung in there because she believed in Susan.

Four months later, Valerie's bank was acquired by another large bank. Over 10,000 people were laid off, including Valerie's replacement. As heads rolled, Valerie, squirreled away in her low-visibility job, was safe. After the dust cleared, Susan (who came out a top executive in the merger) called and asked Valerie if she was ready to take a significant position in the new bank.

Left to her own devices, Valerie would have had no insight into these behind-the-scenes maneuvers; she simply wasn't in a position to see them. Without her mentor, she most probably would have quit in disgust or lost her job in the merger and missed the opportunities she enjoys today.

Women often believe they don't need mentors. They may think, "I do good work. I'll be rewarded on my merits." But in eschewing an experienced advisor, not only do they miss the importance of interpersonal work for career advancement, but they remain ignorant of the rules of hardball being played around them. Indeed, they may remain blind to the fact that a game exists at all.

Despite this skepticism, having a mentor may be more critical to a female's success than it is to her male colleagues'. In an extensive study of individuals who had made it into the senior ranks of organizations, the authors of *Breaking the Glass Ceiling* found that only 38 percent of these successful men had mentors, but *all* of the women executives had them. A mentor doesn't appear to be optional for women, probably because women are less familiar with how hardball is played.

In fact, as organizational psychologist Carol Gallagher explains, one mentor might not be enough. "Surprising as it may seem," she wrote in *Going to the Top,* "most of the senior executive women I studied had no such 'golden bullet' mentor. Rather, they had encountered many advisers and supporters who helped them along the way at various stages in their careers."

Research has shown that if a woman wants to move to upper management, she must make sure she is getting career encouragement. You need a cheerleader behind you. This could be your boss or it could be a mentor. In fact, some research has shown that an informal mentor can also be quite beneficial to your career. According to a 1999 study conducted by A. M. Walsh and S. C. Borkowski, those with informal mentors reported a greater number of promotions and a higher promotion rate than those who did not have mentors. The subjects of this research also reported that the informal relationships helped reduce stress, and that they were more satisfied with their careers. Eighty-six percent indicated that these relationships were professionally productive.

What does a mentor do that's so helpful? Morrison and her colleagues explain what mentors give advice on:

- how to get attention and recognition
- what career moves to make next
- how to conform to the expectations of the organization

Mentors hold up a mirror to help us see ourselves by giving feedback. For instance, if Liz (whom we met at the beginning of this chapter) had had a mentor, she could have avoided or at least repaired some of the damage her resistance to reediting her CEO's film had caused. The mentor might have pulled her aside and said, "Look, Liz. Not only is the CEO the coach, he's the big-cheese coach. And when he says jump, you only ask, 'How high?' "

Then she might have suggested that Liz mend the relationship by returning to the coach and saying, "I'm on the new version of the film. I'll get it done by the meeting. Thanks for your feedback." The mentor would also urge Liz to change her behavior in the future, because her boss would be sure to be watching for other signs of insubordination. As it was, without a mentor, Liz went merrily on her way, believing she was in the right and her CEO was wrong, and she lost her job in the process.

Mentors also nudge you into taking more risks. It can be hard to differentiate between a stupid decision and a strategic venture. With their extensive insight and experience, mentors can help you distinguish one from the other. A mentor also can be your advocate. Having an ally touting your skills and abilities is invaluable in those high-level, behind-closed-doors meetings where your professional fate is determined. On the flip side, when you're attacked in those meetings it can make all the difference to have a supporter in your corner, defending your actions and redirecting the assault.

Finally, you can learn a lot from a mentor. If you work directly for this person, you can watch him or her in action. Often a mentor will explain why a given decision was made, how a problem was avoided, and how a political opponent was defeated—in general, how best to play hardball. All of these lessons are impossible to glean from a formal education.

Moreover, the gender of your mentor can also make a difference in your career. According to research conducted in 1999 by R. M. O'Neill, S. Horton, and F. J. Crosby, women who have female mentors report a greater number of promotions than those who have male mentors but the former also seemed to earn significantly lower personal income than the latter. This could be due to a number of factors, including women not talking about money, male mentors being better positioned within the hierarchy, or the man helping his mentee set higher salary expectations than a woman might. (See Chapter 11.)

It's wise to avoid becoming too dependent on one person. If your one and only loses power or quits, you may find yourself the odd woman out. Try nurturing several of these relationships to cover all your bases. And keep in mind that advice doesn't always come from above. Peers can also help us understand the game. Often we can do some reality testing with politically savvy colleagues who are able to see the opportunities and land mines that are invisible to ourselves.

The successful women featured in *Breaking the Glass Ceiling* had both male and female mentors. Men are usually the ones plugged into the dominant coalition. Unfortunately, allying yourself with a male mentor can create some waves among your colleagues. When men are promoted, we look to their skill. When women are promoted, we look to their bed partners. Even when the relationship with your mentor is squeaky clean, expect that some will see it otherwise.

Women often enjoy the process of helping others grow. As one woman executive told me, "I love mentoring if the person's heart is in the right place. I'll teach her the good stuff and the dirty stuff." Besides, a female mentor can be especially helpful because she has had to learn how to play hardball. She understands your frustration, while a man might judge you as weak, not tough enough. A senior woman executive told me that during a particularly trying period, she would cry all the way home in her car. She mentioned this to her male mentor, the company CEO. "I could tell he saw me as weak because of this, so I never mentioned it again."

When Valerie talked about her manager, Susan, she often mentioned their common issues around balancing work and a family. Valerie clearly saw her boss as a model of organization and had implemented many of the techniques Susan used. A male mentor might view child-care problems as irrelevant or, worse yet, unprofessional.

But where do you find a mentor? You don't request one unless a formal mentorship program exists at your company. Asking someone to be your mentor is much like asking someone to be your friend. It doesn't work that way. But typically you'll have an opportunity to work or talk frequently with more experienced colleagues. When the chemistry seems right and you feel you can ask for advice, insight, or suggestions, then you have the beginnings of a mentor relationship.

When hunting for mentors, keep in mind the following:

- It's better to have several.
- A man and a woman will have different strengths to offer.
- Choose someone highly respected, someone whom you admire.
- Your mentor's access to the dominant coalition can be critical.
- Ideally, you should feel comfortable with your mentor.
- His or her value system should be similar to yours.
- He or she should be willing to give you some time.
- You should be able to get insights from your mentor that you couldn't derive on your own.
- Target mentors from different parts of your organization and other walks of life.

Of course, mentors also get something in the bargain. Usually they enjoy helping an up-and-comer, being the advice giver, and having someone value their knowledge and experience. But mentors are smart enough to know that they are also developing an important alliance. By being your advisor and guide, your mentor is adding another player to his or her team. You'll be expected, as appropriate, to share information and lend support.

Coaches are important for your success. But you need to understand what a coach expects from you, particularly if he's male. Being a good team player can be different than what you might expect. In the following chapter, we'll explore the male version of team play.

A FIELD GUIDE TO COACHES

- Men live in hierarchies: You're either above a man or below him, even if you're his peer.
- When you offer helpful suggestions and ask questions in order to understand the "whys" of those above you, your boss may hear it as disregard for his status.
- Bizarre, illogical requests may be loyalty tests.
- Never say never.
- Coaches want you to behave like a follower, not follow your own ideas.
- Allowing your boss to take credit for your work—as distasteful as it may seem—may pay off in the long run.
- Women will often sabotage other women who receive promotions or accolades. We don't do this consciously, but we do need to become active supporters of other successful women.
- Organizations can be alien territory for women.
- You need a mentor who can help you figure out a game plan for advancing your career.

4

COMPETITION:
The Name of the Game

▼
HARDBALL LESSONS BOYS LEARN

- Competition is fun and stimulating.
- Winners are revered; losers are reviled.
- Competition is the only way to get ahead.
- It's more important to be respected than to be liked.
- "Attack" is part of the competition game.
- Boys who compete aggressively are considered strong and are placed in leadership positions.

▼
HOUSE AND DOLL LESSONS GIRLS LEARN

- Competition and conflict are damaging to relationships and are to be avoided at all costs.
- Everyone wins when we share and compromise.
- Success means we all get along with each other.
- Harmonious relationships take top priority.
- It's more important to be liked than anything else.
- Competitive girls are catty, aggressive, bossy, and unpopular.

▼ ▼ ▼ ▼ ▼ **I**n our free-market economy, businesses must constantly vie for customers. The ongoing debate about foreign trade underscores this simple truth: In order to survive, a company—or an industry—must outperform its rivals. Capitalism is founded on the assumption that conflicts will be resolved through competition, whether it's GM and Toyota locking horns over the automobile market or Wal-Mart and Costco battling over the discount retail crowd. In the day-to-day conflicts between office coworkers, competitive behavior takes its rawest form.

As we'll see, competition is only one of five behaviors people may use to resolve conflict. In a business world based on competition, however, it makes sense that competitive behavior is valued over other behaviors. In this chapter, you'll learn how to be competitive without endangering the relationships that are essential to your success on the job. To begin, let's take a look at the different ways human beings respond to conflict.

According to psychologists Ralph Kilmann and Kenneth Thomas, all people use the following basic behaviors to settle disagreements in their business and personal lives:

- Accommodation
- Avoidance
- Compromise
- Collaboration
- Competition

Yet early training has taught men to resolve conflicts differently from their female colleagues. When conflicts arise, boys are more likely to demand having their own autonomous, independent way. Most often, they resolve disputes using competition:

"I wanna hit the ball!"

"No, I'm gonna be the batter. You're the pitcher!"

"It's my turn. You always get to bat."

"Well it's my bat, so my word goes."

The boy whose will prevails gets to do things his way—he's top dog.

When girls have differences, instead of competing they negotiate in order to preserve relationships.

"I wanna play nurse."

"Wouldn't you like to play Mommy?"

"I know. I'll be the nurse and you bring your sick baby to me."

In their desire to dodge confrontations that might damage relationships, girls are more apt to accommodate, avoid, compromise, or collaborate when resolving conflicts. The one behavior they studiously avoid is head-on confrontation and competition. Yet competition is the name of the game on the playing field and in the boardroom. Clearly, our differing cultural patterns have an impact on how men and women behave in the corporate world. Let's take a closer look at these approaches to understand how gender differences can influence your conflict resolution strategies and your career.

▶ ACCOMMODATION

Accommodation simply means giving in. We let the other person have his way. Sometimes accommodation is useful, as when your coworker feels strongly about an approach and you care very little. You may simply let the issue go.

On the other hand, you might find this strategy detrimental in other situations. Imagine that there's a plum project coming up and you would like nothing better than to take charge of it. You have a rival, however, in the form of Bob, your coworker and peer. He, too, believes that the project would bring him greater visibility and the opportunity for advancement within the corporation. He's going for it.

Even though you might make it known to your boss that you'd like to chair the project, Bob had taken the offensive, setting his competitive machinery in motion. He might try to undermine your confidence by saying, "You know, you're not right for this. You don't have the background. You're too busy." Simultaneously, Bob would build up his own credentials: "I've done projects like this before. I know this territory in a way that you don't. I'll make the time for it because it's a priority."

You find yourself assuming a defensive posture, justifying your position. You reply, "But I can do this. I think I have enough time. I know enough about this project to do it." Yet eventually Bob's attacks become so uncomfortable, and your efforts at defending yourself so difficult, that you simply give up, rationalizing that the project wasn't so important to you after all. It wasn't worth the fight.

The problem here is that Bob saw the resolution of this conflict as the playing out of a game strategy, but you saw it as a discussion. He was taking the offensive position. From his perspective, this was a contest in which he might win some or lose some, but the eventual goal was his surmounting the opposition—you. You, on the other hand, were having a discussion about what is the most fair and appropriate thing to do, given the issue at hand. The notion that this was a game of attack never entered your mind. As a result, you didn't get strategic or think about going on a counteroffensive. Who would do that in a discussion? You were simply talking about the issues.

The unfortunate outcome of Bob's triumph: Not only has he scored his points, but you have also taught him that this full-court press is an effective strategy to defeat you. He is likely to repeat it in the future.

When you accommodate, you communicate your defeated attitude through nonverbal signals. In fact, you literally get "little." The volume of your voice goes down while the pitch increases, so that you sound like a vulnerable child. Even your body conveys the message: Rather than taking up a lot of space, it seems to pull in, making you appear smaller to the other person.

How do you counteract the tendency to accommodate? When you feel that you're under attack, it's important to recognize that you, too, must go on the offensive. You'll find strategies that help in the second half of this chapter.

▶ AVOIDANCE

Avoidance means we ignore a conflict in the hope that it will disappear, usually because we consider confrontation an anathema. Avoidance may be an effective strategy when you ignore your irritation with your boss's management style because you've already landed a new job. When your boss attacks you again, you simply let it go because you're fairly sure you'll be out of there in a matter of weeks. More often than not, however, an irritating situation worsens for having been ignored. When we don't address conflict overtly, it doesn't go away, it just goes subterranean.

Imagine again the plum project. This time, however, the situation is such that you know your supervisor will pick his favorite to do the job. You believe you don't have a prayer; the boss doesn't value your abilities, so you don't even try. Unfortunately, taking such a passive approach can lead only to resentment that may poison future projects. Indeed, hostility that goes underground never goes away, it just gets rechanneled into destructive behavior: You may work slowly or shoddily, or follow your boss's instructions to the letter even though you know he misspoke. These are typical approaches to evening out the score. Such passive-aggressive behavior can further escalate your superior's lack of confidence in your abilities, closing you out of future projects, if not a job.

The personal and professional costs of avoidance are substantial in terms of your loss of self-esteem and advancement. After all, if you never get to work on a project, no one will know that you have a brain! Avoidance is often an inappropriate conflict-resolution style. It's best to move to another, more effective strategy, as we'll discuss later.

It's also important to note that girls use a particular kind of avoidance, especially in communication. Although we were admonished to be sweet, cooperative, and congenial, sometimes we really didn't get along with a playmate. When a relationship was strained by anger, we usually avoided a frontal attack, because that could have damaged the relationship. Instead, we sidestepped disputes by telling others about the conflict. In our book *In the Company of Women*, we explain that researchers have found "more men than women will attack by inflicting physical pain, but women are just as aggressive in their attempts at vengeance. They simply express it through the infliction of emotional pain instead— through indirect, rather than direct, means."

Problems can arise in the business setting from this indirect approach to conflict resolution. Jonathan, the medical director of a large hospital consortium, sent a letter to the chain's physicians asking their opinions on how the organization could better serve their needs.

Unfortunately, Jonathan and regional manager Nancy had agreed previously that all communication to physicians would go out through her—and this one had not. Later, Jonathan revealed he had heard from others that Nancy was furious. He waited for her to say something—he was ready to own up to his violation of their agreement, a small gaffe to him—but she never broached the subject.

"Nancy is someone who sees herself as open, but in reality she holds on to anger," Jonathan confided after this incident. "I don't know why she can't just deal with a problem when she has one." Nancy's indirect approach to conflict has made Jonathan reluctant to have her on his team. To him she seemed dishonest.

Jonathan's reaction is typical. Men often perceive such indirection as manipulative, or resistant behavior: Women are unwilling to "step up to the plate" and deal with the issue in a head-to-head fashion. They may think, "What a catty, gossipy woman." What our male colleagues often fail to understand, however, is that when we express dissatisfaction to others, we are attempting to preserve our relationships with them. Cross-cultural misperception frequently causes us to see the other's gender-culture as having a manipulative intent.

A more direct approach to conflict allows problems to be solved, and it *can* be accomplished without damaging the relationship.

▶ COMPROMISE

When you compromise, you split the prize down the middle. If you and Bob want the project, you may agree to each tackle half of it. In compromising you both win some, but you also lose some: You have an opportunity to work on the coveted project, but you get only half the rewards. The downside of compromise: One may use it to avoid the interpersonal work that occurs when resolving conflicts through collaboration, which we'll discuss next.

Compromise as such doesn't exist in sports (certainly it isn't glorified) unless you consider a tie, allowable in games like boxing. And aren't tie-breakers in football, hockey, and golf called "sudden-*death* play-offs"?

▶ COLLABORATION

When collaborating, two individuals find a way to work out their differences so that both are satisfied with the result. Suppose, for example, you disagree with your coworker on the best way to implement the plum project. You believe that it can be done quickly, say, in one to two weeks. Bob asserts it will take four months to do the job right. You can *compromise* and split the timing down the middle (you both agree to get it done in two months), but by doing so, you may avoid discussing the real issues. And you may come away from the discussion thinking Bob is lazy, while he might consider you impulsive and careless.

In contrast, when you collaborate with one another, you delve into why each of you has such disparate views on the subject. In inquiring of Bob why he feels four months are necessary, he might reveal that he had worked on a similar project previously and it blew up in his face when he didn't give it enough time. If he asks you the same question, he'll discover that you see an immediate problem that deserves everyone's prompt attention. By collaborating, you can both address the current pressing issue while you also avoid the pitfalls to which your colleague fell victim on the last go-round.

Consider how Margaret resolved the problem she was having with her assistant, Ashley. Margaret knew that Ashley regarded long word processing assignments as brainless work; she bristled at them. Yet Margaret had to produce a training manual in two months. She approached Ashley in a typically collaborative way.

"This manual needs to be out two months from now," she explained. "I know your feelings about massive typing assignments. Help me figure out how we can get this done."

In the end, Ashley chose to do a few pages of typing a day and the schedule was met. As the boss, Margaret could have simply given the assignment, but preserving the relationship was equally important, and a win/win approach was more productive.

Collaboration takes time and trust. To have a meaningful discussion you must both care about your underlying concerns, be willing to understand each other, and be open to influence. When you resolve conflicts collaboratively, you can improve your relationships with your coworkers because the level of trust increases. Then they're less likely to sabotage your progress and more apt to work with you in the future.

Women are most adept at collaboration because of childhood experiences. Girls learn to share. Good girls share equally with everyone. On a recent vacation to a small fishing village in Mexico, I observed just how differently girls and boys treat games. Two groups of children were playing ball. The girls gently hit the ball *to* one another, making sure that everyone got an equal number of turns. Down the beach a piece, the boys tackled each other, swiped the ball, and ran with it. Boys focus on doing better than their peers—girls, on being fair to them.

Similarly, at work, women are likely to look for solutions that allow everyone to win. Not to do so would damage relationships. And, as we have seen, relationships are extremely important to us. The collaborative win/win approach is preferable when

- two or more individuals or departments are working together and a team approach is needed.
- the other people involved are knowledgeable and committed to doing a good job. (Ignoring their expertise and enthusiasm could ultimately cause resistance and sabotage.)
- you have the time to include those who will be impacted by the decision or who are needed to carry it out. Inclusion fosters psychological commitment and support.

On the other hand, when we rely solely on collaboration, we may lose out in competitive situations. Because business is structured as a sport, at times we may find ourselves mired in conflicts that can only be resolved competitively. This puts women at a decided disadvantage, but as you will see, not a hopeless one.

▶ COMPETITION

In competition there is always a winner and a loser. If you're vying with your coworker Bob for the opportunity to head the plum project and you're competitive, you may do anything within your ethical boundaries to ensure that you achieve your goal: Drop comments about his incompetence, point out his past cost over-runs to your superiors, or even chip away at his confidence by pointing out his shortcomings—in short, pull out all the stops to undermine his winning the project.

How about just doing a better job to earn the project on your own merits? If Bob and your boss understand the rules of hardball, as I'm sure they must, your excellent credentials may be of little consequence to them. Indeed, Bob will try to weaken your position in any way he can. Even the most superior work can't compensate adequately for a negative smear campaign. After all, when you're in competition, it's you or him, and he wants to be the winner at all costs.

The truth is, men value a team that plays a hard game and gives them a run for their money. Competition is the driving force in male play. A good little boy is one who has embraced competition and strives to win. Men also see work in the same terms: our company (division, department) against the others; my performance against that of my peers. Competition is a bit trickier for women because it can damage relationships. When affiliations are important, competition may be inappropriate for us. On the other hand, men seem to overcome this difficulty, because when the game is over for them, it's over.

Competition is the American way. After a week of dog-eat-dog competition at the office, many men spend their weekends devoted to playing competitive sports and watching athletes duke it out on the football field, basketball court, or baseball diamond. Men revere winners.

To discover how you feel most comfortable resolving conflicts, try the following exercise.

HOW DO I RESOLVE CONFLICTS?

In your journal, draw five columns and label them: Accommodation, Avoidance, Compromise, Collaboration, and Competition.

1. Choose a week in which to observe your own behavior. Chart how often you use each resolution technique by putting a check in the appropriate column.
2. Determine if the problem was resolved to your satisfaction. Follow the check with a P for Positive and N for Negative.

3. At the end of the week, assess which conflict style you use most frequently and which one is most successful for you. They may not be the same.
4. Evaluate whether you'd like to alter your approach.

When you become conscious of how you resolve conflicts, you may choose to adopt other, perhaps more hardnosed approaches, when appropriate.

▶ WHY WE USE THE STRATEGIES WE DO

Boys grow up playing time-bound, goal-oriented games. The clock is ticking and they have only seconds to discuss their options. The coach, team captain, or leader will therefore decide the next move, and the rest will follow. If the team gets the ball over the goal line, they all win. Because of these childhood experiences, men see competition as cementing relationships on their team and establishing relationships with members of the opposing team. Competition is why they bother to play in the first place.

Girls engage in games that focus on getting along, being nice, and receiving approval. There is no time limit in which an activity must be accomplished. Therefore, girls focus on the interpersonal process. And because women strive for intimacy and believe a good relationship is based on personal closeness, we feel that competition and conflict are not only potentially damaging to good human relations but even their antitheses.

For these reasons, competition often doesn't sit well with women. Our preference is to make everyone a winner, but competition means someone has to lose. Women often see competition as intruding into their ability to get the job done. This ingrained attitude can harm us when it comes to playing hardball. The account that follows is an unsettling reminder of how badly we can get hurt when we refuse to compete.

Anna is the director of a human resources department in a large corporation. Her situation, while extreme, typifies power struggles in the business world. Here's how she described a major loss in a contest of wills:

My department was housed in a building far from corporate headquarters. The company was growing rapidly and we needed more space than we had. Unfortunately, we shared our facilities with another department that was expanding too. It was either us or them. One of us had to find new office space, and I decided it would be my team.

It took me a while to locate a suitable site that could accommodate our increasing needs. While I was searching, however, Peter, the manager of the other department, took matters into his own hands. Apparently, he was dissatisfied because we weren't moving fast enough. One Saturday, he had a crew come in and demolish the walls between our areas. They even tore out our bathrooms! Can you believe it?

When my employees and I arrived at work the following Monday, we were shocked. Our offices were a shambles, and we literally had to go outside and enter the building through another door in order to get to toilet facilities. I knew that this was fighting time, but I just didn't have the stomach for it. Even though Peter was my peer, he wielded a lot of power. Somehow, he had the ear of the people upstairs, and I believed I would probably lose this one. Instead of fighting, I got out of there as soon as possible, but I lost tremendous power and respect within the organization as a result of appearing like a whipped puppy.

What I should have done was go up a level to this guy's boss and voice my complaints about what a jerk he was. He destroyed our offices and didn't tell us. He undermined the effectiveness of my department. It took us months to recover. But I just gave up because I didn't want to compete with such an aggressive opponent.

▶ DEALING WITH CONFLICT THE HARDBALL WAY

Women can learn to be competent competitors, but it takes conscious decision-making and practice.

When conducting conflict workshops with women, I frequently ask participants what they'd like to get out of the day. A most common request is, "I'd like to get rid of conflict in my life." Fat chance! That won't happen until the day we die. Conflict is a reality of life, like taxes and death. When you put a group of people together in an organization and ask them to move roughly in the same direction at the same time, they are bound to differ on how best to achieve the goal. Conflict is inevitable. The problem for women is that we tend to cling to accommodative or avoidant strategies when alternative approaches would be more effective.

You may need to learn how to have good, solid conflict by adopting a competitive or collaborative style. *Conflict is important and constructive.* If you can't differ with someone else, your ideas will never get heard, let alone implemented, and you may get trampled in the bargain, as did Anna. Not only does conflict help you deal with a problem, you may win a better resolution as a result of going through it. For example, if you had worked out the conflict regarding the timing of the plum project collaboratively, you and your coworker would have been able to meet your immediate needs while avoiding past pitfalls. To play hardball, it's important to regard conflict as constructive. The follow exercise may help.

SEEING CONFLICT AS CONSTRUCTIVE

Answer the following questions in your journal:

1. Identify a conflict in your life that you avoided at first. Once you got into it, did your relationship improve?
2. Identify a current conflict that you don't know how to resolve. What's the worst possible outcome? What constructive outcomes might you have as a result of working through this conflict? How can you approach the conflict to create a win/win resolution?

In order to make the most of conflict, you may wish to use some of the competitive tools men seem to take for granted. The following hardball strategies can help you do just that.

▶ ATTACK THE PROBLEM, NOT THE PERSON

When you train your sights against an individual instead of his acts, he immediately will become defensive and may either tune you out or retaliate by attacking back. It's much more constructive to criticize the behavior rather than the individual. Make sure to use "I" statements such as "I'm concerned about this project," instead of "you" statements like "You always shoot from the hip." (On the other hand, it's ineffectual to say, "I'm concerned that you always shoot from the hip"!) Also, avoid using expressions such as "always" and "never," which inevitably make people defensive and incidentally can create self-fulfilling prophecies. Really, it's the success of the project that should be your focus. When you attack the problem, you describe what you see.

Read the following two sets of paragraphs. In each, the first speaker is attacking the person, the second is attacking the problem. Note the differences.

1. "Yesterday, when the customer came in, you didn't pay attention to him. Then, when he finally caught your eye, you were rude."

2. "I'm concerned because we want our customers to feel cared for so they'll come back. Yesterday, when Joe Smith came in, you kept him waiting, and when you did talk to him you abruptly asked him, 'What do you want?' I was surprised that you did this. It's not like you. What was going on?"

1. The female head of quality control says to the male head of manufacturing, "What's all this junk coming my way? Your guys aren't doing their part. They're sloppy, lazy, and inaccurate. We have to reject 10 percent of everything you produce."

2. "I'm seeing a lot of glitches with the fasteners coming our way. They are not made to spec. I'd like to talk to you about some of the problems we've been identifying so you'll know how to target your changes."

PRATICE ATTACKS

Read the next two paragraphs and in your journal write how these personnel could attack the problem rather than the person.

1. The nursing manager says to the night shift manager:"Your nurses aren't doing their jobs. They just sit around on your shift and ex-

pect us to pick up everything in the morning when we come in. We're sick of it!"

2. An office worker in a cubicle says to her neighbor: "When I'm away from my desk and my phone rings, you never pick it up. You don't care that my phone is ringing. You're always focused on what's going on with you, and you never give anyone else support when it's needed!"

Now, consider a complaint you may have about a coworker's performance. Write how you would approach him or her, dealing with the problem rather than the person.

▶ USE MIRRORING

When you mirror a coworker, you reflect back to him his point of view without necessarily adopting it. The following are mirroring statements:

- "I share your concern, Sam, about the fact that this is going to cost more than we've allocated in the budget, but I think we can recoup this money by the end of the year."
- "I understand, Toni, why you're concerned that if we stop and analyze this problem we may not meet the target date for the project. I know how important it is to the boss that we meet that date. But I'm concerned that if we don't deal with this problem now, it will cause us difficulties in completing the project later."
- "Randy, I agree with you that Sean's attack was completely unwarranted, but I'm afraid that if we undermine him at this point, it's going to cost us too much in the long run."

With mirroring, you let your colleagues know that you understand, appreciate, and even empathize with their position. You just disagree with the course they've charted. Mirroring statements sidestep defensiveness by affirming an individual's right to his perceptions without belittling them or giving in.

▶ STAND YOUR GROUND

Once, while I was out of town on business, I asked a new female employee to find out from Josh, the manager of another department, the production schedule for the employee handbook. Janet called Josh, but before she could get out her request he yelled, "You guys are always bugging me about your stuff. Don't you think I have anything else to work on? I'll let you know the schedule when I have time." And he hung up.

Because Janet had been with the company only a few weeks, I wouldn't have expected her to press the issue until we had spoken again; Josh was intimidating and she didn't know the political lay of the land yet. But I was impressed when I learned that she walked directly to his office, stood in the doorway, and said, "We need to talk."

Josh headed toward the door but Janet didn't budge. She said, "I didn't deserve to be talked to like that, and I want to get that information now." At this point, Josh became conciliatory, explaining all the pressures he was under. He even apologized. He never treated Janet so gruffly again—although he didn't let up on others.

Janet stood her ground assertively. She didn't accommodate Josh, but without screaming and carrying on she let him know he couldn't push her around or be rude to her. She simply told him firmly and clearly that his behavior was unacceptable, and he respected her for it. Josh saw Janet as a formidable hardball player.

How do you stand your ground? The key is to be strong and assert your needs without being destructive. In *Breaking the Glass Ceiling,* authors Morrison, White, and Van Velsor explain that women have a narrow band of acceptable behavior in which to resolve a conflict. Men have a wider latitude, but, unfortunately, if we become confrontive in a masculine way, we may undermine our own intentions. A woman who is consistently combative will be dismissed as a "raving bitch." Instead, it's better to refrain from giving in but also abstain from attacking.

To understand how the rules differ for men and women, consider the following events that took place while I was employed at a large corporation. My boss, Chuck, had been chewed out by his superiors. He stormed into our suite of offices that happened to be under construction at the time, grabbed a pile of metal door frames stacked in a corner, and flung them across the room. The staff ducked the flying metal.

Had a woman responded in this manner (she would have had to have been awfully strong!), most likely she would have been carried off in a straitjacket by the men in white coats. Her coworkers would have perceived her as a hysterical female who had lost all control and gone crazy. There was no such response to Chuck. Everyone carried on as if nothing had happened after he let off some stream.

Sometime later, Chuck hired a woman to be my peer. For reasons I never understood, Colleen didn't like the assignments he gave her, even though they were typical of the department's work load. Once the rest of the office staff and I heard her screaming at Chuck, "You can't tell me what to do. You have no right. You're trying to undermine me. Leave me alone." His office door was closed, mind you. From that point on, however, Chuck and the rest of the team perceived Colleen as nuts. He didn't want to fire her for fear of being sued, so he moved her to a job in which she did essentially nothing, and where she remained for many years.

Be careful. Taking the offensive can backfire.

▶ STICK TO THE ISSUE AT HAND

Women are brought up talking about relationships, but men are not. Consequently, men feel uncomfortable with discussions about the process of relating. When relationship issues do arise in the course of dealing with women, men are apt to flip the discussion to one involving data and facts. This strategy derails the issue, puts the man in the winning position, and absolutely mystifies the woman as to where she went wrong. I tell the following story to illustrate how women become distracted during conflicts. At a workshop on conflict styles, Frank bragged about how he won a fight with his wife:

Karen: "Get out of this bed! I don't want you sleeping here!"

Frank: "What do you mean, get out? I bought this bed. It's mine. I am sleeping here."

Karen: "How can you say that? This is our bed. We bought it together. It went on *our* credit card."

What's wrong with this picture? For Karen, the problem of whether or not she'll be sleeping with her husband is a relationship issue—it has to do with feelings. Obviously, she's so angry at something he has done, she wants nothing to do with him. Frank, on the other hand, has taken the conflict to "safe" territory, making it a factual, content-based conflict (who spent the money) to avoid the problem in the relationship. Unfortunately, when Karen refutes his assertion, she allows herself to become distracted by his tactics and loses her hold on the issue at hand.

Similar relationship/content conflicts occur frequently among men and women in the workplace. To keep the discussion on track, use the following strategy:

- Recognize whether you're having a relationship conflict, a content conflict, or both.
- If it's a relationship problem, acknowledge the content but stay focused on the relationship.
- If he doesn't want to deal with you, let go or escalate.

Here's how it worked for Mindy and Mark in the business setting. Mindy had a great idea about cutting her department's costs by using external independent contractors to do some of the labor. She had calculated it out and showed her figures to coworker Mark. But the next thing she knew, Harry, their boss, was describing in glowing terms the wonderful idea *Mark* had come up with to cut their department's costs by using external independent contractors. Mindy was angry, and she decided to talk to Mark about the issue of trust.

"Mark," she began, "when I tell you my ideas and you portray them to be your own to Harry, I feel I can't trust you. There's a big problem with us working together."

Mark was quick to deflect her attack. "Well, that wasn't really the best way to cut costs," he said. "I can think of lots of better way to do it."

Mindy was facing a choice here. Either she could allow herself to be waylaid by Mark's criticism and get involved in a factual, content-based argument about cost-cutting strategies, or she could persist in focusing on the relationship problem. She chose the latter, but first she acknowledged the content. "Mark," she countered, "the issue is not whether mine is the best approach. The issue is, I don't feel I can trust you."

At this point, she was fully prepared for a dose of typical female-bashing—which came right on schedule. "Oh, you women are all alike," Mark declared. "So emotional about everything. Let's just keep this professional." That's a man's way of ducking a relationship conflict.

"I'm not emotional," Mindy persevered. "I'm angry. You violated my trust and that's what I want to talk about."

Mark relented, and they had a heart-to-heart talk. If he hadn't, Mindy might have escalated by threatening to go to the boss the next time he pulled such a stunt. Or she might have let go for the moment while making a mental note to refrain from sharing her ideas with Mark in the future.

▶ TAKE OUT THE LEADER

I had a painful learning experience at one point in my career. Working in a large health-care company in which most of the top executives were attorneys, I quickly learned that lawyers exchange views through full-tilt arguments, not discussions. The first several times I presented reports or proposals to this group, I was taken aback by their reactions. It seemed that no matter how innocuous the subject matter, they'd loudly demand:

"Why do you say that?"

"Why didn't you do it some other way?"

"Why didn't you do it sooner?"

My initial response was always female: I looked inwardly to discover where I had erred. I very naturally interpreted the lawyers' aggression as being real and took their criticisms personally, rather than seeing their rejoinders as part of a game of "attack." For boys, part of a sport's fun lies in plowing into the other players, calling names, distracting one another, and piling on. Girls don't usually play "attack."

What to do once the blitz starts? The best approach is to take out the leader. I learned this lesson in an amazing self-defense course designed for women. Impact Self-Defense Training teaches one to defend oneself while under attack by up to four men at a time. I learned to fight viciously. This class dramatically changed how I would fight in a real attack, but much to my surprise it also significantly altered how I deal with the verbal muggers in a work situation. I learned to identify the leader: the most aggressive and verbal, he sets the agenda and pace. I would take him out first. Men are so hierarchical that if the leader is not there to continue the attack, often the others will simply back off.

I decided to apply what I had learned to the attacking lawyers. I used to try to explain my position to the nicest, least threatening of the bunch, since he seemed the most rational. Predictably, that never got me anywhere. To take out the leader, I now knew to single out the boss and deal only with him. When the others chimed in, I ignored them. If I had tried to deal with them all at once or attacked back, I would be doomed to lose the fight. But if I argued effectively with the boss, I had a chance of winning.

To argue the issue, I began by mirroring and validating my boss's concerns. That approach disarmed his defensiveness. To mirror, I'd say, *"I realize you're concerned about the budget and this project will take a long time but . . ."* Then I'd present my side of the picture and wind up with *"In the long run, this will save money because we'll be able to bypass many of the steps we go through now."*

Taking out the leader may feel "foreign" to you, but in the end you'll save yourself a lot of trouble if you go for the chief attacker first. That's how men play the game, after all, and it may be to your advantage to learn to play by their rules in this case.

▶ USE HUMOR

When facing the game of "attack" one-on-one, it's important not to attack back in kind. As we have seen, a woman who goes for the throat often loses more points than she gains, even if she wins the argument. Instead, try humor. It's a great weapon because it shifts the tone from attack to play. Management psychologist Barbara Mackoff explains in *What Mona Lisa Knew* that humor conveys authority by "making light of a situation without humiliating your opponent." It also defuses conflict, provides feedback, and builds support.

I discovered this lesson when I was forced to deal with the head of a division of the aforementioned health-care corporation. Indeed, I dreaded going to the regional headquarters in Houston because every time I set foot in the executive suite, I knew there would be trouble. I would tiptoe past Randy's glass-enclosed office, to little avail. He'd usually see me and yell, "Heim, get in here!" Once inside, no matter what the topic, within minutes he'd find a way to attack me, my boss, and the corporate offices. In truth, the issues were irrelevant, since Randy was blasting me for the fun of seeing me squirm.

I'd lick my wounds all the way back to Los Angeles and even confessed to my boss that I didn't want to go to Houston anymore. He wisely said, "Randy is difficult, I'll admit. But you need to learn how to deal with this type of person."

On my next trip to Houston, I heard, "Heim, get in here!" bellowing down the hallway as usual. But this time, when I sat down I said, "Well, Randy, it's so nice to see you. What are we going to argue about this time?"

He gave me an innocent look and replied, "What are you talking about?"

"Every time I come to Houston we get into an argument," I explained, "so I thought maybe we could just get the topic out on the table at the outset."

Still the congenial host, the division head said, "Pat, I have no idea what you are talking about. It's always such a joy to see you." We continued chatting. I then made an innocuous comment and out of the blue he shouted, "Bullshit!"

With a light tone and a smile that surprised even me, I said, "Oh, *this* must be what we're going to argue about. I've been wondering what it would be."

Randy looked shaken; I had diverged from our usual game of cat and mouse. "No, no, I don't want to argue about this," he said and backed down. We continued talking. He thrusted repeatedly, and each time I parried by acting relieved that we had finally identified the elusive topic of argument. My approach disarmed him. Indeed, this strategy was so successful that he stopped intimidating me altogether and eventually became a mentor.

Humor can relieve stress, put a problem into perspective, and distract an opponent from the fight. Since aggressive counterattack is not a viable option for us, humor can often fill the bill.

▶ NEVER DO CONFLICT BY EMAIL

If you are talking face-to-face with a colleague about a difficult situation and he begins to react in a negative way, you will likely recognize his nonverbal cues and make an effort to maneuver the conversation into safer waters. You might say, "I'm sorry. I didn't mean for you to take it that way. That sounded more negative than I intended." Even if you're on the phone, you can often hear in a colleague's voice that he responded more negatively than you meant.

But if you communicate a disagreement with a colleague in writing, he can take the conflict in a direction you never imagined. Written communication lacks the nuance of verbal or visual communication. Without subtle signals of voice tone or facial expression, it's easy to misread a person's true intent. It is therefore imperative to avoid conducting your conflict in writing—and that includes high-tech forms of written communication such as email.

While expediting the exchange of ideas, use of the Internet has also added an extra layer of complexity to conflict resolution, making what was once private quite public. Most of us have had the experience of sending an innocuous email to someone who, unfortunately, takes offense in a way that was never intended. He may counter with a stinging response, copying numerous individuals in the process. People who didn't have to be involved are dragged into the fray. If you reply via email, the conflict can morph into a huge mess.

If you have a bone to pick with someone, you must resist the urge to compose a quick email stating your complaint. It's difficult because this is just the kind of communication that women often tend toward and that gets us in trouble. Similarly, if someone sends you an email that pushes your buttons or hits you the wrong way, do *not* dash off a hurtful reply. If you feel the need to address the issue, pick up the phone or walk to the office of the person who sent you the email. You might say something like, "It sounds as if you're angry about the situation. Is that what you meant? And if so, let's talk about it."

▶ WHEN THE GAME IS OVER, IT'S OVER

On the playing field, boys are out to destroy the opposition. But when the final score is tallied, they have no problem going out with their opponents for the rest of the afternoon. A primary lesson boys learn is that when the game is over, it's over. Boys separate their feelings about a person from his behavior during the game. Girls, as a rule, do not. Since there are no winners or losers in dolls, the game is never over for girls.

Let's take this into the business setting. Recently I was interviewing the top executives of a computer components company for a team-building session. I talked with the chief financial officer for an hour and a half. He spent the majority of our time tearing apart the new operations manager. "He's arrogant and thinks he knows everything. He tried to threaten my job, and I don't even work for him. He talks down to people and demands instead of asking. He's inconsistent," the financial officer complained. As I stood up to leave, he smiled and said, "You know, I really like the guy."

This makes no sense to a woman. But for the financial manager, the way his peer behaves in his role as operations manager is unrelated to how he feels about him personally.

A woman told me she was in court once, watching the proceedings. The attorneys, both men, were viciously attacking each other. When the court recessed, everyone left except herself and the attorneys. One lawyer turned to the other and said, "You want to get a beer?" She was appalled at the lack of conviction in their anger. What she didn't understand was, the game was over.

Now, imagine two women ripping apart each other's ideas in a meeting. When they walk out of that room, do they still trust one another? Can they continue to work closely together? Would they go out for coffee? Not likely. In fact, it's implausible that women would engage in such behavior altogether, given how damaging it can be to a relationship. You're more apt to find a man tearing into a woman's ideas and then being thoroughly surprised that she took his attack "so personally."

I was talking to an executive about this difference in men and women and I could see, as we talked, that he had a sudden insight. He told me about Marsha, an employee with whom he had

had a serious disagreement regarding a change in companywide policy. He knew it was a major dispute, but he could not figure out why she held on to her anger after he had made the decision. Since he was unaware of our cultural differences, he saw her as a sore loser.

But I knew from talking to Marsha earlier that she perceived his strong-headedness as a character flaw that didn't vanish simply because the decision was over and done with. The angrier Marsha felt, the more her boss distanced her. From his point of view, she didn't know how to take a loss and go on. Since they misunderstood each other, they made value judgments that damaged their relationship.

From observing men in business situations, you can learn that when you've lost a round, it's important to drop the issue so you can play again another day. Men perceive the ability to move on as a strength.

▶ DON'T GET MAD, GET EVEN

While men regard business as just a game, women tend to see their work as an integral part of their personal lives. We don't compartmentalize different aspects of our lives—work in one cubicle, friendships in another. This integration can cause us to be mystified by male behavior.

I once sat in on a meeting at a Fortune 500 company where the top twelve executives were discussing a major project they had just lost to the competition. The president began the discussion by attributing their loss to their rival's underhanded business tactics, and he concluded the meeting with, "We don't get mad, we get even."

About a month later, executives of these two companies met at a conference and arranged to have dinner together. It was a congenial, laughs-and-smiles-all-around feast. I marveled at the executives' ability to genuinely have a good time, knowing that their ultimate agenda was to "get even" with their dinner mates, which they eventually did.

Between the hours of nine and five, men behave in any way they can to secure a project, make a sale, or win the game. After hours, these behaviors are no longer necessary. During a game of company softball or a friendly beer, men may use verbal bantering to establish their position in the hierarchy, but they will drop the subject of business for the evening.

Women find it hard to run hot and cold in relationships. Because we have friendships, and are not simply friendly, we don't switch modes as we go from a meeting to a social setting. We see this masculine behavior as insincere, because we filter it through our own cultural expectations. Indeed, your male superiors will expect you to be competitive *and* congenial as the situation warrants. It's a lot easier to accomplish this feat of duality if you see business as "just a game," the way men do. An important corollary here: Just because a male colleague is "nice" to you doesn't mean he's not after your job too. Beware!

▶ WINNING THE COMPETITION

You can win at hardball without being underhanded or strident, but you do have to be smart about your strategy. Take Michelle's situation. A successful regional sales manager for a packaged pastry company, she was about to clinch a national deal with a large convenience store chain. She was being challenged by a peer, John, who was out to sabotage her coup. To unravel her sale, he was arranging a similar deal with the convenience stores within his territory.

Michelle decided that she wouldn't roll over and play dead. She confronted John and told him she knew what he was up to. She wasn't going to let him win. She told him to drop his plans. Then she unearthed information about his inadequacies and dropped it into conversations she had with their boss. Finally, she managed a "casual" walk by the president's office to give him the good news about her potential sale and to warn him of the impending clash.

"John is going to call you and tell you about his deal," Michelle explained. "I just want you to know about the big picture. My deal is a potentially huge opportunity for our company, and I want to make sure we don't lose it."

As luck would have it, John called just as Michelle finished her piece. While the president listened, he smiled and winked at her, for she had correctly predicted what John would say.

As a result of fighting back on John's turf and on his terms, Michelle won a promotion within six months. Other women might

have been more indirect or might have become defensive and said,
"He's lying. I'm not going to give his misbehavior the honor of addressing it." But instead of becoming indignant or simply hoping
that her deal would come through first, Michelle made sure that
her side would win, and it did.

HOW TO BE A HARDBALL COMPETITOR

- If you can't be both liked and respected, make sure you're re-
  spected.
- Accept that you won't please everyone.
- It's nice if you can collaborate on decisions, but at times you'll just
  have to give the order.
- A direct approach to conflict will often work better in the long
  run.
- You've got to compete or expect to get walked over.
- If you're the target of the game of attack, take out the leader first.
- Remember that for men, business is just a game.
- When the game, argument, conflict is over, it's over, and your rela-
  tionship can revert to its previous form.
- Just because he's pleasant to you doesn't mean that he's not also
  out to best you.

5

HOW TO BE A TEAM PLAYER

▼

HARDBALL LESSONS BOYS LEARN

- Teamwork means sacrificing yourself for the good of the team, even if it means doing things you don't like.
- Good team players don't talk about personal needs.
- You are friendly with members of the team but can switch to another team next season.
- Other members don't have to be likable—just winners.
- Teammates speak the same language.
- Teams always have goals.
- Winning is all, so ruthlessness and cheating are tolerated.
- Team strategy needs to be organized before getting on the playing field.
- Team members need to wear uniforms.

▼

HOUSE AND DOLL LESSONS GIRLS LEARN

- Teamwork means finding a solution that meets everyone's needs.
- Doing your part as an individual is the best way to support the team.
- You are friends with your team—switching is disloyal.
- You need to like your teammates.
- Fairness is all, and it's fair to follow the rules.
- Dress is a form of self-expression.

▼ ▼ ▼ ▼ ▼ **O**rganizations are composed of individuals. Organizations have goals. A constant tension exists between an individual's interests, personal needs, and skills, and what the organization requires of her. We've all asked ourselves, How much of my own agenda should I sacrifice in order to help the rest of the staff meet the company's goals?

If a business is to function at all, staff members must share common goals and cooperate with others who have different skills and perspectives. This teamwork is crucial in the business setting; without it, a company would consist of many individuals blithely pursuing separate, unconnected activities. Nonetheless, given what we understand about male and female culture, it's not surprising that the two genders define teamwork in vastly different ways.

This became clear to me during a team building session with the top management of an accounting firm at which I asked participants to identify their responsibilities as senior managers. One group put "teamwork" at the top of their list. When I inquired what that meant, Rod, a former college football player, proudly stated, "Supporting each other regardless of your own feelings, carrying out company policies even if you disagree, and carrying the ball even when it gets tough."

I then asked the managing partner, Eva, how she would define the team. "Supporting each other, sharing information, and being willing to listen to ideas that may be different from mine," she replied.

Rod's definition focused on doing what is necessary even if you disagree with the boss and the decisions she makes. Eva's definition stressed intimacy and interpersonal supportiveness. Ironically, Eva and Rod found one another's definitions shallow. Eva interpreted Rod's explanation as blind obedience and a way to ignore any problems he or the company might have. Rod concluded from Eva's definition that she got what she wanted from her employees by playing on their emotions.

The troublesome part of this revelation is that both assumed they were talking about the same entity when they used the term *teamwork*. And in truth, their disparate conceptions had caused them problems in the past. Once, for example, Eva had suggested to her staff that they contact clients regarding investment potential. Rod, being the sort who follows the coach's orders obediently, no matter what the cost, took a whole week to contact clients, to the exclusion of all else. His approach made Eva unhappy.

"I didn't expect him to do that all week!" she told me. "It wasn't that big a deal. Rod should have come to talk to me if my suggestion seemed unreasonable."

Eva's expectation that he approach her if an "order" seemed unwarranted, of course, made little sense to Rod. As far as he was concerned, if the coach said it, he should do it. But while he followed blindly, Rod's regular work took a beating: Reports didn't get out on time and other client needs went unaddressed. Everyone loses out when the concept of teamwork is ill-defined. Both Rod and Eva were miffed at their teammate for not doing his or her part in the team effort.

▶ WHAT IS TEAMWORK?

Men grow up learning to sacrifice self for the good of the team. They understand that being a good team player means carrying out the agenda of those above them in the hierarchy. They call this teamwork. Women grow up attempting to find a win/win solution that meets everybody's needs. For them, doing good work as an individual means being a good team player. "After all," women think, "I'm holding up my end, and that keeps the team going." They call *this* teamwork.

The approaches are clearly different, yet the terminology is the same. When men and women don't recognize each other's disparate behavior as team oriented, conflict and confusion can result. How to resolve the teamwork dilemma for yourself? I believe the best solution is to first adopt the male approach and do what the coach asks, but then hold true to the female view and offer your own insights and perspective. To do that, first you must do what is asked of you. But then you can say, "I've done what you told me, and I've written up a couple of strategies that I think could even broaden your approach."

Nevertheless, to many women the male version of teamwork is a mystery. A woman might be cooperative and thoughtful (her version of teamwork) but still get zapped for not being a "player." Sherry, for example, spent several weeks visiting various departments in her company to collect money for the poor and homeless during the holidays. She didn't ask permission but took the initiative without her boss's blessing. Rather than garnering praise for her gumption, Sherry was criticized for not being a team player. Her boss saw her as a "loose cannon." In order for the hierarchy to function properly, everyone must be in his or her assigned position.

Had Sherry gone to her boss first with her good idea, he could have made the collection part of his PR effort. He might have said, "Let's make this the Real Estate Division's contribution for the holidays." As it stood, Sherry's generous and heartfelt (but individual) act worked against her position in the company.

At the end of one workshop, Jill told me she was afraid that she might be fired. During her recent performance appraisal, her boss had told her she wasn't a team player and that if she didn't become one she'd be out of a job. When she asked if he could explain what he meant, he simply said, "No."

I've often wondered if he was setting her up or if he had so internalized the concept of teamwork that he couldn't put it into words. I explained the male version of teamwork to Jill. Then I added, "Even if you were a great team member from the female perspective, your boss could not value your behavior. But you don't have to give up your bright ideas and become an automaton. You may have to adhere to your boss's wishes first, before you try to add your own. In fact, you may need to maneuver it so that he eventually appreciates what you see as a great opportunity. If you play the teamwork strategy right, he may even come to believe that your idea was originally his, which he might perceive as a positive development."

One of my clients was able to do this deftly while I looked on. Laurel was a physician on staff at a large hospital. Joseph, the institution's medical director and her boss, asked her to implement a new program he had devised in which doctors would set goals for themselves and then be paid according to how well those goals were met.

Joseph wanted Laurel to write a memo to that effect to the rest of the medical staff, but she knew that approach would be ineffectual. When physicians have decisions announced to them, they frequently resist. Rather than butting heads with her boss, however, Laurel replied, "Joseph, you were so successful in the last decision when you involved the medical committee. Your approach worked so well. What do you think of using the same strategy with this issue?"

Laurel was skillfully able to bring Joseph around to her position without stepping out of her role as the supportive team player who does what the coach says. And Joseph agreed.

To understand what your coach and your team consider teamwork, consider the following situations.

TEAMWORK DILEMMAS

1. Your department is falling short on profits. Your boss suggests you need to cut costs. Do you:
   A. Get out the expense sheet and begin to look at ways to slash departmental expenses?
   B. Ask the boss why he thinks expenses are the only thing the department needs to look at?
   C. Identify ways of cutting expenses but then suggest some ways of enhancing revenue that would strengthen the bottom line?

If you answer A, you're behaving blindly. If you answer B, you'll probably make your boss angry. If you answer C, you'll solve the problem. You'll be doing what your boss wants without questioning his authority, yet you also show your ability to think and contribute to the organization.

2. Your boss has decided to figure out why customers are unhappy with a product the company sells. He wants you to create a form listing reasons why the product might be returned. You're concerned that the real reason people return the product is more complex than can be assessed on a simple check-off sheet. Do you:
   A. Create the check-off sheet and mutter?
   B. Try to explain to your boss why his idea won't work?
   C. Create the sheet but then place some follow-up calls to customers to ascertain if information is accurate and complete?

Again, C is the best answer. You'd really be showing your teamwork savvy if you reported back to your boss as follows: "I'm so glad you suggested the feedback form. I've done some follow-up research and found that when customers call for service they get transferred so many times, and ultimately to the wrong department, that they get ʈfed up and return the product. Nothing's wrong with our product, but we've got a big problem with the phone system!"

▶ GROWING UP ONE-ON-ONE OR IN A CROWD

The men you work with grew up in a crowd. Most of their games required a group. As kids, they learned to maneuver among many and, like Rod, to sublimate their own points of view and agendas to those of the team without bringing up their interpersonal needs or feelings. (If a boy complained that he wasn't getting enough recognition for catching fly balls, for example, he would be chided for being a "crybaby.") Now, as adults in business, men's focal point is not relationships; instead, all eyes are on the goal, and each does what he can to help the team win.

You, meanwhile, were probably back in the house, playing with your best friend. Your play was highly interpersonal, and your primary agenda was to get closer to your pal. The play of girls doesn't have an external goal line; girls enjoy the process of being together and sharing intimacies. Women feel this relationship component to be very important at work, but men can become mighty uncomfortable when talking about personal issues.

Charlene told me that she was having difficulty getting along with her boss. She felt he was cold and distant and she feared he didn't trust her. "I'm going to make an appointment next week to talk to him about these issues," she said.

"Watch your step," I cautioned. "Your plan might backfire because you may have grown up discussing the interpersonal realm, but chances are your boss didn't."

Conversations about feelings are often strange and uncomfortable to men, especially in the work environment. Charlene's boss may not have had a problem with her to begin with. His distance might have reflected his idea of businesslike behavior; to him, work is not a social setting. Forcing him into a discussion may actually create a problem by heightening his feelings of discomfort.

He may see Charlene as a "wimpy" female who always wants to hash over "feelings." This may cause him to distance himself further, compounding Charlene's sense of alienation.

Rather than looking to her boss's interpersonal warmth to determine if all was well, I suggested to Charlene that she might better assess her position on the team by noting whether he had given her opportunities to "carry the ball." It's also a good idea to discuss specific work projects. By talking to her boss about her work instead of their relationship, she would most likely improve their communication, and he would feel more comfortable with her.

As a general rule, it may be wise to avoid bringing up personal feelings unless a male boss initiates the discussion. Even if a boss lets down his guard and "gets personal," it could backfire later when he feels uncomfortable or vulnerable for having done so. Indeed, if your boss does talk about his feelings, it's best never to bring them up later. Simply sit and listen without comment. Let it pass.

In their crowd, boys learn that feelings have nothing to do with work and reaching goals. If relationships sour, they continue toward their objective, even if they sabotage one another at a later date. This is in marked contrast to a "team" of girls, focused on the interpersonal realm. If relationships go bad among girls, it interferes with their ability to support one another, work together, and get the job done.

Katie had done her part to make sure a program was launched. She met every deadline that was required of her and produced a training manual in record time. Despite her terrific performance, she was surprised to hear that her coworker Matt was complaining she wasn't trustworthy. "What does he mean he can't trust me? I did everything I said I would do and then some." When she told me about this incident, I asked her if she had discussed the project and Matt's role in it with other people in the department.

'Sure," she said with surprise. "What does that have to do with it?"

According to Charol Shakeshaft at Hofstra University, men and women define "trust" differently. In fact, just like being a "team player," issues of trust are often gender defined. Men trust someone whom they perceive will not ridicule them or divulge what they say to others. Women see trust as carrying out your word or your promise.

"In talking about Matt to others," I explained to Katie, "he may have felt diminished and as if he had lost position in the hierarchy." To maintain trust with male team members it's important to realize that they are constantly assessing where they stand in the hierarchy and how your communication impacts that. And by the way, it's a good idea to never bad-mouth a team member. If you have an issue with another, you should talk directly with that person.

▶ YOU CAN'T WIN IF YOU'RE THE LONE RANGER

If you want to be successful in an organization, you need to be valued for what you're doing. Teamwork implies working with others. Even if you perform good works like Sherry did, collecting money for the homeless and needy, if you don't do it under the auspices of teamwork, your male colleagues won't appreciate your efforts. Most men do not value lone actions. The rugged individualist might make it as an entrepreneur and create his own team (who will then do what he says), but he will have difficulty fitting into an organization.

The director of education in a hospital once complained to me that a very powerful and arrogant doctor there made her life miserable. He was demanding, unappreciative, and imperious.

I suggested that Liz might want to get Dr. Logan on her team because he was powerful and was able to convince the administration to spend money on pet projects. "Have you seen any opportunities to do so?" I asked.

"Well, as a matter of fact," Liz replied, "this doctor needs to be recertified in CPR. He asked me to offer an evening class so he wouldn't miss seeing any patients during the day."

What a prime opportunity to lure Dr. Logan to her side. "What are you going to do?" I asked eagerly.

"I would never do what he asked! I'm scheduling that class during the day because he's such an ass," Liz retorted. "To give in to that boor of a human being would only reward him for his abuse."

Although I understood Liz's response, I knew that it certainly wouldn't get her very far. If Liz had arranged a special class just for Dr. Logan, she would have been further along in enlisting his support. And one day, he might have been inclined to reciprocate the favor. But the larger problem was that Liz didn't know she needed a team.

As women, we often see ourselves as independent agents, hired as individuals to do a job. We often fail to recognize the larger network of relationships on which business is run. The "I'll scratch your back if you'll scratch mine" approach appears wrong to us. The real agenda for women is doing what's right rather than helping each other to build power bases for personal aggrandizement. We cringe when we hear statements like "I'll support your efforts to create a new website in your project if you'll support me when I push for two new positions later this year." We'd prefer for decisions about the computer network and the new positions to be made on their own merits.

But in reality, such deals exist and greatly impact business decisions. You can either ignore them and lose a lot or learn to use your connections and get what you need more often. Think of it as chips in the game of poker. Through this reciprocity, as you build or lose social credits with them, others will either cooperate or attempt to undermine you. You may do a favor for a coworker because it's "right," but most men would expect you to cash in a chip for a favor in return.

Women frequently tell me that they just want to do their jobs. They "hate playing all these games." Often, however, they can't get the job done if the team doesn't support them. We work on a playing field, and in the game of hardball we can't make it without teammates.

▶ HOW TO BUILD A TEAM

It's critical to master the art of building a team. If you can't build one, you could be perceived as being unable to handle more responsible positions or projects. If you can, your department will be effective, you'll get the job done, and you'll become known by a broader range of people. The higher one gets in a company, the larger the stakes, and the more absolutely essential it becomes to build effective teams. Team building is highly related to future opportunities.

Before you set about building a team, you'll need to identify your key goals: you'll need to create a computer system that networks three geographical areas; a training manual for managers; and counseling support for families of terminal patients in a nursing unit.

Now that you know where you're going, assess who can help you get there. Get involved in networking. Consider people beyond your department or those high up in the hierarchy. You may need Rebecca in reproduction and Francine, the president's assistant. Sunny, the receptionist, may also be extraordinarily helpful.

Next assess who is likely to prevent you from reaching your goals for any of the following reasons:

- They'll lose power.
- You'll gain too much power.
- They don't like change.
- They see nothing wrong with the status quo.

Consider networking with as many of these critical players as possible. Can you share power and glory with potential saboteurs? Can you make it uncomfortable to continue with the status quo? Can you make it more comfortable to try your new way? For those who are predisposed to supporting you, assess what kinds of favors (chips) you can exchange to keep this loyalty. Your general strategy: How can you reward those who are helping and make it uncomfortable for those who are not?

TEAM-BUILDING ROUNDUP

Identify a goal you want to accomplish.

1. List the players who can impact your goal. Create two columns: those who can help make the goal a reality and those who can prevent it from ever happening. (Some people, such as your boss, may fit under both categories.)
2. Analyze each player's present stance with respect to you and your goal. Who can make it happen and is already on your side? Who can make it happen but wants to thwart you?
3. How can you get those opposed to you on your team?
4. How can you maintain the support you already have?
5. How can you dissuade those in a position to stymie your project from doing so? Can you trade on chips? ("When I

present my new ideas on promotion, I hope I can count on the kind of support I was able to give you the other day for your new project.")

▶ FRIENDSHIP VERSUS FRIENDLINESS

Relationships with team members may differ considerably from friendships. When we women commit to supporting someone, we do it with a vengeance that is foreign to most men. Our fierce loyalty can sometimes get in the way of our playing hardball by clouding our decision making and our ability to be strategic for fear of alienating a friend.

Women have friendships; men are friendly. The behaviors initially appear to be the same, but the underlying rules differ. For women, a friend is a friend in all situations: in a meeting, at lunch, when the boss is displeased with your performance, and when you have competing needs. But the friendliness that men practice comes and goes as needed. Women grow up with a devotion to their best friends. Men switch sides and loyalties as easily as they shed one team jersey and don another. Consider how effortlessly trades are made in baseball at the end of each season!

Tara, president of a medium-sized company that provides temporary personnel services, almost fell victim to the loyalty trap. Much to her consternation, she was being recruited for a top executive position in a large national organization that was one of her major competitors. The job intrigued her, the pay would have been great, and she didn't even have to move. Yet when I asked why she seemed so reluctant to take the position, Tara explained, "I've always seen this large company as my enemy. Over the past several years they've made a concerted effort to woo away my company's customers. To work for them would be disloyal."

I pointed out to Tara that this was a very female way of looking at the situation. "I know," she admitted. "The recruiter, Simon, thinks I'm crazy." Eventually, the logical, career-oriented part of Tara's personality won out. She took the job and in the first year saved the new company $1.25 million.

One of our great strengths is our loyalty to friends. But businesses are hierarchies, and mixing friendship with hierarchical relationships can lead to no-win situations. I've seen women's commitment to friendships hold them back in their careers. Anne was given the opportunity to advance and become a supervisor, but she declined the promotion because she felt disloyal leaving her friends. Even worse is the prospect of competing with a chum for a position. I have seen women adamantly refuse to apply for a promotion because they know a buddy is interested in the job. Men see such competition as part of the game: "May the better man win." Most woman perceive it as betrayal.

With experience and training, however, we can overcome the tendency to place friendship above business decisions. I was once asked by the CEO of a computer software company to work with his president. Lucy was a brilliant strategist and a genuinely good human being who cared about her employees. But the fact that she had become good friends with one of her vice presidents was causing a significant problem in the organization.

Alan was a charismatic charmer who had hooked Lucy with the force of his character. He was performing poorly, but Lucy had difficulty giving him honest feedback because she was his friend. When he complained that she was being too hard on him, she retreated even further. The situation only got worse. He griped about her to his employees, and tried going behind her back to air his grievances with the CEO.

When Lucy and I met, I explained the difference between friendship and friendliness and suggested she back off into friendliness. Finally able to conceptualize the problem, Lucy began to change. She set up weekly performance assessment meetings, followed by monthly written reviews of Alan's goals and accomplishments. She asked me to sit in on one of these monthly sessions.

Lucy began by discussing the accounts receivable, which had climbed to an all-time high. "This is a much higher rate than you and I agreed on three months ago," she said to Alan.

"Come on, you know how hard I've been working," he shot back. "We're trying as hard as we can to get the accounts receivable down. You're not being fair." Alan knew that fairness was a real issue for Lucy; she was always second-guessing herself about impartiality. This was a true test of her mettle; could she resist the friendship/fairness button?

"You and I made an agreement about the accounts receivable," she replied matter-of-factly. "And you broke the agreement." Alan could no longer count on a knee-jerk response from Lucy. Eventually he quit his job because he was no longer able to manipulate her and get away with his nonperformance.

The loyalty that we develop as women is to be lauded in those relationships among equals that are built on long-term commitment. But loyalty can interfere when you have to play hardball: It is difficult to appraise a friend's performance, give a friend a tough assignment, or openly disagree with a friend at an important meeting. By being friendly instead of making friends, men can quickly form and reform alliances when necessary.

How can we women learn to do the same? Try the following three-step approach:

1. Express yourself. Talk with your female friends about the importance of being able to disagree.

2. Take it up a level. Explain that the issues are not about damaging relationships but about the content of the disagreement. "I don't want you to take it personally" can go a long way in assuaging hurt feelings.

3. Move on. It's important to be able to disagree and then move on from there without jeopardizing the relationship.

Such behavior is not always easy for women to take. A man may vehemently disagree with a female colleague in a meeting and tell the boss her idea is no good. His colleague is likely to feel deeply betrayed by this behavior unless she understands it as a normal part of competitive hardball.

If you should find yourself in such an unpleasant situation, stay focused on the fact that this is a game for him. He's being competitive in the only way he knows how. It feels and sounds like a personal attack and a betrayal of friendship, but it isn't. It's just not convenient for him to be friendly right now.

Instead of thinking, "What did I do to this guy to make him turn on me?" you need to come up with ways to argue back: "What do you mean, I don't have experience? I did three projects like that before I came here." Then, rather than becoming defensive, go on the offensive in face of an attack: "You're just unaware of my experience. If you were more informed, you wouldn't say that." When you walk out of the meeting, drop the topic. The argument never happened in terms of your relationship and shouldn't affect it positively or negatively.

The following exercise should help you prepare for a challenge from a coworker.

DEFLECTING A SURPRISE ATTACK

Think of a time when you received a surprise attack from a friend.

1. What was your reaction? "I didn't deserve that." "Why is he attacking me?" "I thought he was my friend." Write down your honest thoughts.
2. What alternative self-talk could you use in that situation? "He doesn't know what he's talking about." "I'm the best person for the job." "What can I say to shoot down his negative comments?" Write down your thoughts.

▶ PLAYING WITH PEOPLE YOU DON'T NECESSARILY LIKE

To win a game, boys know they need team members with certain attributes: agility, coordination, a strong throwing arm, a good eye, toughness. Similarly, when choosing a team to work with, men will look for the qualities they need to reach the goal, without regard for whether a team member is a good human being.

Women, in contrast, choose to be with people who are "nice." If we feel we can't trust a colleague, we want nothing to do with him. As a result, we may unintentionally limit the resources available to us.

Brenda managed the personnel department in an aerospace firm. For several years she lacked the financial backing to implement some of the programs she considered vital. Her major stumbling block was Todd, the budget manager, who restricted what she could budget in certain categories and then further dictated how she could spend the money. He wasn't nearly so stringent with managers who were his buddies.

When Brenda complained to her boss, he shrugged off her

grievance, saying, "Brenda, you have to learn to fight your own battles."

At a workshop on women in business, I suggested to Brenda that she strike up a friendship with Todd. She bristled at the idea. "I can't stand the guy. He's a bully who just likes to throw his weight around."

I pointed out that personality had nothing to do with it. "Todd may be a bully," I explained, "but you need him if you're going to get the money you require to pursue your goals."

Brenda reluctantly agreed to give it a try. Three months later when I ran into her, I realized she was beginning to learn the rules of hardball. "I started being very nice to Todd," she said. "I helped him out with a sticky personnel issue and we've even been out to lunch a couple times. He's not someone I'd choose to spend a lot of time with, but having him on my side sure makes things a lot easier."

Many men don't find themselves in this tug of war. To work well with someone, they need only be friendly. They don't feel the need to let others into their interpersonal world of feelings and relationships. It's habitual to keep others at arm's length. Personal feelings are beside the point. This can feel hypocritical to women because of our feelings about friendship. But in hardball, all you really need is friendliness. Getting to the goal is the only issue.

▶ I DON'T WANT TO LEARN FINANCE

Being a team player also means doing things you don't particularly like. You participate because you're part of the team, and the good of the team is your first responsibility.

Once I was trying to schedule a workshop at a hospital. The director of nursing said to me, "Well, Thursday morning is the finance meeting. Nursing is invited but we usually don't go, so let's schedule the workshop then."

This seemed odd to me, because a hospital's financial resources are usually a major bone of contention, especially for nursing.

So I said, "Tell me, Dorothy, why are you skipping the finance meeting?"

"Oh, they're so boring," she replied. "I don't know what they are talking about half the time, and the other half, I don't care."

I am quite sure those meetings *were* boring, but important skirmishes took place there and much could be won or lost. If the director of nursing wasn't present to represent her team, the nursing department would be the big loser, especially since Dorothy wanted to institute a pet project—a new counseling service for terminally ill patients—that needed financial backing.

When I voiced my opinion, Dorothy said, "Look, I went into nursing to care for patients. Those finance people speak a foreign tongue. I'd rather leave them alone to play with their numbers." But she shouldn't, because if she does, her team will lose access to information and money.

Liz, the director of education whom I mentioned earlier, did learn to carry out unpleasant tasks for the sake of the team. After our conversation regarding the loathsome Dr. Logan, she decided to offer a special evening CPR course. Before she advertised it, she checked it out with him to see if it cleared his calendar. She mentioned that she had set this special date just to suit his needs. He attended the class and as a result was more courteous to Liz than he had ever been. Liz later said to me, "I didn't like doing it, but I can see the payoff it got me."

▶ KNOWING THE TEAM'S GOAL

Even though you're a doctor, a lawyer, a financial analyst, or an office manager, you're also a salesperson. Sales may not be part of your job description, but the degree to which you can sell your ideas will determine how successful you will be in realizing them. Teams always have goals; it's their raison d'être. Thus, when you sell your ideas, you need to show how they will help your team meet its stated (and unstated) goals.

Isabelle was the human resources director in a manufacturing company focused on getting "parts out the door." What mattered most to the company was how many parts were shipped in a given month. The organization was chronically behind in its shipments, which meant it was chronically behind in making money.

By interfacing with employees, Isabelle had become acutely aware that their morale was abysmal. Consequently, she called a meeting of the executives and presented a program to boost morale by instituting an employee-involvement program to identify and solve problems. As she talked, however, she could see the executives' eyes glaze over. She and her idea were dismissed before she was able to present her plan in its entirety.

"I'm frustrated and angry that the executive committee was not open-minded enough to care about employee morale," she said in a meeting with me.

"Well, what *do* they care about?"

"All they talk about is parts out the door," she complained.

"In that case," I advised, "you need to show your team how you can help them reach that goal."

A couple of months later, Isabelle unveiled her idea to increase productivity. She shared research on the correlation of employee involvement, attitude, and productivity. "They looked at me entirely differently," she told me. "They listened and even asked questions. And then they adopted my program."

Fortunately, as Isabelle learned, you can usually put your ideas across in such a way that you can do the right thing and win.

▶ WOMEN'S INVISIBLE WORK

Emily had watched her colleagues labor away on a project that eventually just fell to pieces. It was a big disappointment for her department that she swore she would avoid in the future. Six months later, her team was given a similar assignment. Having observed the earlier failure, she wanted to make sure that her team didn't fall into the same hole. She invited several of her colleagues to speak with her current teammates to share the hard lessons they'd learned from their debacle. As a result, Emily's team succeeded where the other had failed. Ironically, however, since no problems occurred on this new project, Emily's efforts at smoothing the way went unnoticed.

Women bring many strengths to their work teams; often they are the team glue. They connect people to prevent reinventing the wheel. They help individuals communicate with one another. This social activity can actually prevent problems, as it did for Emily and her team. However, it's human nature not to notice when things go well. We just take it for granted, and that hard work becomes quite invisible.

Indeed, as Joyce Fletcher at the Center for Gender in Organizations at Simmons Graduate School of Management explains, such relational work is *not* seen as strategic or important in many organizations. Technical skills are valued, so "women's work"—the fostering of social connections and communication—often disappears. It's a lot of behind-the-scenes labor that is neither recognized nor compensated.

Fletcher suggests that it's important to get credit for this valuable work. Talk about it. You might, for instance, mention to your boss and other powers-that-be the importance of the connective tissue within and across teams. Talk up what you have done in terms of this social "grease" with those who can impact your career. It's time to render this invisible work visible by naming it and recognizing its importance.

▶ DO YOU WANT TO WIN OR DO YOU WANT TO BE FAIR?

Men like to win; women like to be fair. While boys are told "it doesn't matter whether you win or lose, it's how you play the game," very few ever believe it. If you're going to play a game, the whole point is to win. For girls, on the other hand, relationships are what matter. Being fair enhances closeness and equality.

As a result of this early training, men and women come into business settings with different approaches to doing the "right" thing. For men, acting correctly means doing whatever it takes to achieve a goal; for women, it means doing what's fair for all. Because these motivations are so central to us, we frequently don't notice that our colleagues are working from a different frame of reference.

If your company is forced to down-size, chances are you will become immediately aware of just how different these frames of reference can be. I recently worked with a medium-sized tool and die company that was laying off about sixty employees. The senior managers had come together to plan the layoff and to discuss employee severance packages, as well as how employees were actually going to be told (one-on-one, small groups, or one large group). Corinna, the human resources director, and Heather, the director of information systems, were the only women on the nine-person team.

"I think one month's severance pay is the fairest sum," said Corinna, when the discussion rolled around to payoffs.

Heather concurred. "We should let the employees know one by one," she added. "That would be the least painful and most respectful way."

But the men, including the president, kept coming back to the minimum they could offer without getting the company into "legal hot water." In fact, the men thought it best for security if the laid-off employees were escorted from the building by a guard, since they might be incensed at their rotten deal and attempt to retaliate.

"It's not fair to treat loyal employees this way," Corinna and Heather protested. For the men, however, fairness had nothing to do with it. They wanted to do what was right in order to win, and to them winning meant keeping as much money for the company as they could get away with without being sued.

Despite our inclination to the contrary, winning often takes precedence over fairness in the game of hardball. In a company where I worked, a manager fired a long-term employee without cause. He then used that man's salary to start a major project bringing him high visibility and a possible promotion. The manager saw it as a good strategic move and felt the employee would be able to get a job elsewhere.

In the ensuing water-cooler discussions, the female employees tended to focus on how unfair it was to fire a worker without cause. They considered the manager cruel and ruthless. The men, on the other hand, speculated on the manager's new project. They thought he had made the right move; furthermore, they stated, "If you can't stand the heat, get out of the kitchen."

These profoundly different viewpoints leave us feeling uncomfortable and suspicious of the other gender. What can you do about these feelings? It's best to remember that men are from another culture. They may do things differently, but that's just their way. It's important not to take their approach personally because it's not personal, it's cultural. But how do you achieve what you're after—let's say equity, in the case of Corinna and Heather and the laid-off employees? At times like these, it's best to present one's ideas in a way that men will value them. It may be wise, for example, to couch the "fairness" agenda in "winning" terms based on the company's goals.

For instance, Corinna might have said, "You know, from the data from outplacement companies, we've learned that employees who go through an outplacement process are less likely to sue for unfair termination. If we treat these laid-off employees fairly, we'll be the big winners in the end."

▶ CHEATING

Some years ago, I read about an incident that occurred at my alma mater, the University of Colorado. During the final game of the football season (and football is big at Colorado) the team was down to the last play and final down. The ball was on the one-yard line. If the team could get it over the goal line, they were going to the national championships. They were unsuccessful in this attempt, but contrary to the rules of the game, the referee mistakenly gave them another (fifth) down. They took advantage of his error, scored, went to the championships, and won.

I was so appalled by this I really didn't think the story could be true. Some time later, while speaking in Boulder, I ran into the sports editor of the local newspaper and asked him if this incident really happened.

"Yeah," he confirmed, "sure did."

"I can't believe the team would take advantage of such an obvious mistake on the ref's part," I exclaimed. "How could they really feel like champions when they didn't earn it honestly?"

"Well, they were given the down. Why wouldn't they take it?"

Boys learn that fouls are part of the game. You break the rules and try not to get caught. There is no parallel in female culture. Behavior is either right or wrong, good or bad. This was brought home to me during a gender differences workshop with a group evenly split between men and women. I asked the men to tell us the lessons they had learned playing team sports.

"How to be a leader," one said.

"Taking criticism," said another.

Soon the lessons were flying thick and fast.

"How to lose."

"Doing what the coach says."

"Taking a hit."

"Looking aggressive even if you're not."

They had listed about a dozen when three men simultaneously said, "To cheat."

The women in the group gasped. One of them spoke up. "I'm shocked. What do you mean to cheat? You'd better explain." The other females nodded and murmured in unison.

The men, meanwhile, were surprised by the women's reaction; cheating seemed so obviously part of the game, it was hardly worth discussing. Eventually one participant said, "Whenever the referee, the umpire, the opposition, whoever, turns his back, you get away with what you can. That's how the game is played."

That's even true in professional sports. During a recent Oakland A's game, a player was talking to the commentator about throwing spitballs. "I didn't get caught so I wasn't cheating," he said. For him, bending the rules was all part of the game. Holding and face masking in football and fouling in basketball are all expected modes of cheating in sports.

To women, however, rules dictate how one should conduct oneself. It's fair to follow the rules. But for many men, rules are rules only if you're caught breaking them. Indeed, women usually believe that if cheaters get caught, the system will deal with them properly. That's not always the case. I knew a man, for instance, who had just gotten his first job out of graduate school. Jeremy was sent back to his hometown on a business trip. The last night of his stay there, his old high school buddies joined him in his hotel room and ran up a huge room-service bill.

Jeremy returned to work contrite and shamefaced. He was embarrassed to tell his boss about the bill for fear of losing his job. Finally, when he got up the nerve to confess, his boss said, "Here, let me show you where to hide it on the expense form."

Men apply this hardball lesson to business every day. I was surprised once when an executive in a company where I worked told me with relish how he had bought an entire set of luggage and had put it on his travel expense form. His boss, he said, never caught on. I wasn't astonished that he had done it, since he was a pretty sleazy character, but I was shocked that he'd tell me about it with such pride.

Early on in my work life, I made a rare visit to my boss's manager. While we were discussing another matter, he took a call from a supplier, Jack, confirming a meeting at four that afternoon. Five minutes later, Michael, one of Jack's competitors, called. My boss told him that he had definitely bowed out of his commitment to Jack. As he talked with Michael, my boss smiled and winked at me, indicating "I'm really putting it over on this guy." I remember blushing. Mortified for this manager, I was utterly mystified that my boss would lie so blatantly in front of me and not be embarrassed about it.

To women, cheating is a moral issue. But it looks and feels entirely different to men. As Jinx Melia explains in *Breaking into the Boardroom,* "The Japanese language contains words used only by males and others used only by females. If the same were true in English, 'bluff' would be a masculine verb." When it suits their purposes, many men don't hesitate to bend the truth.

Where do you draw the line between cheating and stealing, hardball tactics and corruption, sleaziness and crime? Corporate corruption at Enron and Worldcom are good examples of what can happen when cheating gets out of hand. And the government—and society in general—fluctuates as to what's acceptable and what isn't. Although I have my own standards of behavior, I believe it would be presumptuous of me to dictate proper business ethics. Values are set by the time one reaches adolescence. You need to be true to your own values in determining the lines you won't cross, no matter what the cost.

Nevertheless, even though you may strongly believe in always telling the truth—as I do—sometimes you may find yourself in a situation where you have no choice but to bend the facts a bit. You may even be forced to do so for the sake of your organization's solvency. Sharon was the vice president of patient services at a hospital in a very affluent community. Shortly after signing a five-year contract for space in a nearby office building, the hospital changed its long-range strategy and no longer needed the space. Sharon's boss, the executive director, assigned her the thankless task of getting out of the lease.

Sharon first tried offering the landlord a financial incentive. No go. Then she cajoled and argued, to little avail. Finally, she had the following plaque installed on the door of the offices: ADOLESCENT PSYCHIATRIC TREATMENT CENTER. A few days later she put a handwritten sign under the plaque: "To the tenants: We will soon be opening our treatment center for mentally disturbed teenagers. If you find anyone using drugs in the bathroom, writing graffiti on the walls, or harassing you or your clients, please let us know. Bay Hospital Administration." Within two days, the hospital was out of the lease.

How expert you become at bluffing is a decision you must make yourself. Although I'm not suggesting that you move whole-sale into the world of lies and deceit, I do believe you must be aware that others cheat and bluff during games of hardball, and at times you may need to adopt these strategies yourself.

▶ SPEAKING THE LANGUAGE

Every team develops its own language. In addition to acting as shorthand, team jargon marks who's 'in' and who's "out." Indeed, corporate language is fluid. If, for example, the president begins using a new buzz word, you can be sure the rest of the staff will pick it up in short order. (If a secretary were to initiate it, however, no one would notice.) Acronyms for business functions such as R & D, ROI, ECO, SEC, STAT, STET, MEDS, IPO, and RAM all depend on professions, industries, and organizations. The more you can sound like one of the "in" group, the more likely its members will consider you an integral team player.

If you don't speak the same lingo as other team members, you won't be treated as an equal. In addition, you may feel confused or may lose an opportunity to make a valuable contribution. If nursing director Dorothy really wanted to become a powerful player, she not only needed to learn that ROI means "Return on In-vestment" but she also had to be able to argue that the new serv-ice she wanted to institute, counseling for families of terminally ill patients, would have a high ROI because family members would feel positive about the hospital and come back for future services. If she can't speak the budget director's language, she won't be on his team. And consequently she would be unable to sell her ideas or meet her department's needs.

At times, your right to be a member of the team will be tested by whether you can speak its language. Not too long ago, I was sitting in on a meeting at an airplane manufacturing company that hired me to do team building with their executive staff. A new member of the executive team clearly wasn't sure about having a woman involved in the development process. To test me, he began talking about whether the high number of ECOs had anything to do with a gap in communication.

Fortunately, I had worked in aerospace for a couple of years and knew about engineering change orders—ECOs. If, on the other hand, I had had to ask this man to define his terms, I would have destroyed my own credibility, and he would have possessed all the necessary ammunition to exclude me. I answered that his supposition was probably right, he visibly relaxed, and that was the end of that.

If you find yourself at a meeting where computerese is the only language spoken and you're an illiterate, what do you do? If you're a woman, most likely you'll find a way to blame yourself for your ignorance. You may think, "I'm not equipped to be at this meeting. . . . I should never have been chosen," or, "I should know this but I don't." The typical male response, on the other hand, is to go on the offensive: "I don't know what in the heck you guys are talking about! How 'bout if we speak English for a change?"

If you're among peers an effective approach might be to say, "You're all using computerese, and I don't understand the language. Could you explain or use common terms that a layperson would understand?" If, on the other hand, you're at a big meeting or find yourself the low person on the totem pole, you can't ask for explanations without drawing attention to your ignorance. In that case, it's best to list the terms you don't understand and ask a trusted colleague after the meeting. And make sure to bone up on computer jargon for future meetings.

▶ MANEUVERING BEFORE AND AFTER A MEETING

Meetings are one of the most visible arenas in which you are expected to display your team affiliation. Yet the inner workings of meetings are often a mystery to women, particularly since most of us ignore the fact that *real* meetings actually happen before the meeting ever takes place and after it's over. Failing to understand this aspect of team play can undermine your progress.

Take Amy. When she became the medical director of a large community clinic, she decided that the clinic could offer better care and save money if it hired specialists instead of sending patients out to see them. But to do so meant a major restructuring of the medical staff. Amy presented her plan at an executive staff meeting. "While my colleagues seemed to get the logic of it," Amy reported, "they still fought me." She came to me seeking advice on how to meet her objective. I was sure from her explanation that the men on her team had felt blindsided.

"Did you, by chance, present the idea for the first time in the meeting?" I asked.

"Of course," she replied, surprised that I would even ask.

Amy had made the common mistake of assuming that meetings happen in the meeting. She didn't understand that men resist being influenced in public situations—it puts them one down in the hierarchy. They're more amenable to being swayed in private, since they're not as vulnerable to being shown off as wrong in front of their colleagues. She also failed to realize that she needed to get her team organized before she went onto the playing field. If she had button-holed each of the "players" ahead of time, explaining her idea and the personal advantage to each of them in supporting her, when the meeting itself came around, her plan would have been accepted with greater ease.

Women are often astonished that they have to go through this process and they may attribute ill intent for why men don't have the meeting during the meeting. "What's the point of having a meeting if you don't do the business there?" they will ask me. Others say, "It feels so slimy and political . . . like the 'smoke-filled room' of yore. Why not just have everything out in the open?" Rather than having this negative twist, it's important to understand that the drive behind the meeting-before-the-meeting is neither exclusionary nor negative but rather an attempt to save face in public.

If you've got a great idea you'd like to implement, you need to do your homework. Before you arrive at the appointed hour, consider who will be there and who will have a say. Certainly, a key person to get on your team is your boss. Secure his or her buy-in and commitment before the parley. You won't have a prayer if you try to do it during the meeting.

Also keep in mind that the rest of the meeting takes place after the fact, in informal gatherings at lunch, in the hallway, and in the restroom. To the degree that you can, you need to participate in these groups. Whether your idea really gets carried out may be determined there.

Obviously, what happens at the urinal can be off limits to you unless you're someone like Jackie. I was preparing to work with the board of directors of a national medical society. The chair brought me up to speed about Jackie, the only woman on the board. He described her as "'tough as nails." It seems that during the break at a previous board meeting, four of the members, including Jackie, were walking down the hall discussing the politics of the organization. The three men made a turn into the men's room. Jackie followed right along behind them. They were stunned and asked her, "What's up?"

"You weren't going to have this discussion without me, were you?"

The chair told me that the men are now very careful about discussing board issues in the restroom because they're afraid Jackie will come in. Sometimes we think there's nothing that can be done about a situation, but often you can push the limits beyond what you expect. I believe Jackie's tactic worked well because she was a well-respected member of the board. But gestures such as hers need to be used sparingly and with aplomb.

▶ USING MEETINGS TO YOUR ADVANTAGE

Of course, much jockeying for position and hierarchical activity occurs during the meeting itself. Knowing the unspoken hardball rules of meetings can help you use them to your advantage.

First, know your place in the hierarchy. If you're among peers, you can ask questions and challenge in a way that you can't if your boss invites you to a meeting she normally attends. Check out the corporate culture of meetings in your organization. I was seated next to a studio boss at a major fundraiser recently, discussing how men and women use language differently. He cut me off and told me that the person he listens to is the one with the strongest point of view, the one who can argue his or her case most vehemently. This style may or may not fly in your company. Observe others and how they behave. Experiment with different behaviors. In some companies a senior executive will bring a junior member along to see if she's got a brain and can speak. In others, the junior executive is expected to keep her mouth shut and observe. If you're not sure which it is, ask your boss what he wants you to do.

You can control a meeting by controlling the seating. The ends of a rectangular table are positions of power; people seated there give the impression of presiding. If you'd like to control the meeting's agenda, get to the conference room early and take a position at the head or foot of the table. On the other hand, if you want to equalize power as King Arthur did, use a round table.

One of our greatest female strengths is our ability to read nonverbal cues: who is with us, who will resist, where the coalitions are, and so on. We can use these observations to our advantage during the meeting. Despite our astuteness, however, some women may unwittingly undermine their position by trying to flatten the structure. They may challenge the power brokers, contradict the boss, or even argue and ask the deadly question "Why?" Failing to abide by the hierarchical structure within a meeting can cause you to lose points and position.

Intrateam meetings differ from interteam gatherings. In the former, you may be able to argue with your teammates about the best approach. In the latter, however, your team will want to present a united front. This is not the time to bring up ideas of your own. You need to know and show which team you're on. During interteam meetings you may also face the following dilemma: Do you behave like a man—that is, lock down and be closed to influence—or do you leave yourself open to be influenced and be perceived as a traitor to your team? In this case, it's best to feel out the values of the person above you in the hierarchy. If your boss wants you to toe the party line, and you don't, it will cost you. If your boss is open-minded, it won't.

For other verbal and nonverbal strategies that can help you appear powerful during meetings, see Chapters 7 and 8.

▶ THE TEAM UNIFORM

For women, clothing is an expression of self. Because women see attire as a means of communicating who they are, if I were to suggest that a woman's outfit is inappropriate, it's tantamount to saying that she herself is inappropriate, somehow "wrong." On the other hand, I hear many women complain about the beautiful but unworn sweaters or ties they buy their husbands. The women are thinking fashion, but the men are thinking team.

Since men usually dress in a routinized (some might say boring) way, we often make the mistake of assuming that dress is unimportant to them. And while it may be true that most men are relatively unaware of or unconcerned with fashion, they are acutely mindful of how their team dresses. To many men, work clothing is nothing less than a team uniform.

I recently ran into a former colleague, Eva, who had just returned to the work force after staying home and caring for her children for several years. Eva was taking this precaution because she was convinced that her husband, Paul, a senior executive in one of New York's largest banks, might soon lose his job.

In this bank, men had traditionally worn ties with diagonal stripes—until the bank hired a new president who wore nothing but paisley ties. On his first day, the president met with his direct reports, one of whom was Eva's husband. The next day, every man in that group was wearing a paisley tie—except Paul.

Now, it seemed a bit extreme that Eva would start working again because she was worried about her husband losing his job over a seemingly insignificant article of clothing. But within two months Paul was unemployed. Most probably there were other factors involved, but Eva was a political animal and knew that her husband, intentionally or not, had sent signals about whose team he was on.

Team uniforms exist in virtually all institutions and may differ radically by organization, industry, and even area of the country. In factories, machinists wear work coats; in hospitals, doctors wear lab coats; in offices, executives often wear conservative suits but support staff may wear more casual attire. The banking, insurance, and marketing industries tend to expect conservative dress. Publishing, retail, and advertising allow more leeway. In fact, if you routinely dress in a conservative suit in the fashion or art field, it may actually limit your career advancement.

Implicit and formalized dress codes are defined by each company. Early on in my career, I was given the assignment of introducing new executive trainees to the rest of the staff. One of our stops was the CEO's office. We went up to mahogany row, entered his wood-paneled office, and sat on his leather furniture. The CEO entered looking like a CEO out of central casting and began talking about the future of the company.

Suddenly he stopped and said, "I must clarify why my jacket and pants are a different color." It was as if somebody had flipped the channel in the middle of a program. The CEO went on to explain. "Today is Friday, and on Fridays, jackets and pants don't have to match." I had worked at this company for over a year and had never noticed this unwritten custom. (Of course, I had on my very best suit, which was the same color, top and bottom.)

At first, the CEO's comment seemed bizarre. Then I realized he was telling the new trainees, "You must wear a conservative same-color suit four days a week. This is the casual limit on Fridays." Of course, these days, "casual Friday" has taken on a whole new dimension—polo shirts and khaki pants, sweaters instead of sport coats, and in some companies even shorts and T-shirts are seen.

The fact that no one discusses the team uniform with women further minimizes the apparent importance of dress. This became particularly evident when a former colleague who had recently taken an executive position in a financial organization asked me to give a management skills workshop for the company's supervisors (twenty-three women and two men). While discussing the content of the upcoming workshop he told me, "We have virtually no women above the supervisory level in management. I think it's a crime. I want to do something about it, but these women dress like hell. In this organization, once you reach the management level you start meeting with clients. There's no way these women are going to get promoted, dressed the way they are. I'm new here; I can't tell them. Can you?"

During the management workshop I talked about nonverbal cues and attire. When I asked the group how they were supposed to dress, they replied, "Professionally." So I prodded further. "What does 'professionally' mean to you?"

"Like we're dressed now," one woman said. Most of the others in the group nodded.

With the exception of the two men and one of the women, all attendees wore functional wash-and-wear polyester skirts, pants, and blouses. While the clothes were comfortable and easy to care for, they did not reflect the image that a financial institution wanted to send. So I asked what the team uniform was: "What are the guys at the top wearing when they meet with clients?"

"Oh, that's easy," another woman replied. "Navy blue suit and white shirt."

"Well, it seems to me," I ventured, "that if you want to be part of the management team, you need to wear the uniform." While a navy blue suit every day probably wasn't necessary, clearly the message was "dress conservatively." The following week, when I returned for our next workshop, at least half the women were dressed in suits. They had gone from looking like a bunch of clerks to a group of professionals. I don't know if any were promoted, but my guess is that they had cleared an invisible hurdle and had at the very least become promotable.

If you haven't received any feedback from above about your dress, it's not necessarily good news. Like my former colleague, many executives would like to help women but are reluctant to say anything, often fearing if they comment on women's dress and not men's, they will put themselves in a legally vulnerable position. As an outsider, I had been explicitly told that without a change in dress, these women were going nowhere fast. But they were never informed, nor would they ever be.

But what if the people around you dress differently from those at the top? One of the executive trainees I took to meet the CEO was a woman in her early twenties. She was the only young woman outside the secretarial pool in her first job placement. Because she needed clerical support from the secretaries, she was caught between needing to fit in with them and needing to fit in with management. When she wore her suit, the secretaries heard her saying, "I'm superior to you." But given her position and the CEO's not-so-subtle message, she knew she had to wear a suit. She struck on the strategy of removing her jacket in the office but putting it on when she attended meetings, walked the halls, or went home.

THE EXECUTIVE SUIT

Do you know the uniform in your organization? If you look about you, especially near the top, you'll often find that a consistent picture emerges. Take a walk through the executive area and make mental notes about what men and women are wearing.

1. What are the trends in colors and attire?
2. Is the message conservative, trendy, artistic, or individual?
3. How can you adjust your wardrobe to fit in?

▶ DRESS TO WIN

Women often exempt themselves from uniform rules because they find them illogical. But if you look for logic in the rules, you won't find it—wearing a team uniform can be just another loyalty test. Knowing the uniform can be a helpful guide, but if you're wondering which way to go, your best bet is to err on the conservative side.

Research reported in the *Wall Street Journal* disclosed that "female executives whose attire was described as 'extremely feminine' were typically paid less and promoted less frequently. The highest paid women, on the other hand, were those whose dress was described as professional, dull, conservative, non-sexy, or non-frilly." The article went on to report that women who wore more conservative or traditional clothing were twice as likely to receive promotions as those who wore frilly or sexy clothing. It's not the most exciting way to dress, but it can determine what opportunities become—or do not become—available to you.

The way you dress determines the overall message you send. In general, the most important rule of thumb is: *Dress for the job you want, not the job you have.* When your boss scans the environment for the appropriate person to fill a particular position, you'll look as if you already belong there. But other factors are also key in choosing clothes.

Even if your company has a casual policy, be careful. A study was conducted using a man and a woman of approximately the same age. First they were dressed in similar dark suits. When subjects were asked to identify who was the manager, they chose the man and the woman in equal numbers. When this pair was dressed in polo shirts and khaki pants, the man was overwhelmingly identified as the manager. You may want to consider wearing a blazer or jacket over those khakis if you want to communicate authority.

In fact, power is best communicated by a dark suit (blue, gray, or black). National political campaigns are a great place to observe this rule in action. Seven candidates are on the stage together, all wearing a blue suit and a white shirt. The only variations are the pattern and the color of the tie. These men aren't dressed alike because they all have the same fashion coordinator but because they know the powerful impact of this combination.

But you won't always want to look like a powerhouse. At times that may intimidate others to such a degree that you'll be excluded from the inner workings of the office. If openness is what you want to communicate, softer colors such as camel, beige, light blue, or pink will cause others to feel more comfortable with you. The hierarchy in terms of conservative dress is as follows:

- dark suit
- lighter suit
- mixed-color skirt/slacks and jacket
- dress

Avoid the following:

- T-shirts and/or jeans
- sweater dress
- midriff-baring tops or pants (ever!)
- sandals or workout wear
- miniskirts
- very high heels
- jewelry that moves or makes noise
- big hair
- long, brightly polished nails
- unnatural makeup
- low-cut tops or other tight, figure-enhancing apparel
- purses (Tuck anything you need to carry into skirt or jacket pockets or your briefcase)

Depending on your industry, you may need to dress more creatively. In that case, brighter colors and more fashionably cut clothes may be in order. Indeed, female executives in the upper echelons may elect to dress in high-fashion outfits; they've won and can now determine their own rules rather than follow previously established norms. But remember that dressing in a way that draws attention to your sexuality—miniskirts, high heels, tight sweaters, lots of skin—can subvert all your hard work. Once a woman's sexuality becomes the focus, her work fades into the background.

As for makeup, it should look natural, like you. Don't draw attention with bright blue eyelids or inch-long eyelashes; the focus will become the makeup and not your abilities and successes. At a certain age, makeup may no longer be optional. You'll know the moment, because when you get there, coworkers may ask, "Oh, you're not feeling so well today, are you?"

One woman said to me, "All this stuff about dress seems so ridiculous. I just want to dress in a way that allows me to be comfortable." I couldn't agree more. But keep in mind that you need a team to win, and in order for your fellow team members to know you're on their team, you need to dress in a way that doesn't single you out as being different.

TEAM POINTERS

- You need a team in order to win.
- Men often are uncomfortable discussing interpersonal issues; focus on the work when you talk to them.
- Men are friendly, but they won't necessarily be loyal to you even if they're your buddy.
- It's important to choose whether friendship or friendliness is the appropriate relationship.
- Because you need strong players on your team, you may need to play with people you don't necessarily like.
- Attend important meetings even if they are boring.
- Sell to the team's goal.
- Realize that your agenda to be fair may not be shared by all members of the team.
- Be aware that for many, cheating is part of the game.
- The real meeting happens before and after the scheduled meeting.
- Learn to speak the language of the powerful teams.
- Recognize your team uniform—and wear it.

6

HOW TO BE A LEADER

▼

HARDBALL LESSONS BOYS LEARN

- To be a leader, you have to give orders and make them stick.
- There's only one leader, and his word goes.
- Power is the ability to push your agenda through.
- Wielding power is natural, desirable, and masculine.
- If you don't have all the answers, at least you can act as if you do.

▼

HOUSE AND DOLL LESSONS GIRLS LEARN

- There are no leaders.
- Negotiate: Ordering people around costs relationships.
- Girls can't be overtly powerful and feminine at the same time.
- It's important to admit all your shortcomings.
- Keep power dead even.

▼ ▼ ▼ ▼ ▼ **G**reat leaders make leadership look so easy. They announce a direction, and the team eagerly follows. But anyone who has ever been in a leadership position knows it's a real balancing act. If you're too controlling, people will feel resentful, like mere cogs in a wheel. They may dig in, move at a snail's pace, sabotage your efforts, or worse. If you're too warm and open, your department may love you and everyone in it, but it's unlikely that much will get accomplished. It's the balance that makes all the difference and yet is so difficult to achieve.

▶ LET THE MANAGEMENT STYLE FIT THE EMPLOYEE

In *Management of Organizational Behavior,* Paul Hersey and Kenneth Blanchard advocate a *situational leadership* approach to resolve this dilemma. Indeed, according to their model, there is no single style of leadership: The best managers choose and adjust their style to the individuals they supervise and the situations in which they find themselves. To treat the superb, dependable, knowledgeable employee as you would a recalcitrant who only works when you watch her would do both employees and your organization a disservice.

According to Hersey and Blanchard, the principal components of leadership are directiveness and the cultivation of relationships. These exist on continuums. In the case of directiveness, some employees need little direction and would be insulted if constantly told what to do, whereas others require more guidance. At the extreme, directiveness means the hierarchical command and control approach (often used by men) that dictates who, what, when, where, and how to accomplish a task.

Similarly, the relationship component speaks to the fact that some employees need constant reassurance and feedback, while others are competent and confident and require only an occasional pat on the back. At the extreme, the cultivation of relationships means that no decisions are reached without negotiation—a flatter, more feminine approach.

These dimensions drive a progression of four management styles: directing, coaching, supporting, and delegating, directing being the most controlling and delegating being the least. The employee's *competence* and *commitment to a task* dictate which style you choose. Let's look at these in greater detail.

Directing

A directing style is appropriate when an employee has low competence, low commitment, or both. This is a one-way communication: The manager explains to the employee how to go about achieving the task; the employee does it, and that's that.

Imagine, for example, that you've hired Carol to run the reception desk. Since she knows nothing about it, you show her how to work the phones, check identities, have people sign in, assign them a security pass, and call the person they're coming to meet with. To ask her, "What do you think you should do?" or to simply leave her alone at the desk with no instruction would set her up for immediate failure and an office in chaos.

Many women feel uncomfortable with a directing style because it implies hierarchy and presupposes that the leader is entitled to make all the decisions. (Men, on the other hand, may fall into this authoritarian "command and control" approach more naturally because it echoes their early play experiences.) Although men may choose this style out of habit, women may feel comfortable adopting it under certain circumstances. Directing (or "command and control") is valuable especially when:

- You need to take charge of an employee or situation.
- Time is limited.
- No alternatives are possible (as when a new policy or procedure is handed down from above).
- You must win this one or your job, your department, or the company will go under.

It is important to think of directing as temporary. In the long run, competent workers learn their tasks and don't need or like being told what to do. On the other hand, if a worker can't or won't learn under your guidance, she may be ill-equipped to handle the job, and you'd best be rid of her. The agenda of the directing style is, "Get better or get out."

Coaching

During coaching interactions, the manager is somewhat directive (because the employee is learning), but two-way communication exists. The manager solicits her employee's ideas and opinions in problem solving, yet the ultimate decision still rests with her.

In Carol's case, as she catches on to her job, you would begin involving her in decision making. But if she comes up with an idea that you know won't fly, you would explain why the idea is faulty and talk about other, proven alternatives. In a coaching style, your goal is to help Carol learn to make good decisions and solve problems. Female managers frequently use coaching because it falls within the parameters of a flat, collaborative approach.

Supporting

The manager still works with her employee, but now allows her to take the lead in determining a plan of action or in solving problems. Dialogue (especially questions on the part of the manager) moves the action forward. A good manager supports and trusts an employee who has gained greater competence and commitment to a task.

In our reception desk example, imagine that Carol has mastered the workings of her job. As her supervisor, you may now want her to take the initiative in solving problems. If she comes to you asking what to do about an irate visitor who swears at her, you might answer, "We've discussed this in the past. What do you think?" You may be sure that she has the answer.

A word of caution here: Managers often have difficulty moving from coaching to the supporting style. When competent employees seek their advice, these managers find it easier (and perhaps are more accustomed) to simply give answers rather than asking, "What do you think?" Employees, too, may find the coaching style safer. It can be frightening to fly on your own for the first time.

Women managers frequently use a supporting style because it, too, suits their need for give and take in working relationships.

Delegating

When an employee is fully competent and committed to her task, the delegating style is appropriate. In this case, the manager gives her employee responsibility without input or direct supervision. As Ken Blanchard has said, when in a delegating style, "Don't just do something, sit there." Delegating (like directing) involves more one-way communication, but this time, rather than dicta coming from above, it's the employee who reports back to her boss on her progress or bright ideas.

Problems arise when managers feel they need to be involved in all aspects of their department. Bear in mind, however, that if employees can function at the delegate level, it frees the manager to become involved in strategic thinking and networking that can further her career. (If you're so enmeshed in teaching your employees the basics of their jobs or in day-to-day directing, there's little time for this kind of activity.)

Once reception whiz Carol has developed confidence, you can depend on her to make decisions and solve problems on her own. She may need positive feedback from time to time, as we all do, but not as much as previously.

Women gravitate to coaching and supporting managerial styles because these are the most collaborative. But to be good managers, they also need to use the directive and delegating styles. And no matter what style they choose, bear in mind that all employees need clear goals from their leaders.

▶ GROWING EMPLOYEES THROUGH PRAISE

Male coaches are more apt to criticize than praise. Women, however, use praise to encourage their employees to excel. Indeed, women praise instinctively. Appropriately applied praise can be a powerful management tool.

Praise and positive feedback are helpful in moving employees along from a state of needing constant direction to the ability to take responsibility for their own decisions. When you praise behavior you approve of, your employee is apt to repeat the task to your liking. This is the simple principle of *operant conditioning*.

Ken Blanchard explains how operant conditioning works by describing how trainers taught the whale Shamu to leap in the air. At first, Shamu swam randomly in her tank. But every time she swam over a submerged rope, her trainers rewarded her with a fish. Soon, Shamu understood that swimming over the rope was a good thing to do. Then, her trainers suspended the rope in the middle of the tank. When Shamu swam under it, her trainers did nothing. When she swam over it, she was rewarded. Before long, she learned to swim only over the rope. Her trainers raised it to the surface of the water and eventually above the surface, with similar results. Eventually, Shamu jumped over an imaginary rope.

We humans aren't much different. As an employee moves in a direction you'd like him to take, he will learn from your positive feedback. If you wait until he has actually accomplished the goal before you dish out the kudos, you may be waiting a very long time! Praise the well-thought-out effort and the steps along the way to achievement, not just achievement itself. This is especially true of employees whom you're encouraging to take more initiative, particularly if they've had a setback or two.

When you praise, be specific about the behavior you liked. Rather than saying, "Great report, Jessica," say, "I appreciate that you kept it short—under four pages. You gave me all the data available and did projections, too. Good job!" Employees are likely to repeat behavior you have lauded.

Be sure, however, that you don't overpraise, as your employees will become habituated to positive feedback and it will lose its punch. In fact, I recommend that you praise irregularly. Think of it this way: If your group performs well, you might reward them with bagels on Monday. They'll be sure to repeat their excellent performance. So you bring the same treat the following week. By the third Monday, they'll be wondering where the bagels are. When employees expect the praise, it doesn't have the same impact as when you give it sporadically and candidly.

Should you sweeten criticism with a dollop of praise first? I like to think of this as the sandwich method: you deliver the good news, the bad news, and then the good news again. Women tend to gravitate to this indirect communication to preserve the relationship. With the sandwich method, however, the employee often only remembers the beginning and the end of the communication and misses the meat in the middle. Consequently, feelings are spared but the employee neither hears nor deals with the bad news. It's more effective to start with the bad news and end with a statement such as: "I believe in you and your ability to solve this problem."

▶ MANAGING PERFORMANCE PROBLEMS

What happens when an employee gets into hot water? That's the time to go into a regressive mode. That is, determine the management style you've been using and back up one step. For example, if you've been delegating, you may find the situation requires supporting. In that case, you would start asking questions such as, "What's going on with you? Your work has been slipping lately." You might discover that Carol has had personal problems at home, is bored with her job, or is angry at you. Ideally, you'll find the problem and help your employee work out a solution.

But if talking makes no difference, you may need to back up still another style, into coaching. In that case, you might say, "We've agreed on these goals, but you're not accomplishing them." Meet informally every two weeks, with a follow-up meeting scheduled on the calendar, to discuss your employee's written plans and goals and to create new plans of action for the coming two weeks. If you're still not getting the performance you expect, pull in the reins even further to weekly meetings. These written work plans and your formalized evaluations can serve as documentation if you must terminate the employee in the future.

Finally, if all else fails, you must back into the directive style. Then you would say, "Let me tell you exactly what to do today. If you have a problem with this, come to me and I'll tell you what to do instead." Most certainly, your employee will hate this, especially if she knows how to accomplish the task. In fact, she may quit. Nevertheless, in cases of incompetence or lack of commitment, it's important to stick with the directive style. The employee needs to improve or get out.

YOUR SITUATIONAL LEADERSHIP STYLE

Choose the appropriate management style in the following situations.

1. Your employee has been on the job for six months and has learned how to do the work. Today she comes to you with a question that you know she can answer on her own. Do you:
   A. Discuss options with her but tell her which option you'd take?
   B. Tell her to figure it out herself?
   C. Tell her what to do and monitor her closely?
   D. Ask her what she would do?

2. You've hired a new employee who is eager to get into the profession and to be a star, but he is inexperienced in this line of work. Do you:
   A. Give him an assignment and check in a week later to see if he has done it?
   B. Discuss different ways to approach the work and then suggest to him which would be best?
   C. Tell him exactly what you expect, then monitor to see if he's performing?
   D. Ask him about his ideas and then let him run with the ball?

3. You've been on vacation for two weeks. You return and find your boss needed a major assignment completed in your absence. He gave it to your employee. Although she has never done this kind of work before, she is making good progress. Do you:
   A. Take the assignment back and do it yourself?
   B. Leave her alone and check in with her periodically?
   C. Discuss her approach and give your ideas about how to proceed?
   D. Talk it over with her but tell her how you'd like it done?

4. Your employee is able to do her work but often needs feedback from you. Lately her assignments have been coming in late and full of errors. Do you:
   A. Leave her alone because she has been dependable and will probably get better?
   B. Review with her what the problems are and write a plan of action, then meet the following week to discuss?
   C. Sit down and clearly explain what you want and when you want it?
   D. Ask her how she plans to resolve this problem?

Applying Hersey and Blanchard's model to these questions the correct answers would be.

1. D. A supporting style works best here because the employee has demonstrated her competence and commitment.
2. C. A directing style is recommended because the employee is an inexperienced novice.
3. B. A delegating style is appropriate for an employee who can handle work independently.
4. B. A coaching style is needed, since the employee requires more guidance to improve her performance.

If your answers differ from these, assess what style you most frequently use. Think about how to integrate the less familiar (but more appropriate) approaches into your management routine.

The situational managerial style is the ideal, but it doesn't always prevail. Indeed, most often management styles are split along gender lines, based on what we learned as children.

▶ WHAT GIRLS DON'T LEARN ABOUT LEADERSHIP

From early childhood, girls are trained to operate in collaborative rather than directive managerial styles. Moreover, the message often conveyed to them is that men and not women are in positions of power.

Boys have the opportunity to practice directive leadership when they get to be team captain. As Deborah Tannen says in *You Just Don't Understand,* the key here is "giving orders and making them stick." A boy is expected to assert his authority and show his power, not to negotiate. Men grow up to value a leader who gives direction. Ideally the direction is good, but even if it's not, they're not likely to question it. In fact, they often value a leader who is strong over one who is right. The *assuredness* is most important for them.

The flat organization in which girls grow up develops and nurtures intimacy. Certainly some of us started out as highly directive little individuals (behavior that is usually labeled bossy in a female), but most of us learned quickly that this cost us friends and playmates. In girls' play, direction is not set by a power figure but is negotiated. A primary goal is to include everyone in the process. There is no single leader, and even if one girl distinguishes herself as official leader, she doesn't act the part. Some girls are more persuasive than others, but they're still not considered the boss. It is for these reasons that men may feel more comfortable in directing managerial styles, whereas women feel more at home as coaching or supporting managers.

The limited image of woman as leader is further reflected in the books children read. Katharine Heintz studied Caldicott Medal winners from 1971 to 1984, children's books that had been recognized by the American Library Association for excellence and distinction. Although the books were written equally by men and women, the equality stopped there. "Males were often shown leading activities and controlling the actions of others, but females were shown being led or told what to do."

In the books honored during that 13-year period, 29 male protagonists were involved in leadership activities, but only 3 females led. In fact, males outnumbered females two to one in all activities, including amorousness, primping, and posing. So what were the females doing? Fifty percent were homemakers and 25 percent, witches. The other occupations girls could aspire to included being a dancer, singer, musician, queen, and fairy. Does this reflect career opportunities in your neighborhood?

Children's books shape expectations by teaching youngsters what their future may hold. It is clear in these top children's books that leadership in an option mainly for boys.

As a result of this early training, women feel especially uncomfortable in taking on the leadership role if men are present and rarely move into leadership if a man is there to do it instead. Even when a woman is the most capable, knowledgeable person for a particular position, she defers. In the long term, this pattern of behavior is dreadfully damaging. If a woman doesn't assume the mantle of power, her career will be shaped by others. Her skills and abilities will never be fully utilized.

Women's deference to men has been borne out in research studies. In one investigation, subjects were tested for dominance and then put into pairs to make a decision. When the pairs were of the same sex, the most dominant person became the leader. But once genders were mixed, interesting interactions resulted. If a dominant man was paired with a weaker woman, he became the leader 90 percent of the time. The surprise came when the dominant individual was the woman. She took the leadership role only 20 percent of the time, but even as a subordinate, she still exerted her power—she appointed her weaker male partner the leader, saying, "Why don't you be in charge?"

▶ WHAT GIRLS DO LEARN ABOUT LEADERSHIP: FLATTENING THE STRUCTURE

Some years ago, I came across a short report in the *Los Angeles Times* that typifies a female leadership style. California Supreme Court Justice Joyce Kennard joined her staff in taking four days without pay. "I feel I owe it to my staff," she said. "How can I ask them if I were not going to be subject to the same sacrifice?" The article noted that Kennard was the only justice among the seven on the supreme court, or among the 88 on the state court of appeals, to agree to a voluntary money-saving furlough program that would help defer future cutbacks and layoffs.

Above all else, in this selfless act Kennard demonstrated her need for fairness and her belief that she was no different from her employees. In this case, she sought to keep the power dead even.

The feminine leadership style can work under certain circumstances. Indeed, some women in positions of power are able to recreate flat organizational structures in which they are mostly coaching or supporting. Frances Hesselbein did as much when she became the executive director of the Girl Scouts of America. "I can't stand to box people in," she reported to Warren Bennis in *On Becoming a Leader*. "Everyone's in a circle. It's rather organic. If I'm the center, then there are seven bubbles around me, and the next circle would be group directors, and then team directors, and so on. Nothing moves up and down, but rather laterally, across. It's so fluid and flexible that people who are used to a hierarchy have a bit of trouble adjusting, but it works well."

As it happens, Hesselbein was the first Girl Scout chief executive to come up through the ranks. She had spent her entire professional life in organizations of women. In her position as executive director, she created a structure more consistent with the way women prefer to relate.

But precious few organizations operate this way. Most are structured as hierarchies in which flat organization is the exception, not the rule. Indeed, I have found that the power-dead-even rule is especially problematic (for widely disparate reasons) in situations in which women are in a leadership position. Let's look at these cases individually.

▶ HOW OUR DIFFERING STYLES AFFECT LEADERSHIP DECISIONS

Boys enjoy being challenged. Indeed, they're less concerned with being liked than being respected. They'd just as soon have things their own way and be the winner than be the most popular guy in the group. Once they've won, others will look up to them and do what they say. That's reward enough.

Girls, on the other hand, because of the primacy of relationships, need to feel liked. You'll often find clumps of girls comparing notes about favorite playmates. In fact, an important social goal of most girls is to be "popular," which implies being liked by many.

Our early training can become a significant problem for women in business, and particularly for those in management. As the manager makes decisions all day long, she not only weighs the objective factors of her moves, but she also calculates how others will respond to her personally: Will they dislike her for enforcing an unpopular but necessary policy? Her competitive edge may be blunted by the need to maintain good relationships with colleagues and employees. Clearly, most men aren't burdened with these concerns.

Laura, the manager of a department of consultants in a large financial services company, ran into just this problem. It was performance appraisal time, and she was in agony. Several of her highest achievers clustered around the top of the five-point scale. The human resources department had limited the number of excellent ratings managers could give to 10 percent, and Laura's department had exceeded the quota. Despite her misgivings, she had to assign some of her best consultants fours on their reviews. She dreaded handing back the assessments.

In talking with her, it was clear that Laura was deeply concerned about what the less-than-perfect reviews would do to her relationship with her employees. "They'll be so angry at me, and I can't blame them," she moaned.

To make the situation even stickier, a couple of Laura's more savvy consultants had intuited how sensitive she was to her staff's negative responses. They used this insight to their advantage, accusing her of being unfair or uncaring (two hot buttons for her). As a result, Laura was more likely to give these consultants higher scores in order to avoid their strong negative reactions. The quieter, more agreeable consultants would be the losers.

Laura's need to be liked had caused her to lose the respect of her employees because they saw her as incapable of making hard but fair decisions. This typically feminine need can be significantly detrimental to your career. You may avoid tough decisions such as firing an incompetent employee, cutting the budget and jobs, or demanding that employees stay late to finish a project for fear of displeasing anyone.

Admittedly, this is the difficult part of management for women. After time, however, we grow into being able to separate our need to be liked from doing a competent job. Often this occurs after many painful incidents in which we learn that the cost of being everyone's friend is just too great. Besides, when we're tough but fair with our employees, even though we may not always give them what they want, we see that eventually they come around. If, on the other hand, we're arbitrary (sometimes we're tough and other times we're soft) or unfair (only our favorites or the loudest complainers in the department get to win), then the simmering long-term resentment engendered by our behaviors will eventually boil over into outright sabotage.

The trick is to realize that it takes time to see the pattern: *They're angry now. I had to make this decision. But they'll come around.* When you do what you must, your employees may not love you, but they will respect and follow you.

Be careful, however, not to undermine yourself with negative self-talk such as, "They hate me. I'm a bad manager." Instead, support your own decisions. The following exercise may help you monitor your inner dialogue and keep it from degenerating into self-criticism:

EAVESDROPPING ON YOUR SELF-TALK

Try to become aware of negative self-talk when you've made what you feel is a fair but unpopular decision.

1. Listen to your internal dialogue. If you catch yourself being self-critical say, "Oh, c'mon. You did what you had to."
2. If you catch yourself using positive self-talk, give yourself a mental pat on the back.
3. If all else fails, place a rubber band on your wrist. If you can't seem to get out of a negative frame of mind, give it a snap every time you find yourself slipping into self-criticism. This aversion therapy (a slap on the wrist?) will grab your attention, if nothing else.

In Chapter 9, "Making the Most of Criticism and Praise," we'll discuss the power of self-talk and how to make it work for you.

▶ ASSERTING AUTHORITY AMONG MEN

Inge was the first woman promoted to be a regional vice president in a large insurance company. All of her direct reports were men who had never worked for a woman before. In advance of her first staff meeting, she sent out an email asking for input on what they would like to discuss. Inge never realized that this had upset her staff until I met with all of them during a gender differences workshop. When I described the issue of having a meeting before the meeting (see Chapter 5), her male employees erupted in questions.

"Is this what you meant when you sent out that memo asking what we wanted to talk about?" one asked.

"We didn't understand what was behind the memo, and we were all emailing each other, trying to figure it out," said another.

Inge was stunned. "I just wanted to know what would be helpful for us to cover," she explained. "There was no hidden agenda."

A hidden agenda? Apparently not. But there were hidden gender differences. Inge was leading like a woman: soliciting input and engaging her employees in the decision-making process. Her male employees had never encountered this style, and, not surprisingly, were thrown by it. They were used to having someone to push back against as a way to define their positions in the hierarchy. Inge's request felt disconcertingly "mushy" to them. And, as a consequence, she seemed less boss-like to them. In my experience, men often settle in very nicely with a manager who invites input, but initially, without understanding what it means, they often attribute a puzzling yet negative intent to the behavior.

Assert Your Authority and Stick to Your Limits

A manager like Inge would drive many a male employee to distraction. Men expect that those above them in the chain of command will be directive and exert the authority inherent in their position. Instead of perceiving Inge as open-minded, a man would often hear her as being indecisive: "Why doesn't she just tell me what she wants and I'll do it, instead of playing all these games with me?" The average male employee wants a woman manager to be the coach so he can follow.

Besides, all employees test limits when they settle into new relationships. Men in particular will push against a boss's authority to find their place in the hierarchy. Moreover, they test limits more overtly, quickly, and aggressively with female superiors, especially since they have learned that women often back down for fear of damaging the relationship.

It is, therefore, encumbent upon you to set limits with your male employees and stick to them consistently. If you vascillate in your resolve, your male employees will push all the more, in the hope that they've finally found the issue over which you'll capitulate. They may see themselves in the driver's seat (since equality is not an option, they have to be above or below others in the hierarchy) and may make demands accordingly. Sticking to your limits may feel uncomfortable from time to time, but weakness and inconsistency can be a big mistake.

Glenda caught herself before she was pushed beyond her limits. The manager of a research department, she interviewed many assistant researchers but decided to hire Dennis because he had excellent technical experience. In the month between Dennis's hiring and his taking the job (he had given thirty days' notice at his old company), he began phoning Glenda with requests. The first week he called saying, "I'm really excited about this job. I'm going to do so much computer work. But you know, I realized I'll need two computers to do it well."

"Gee, we don't have a lot of computers," Glenda responded. "Maybe I can arrange for you to share a second computer with someone else."

"No, that won't work," Dennis countered. "I need two fully dedicated computers. After all, you told me how important my contribution would be. If you really value it that much, I'll need the two computers."

Glenda set about fulfilling Dennis's wish. But within a week, she received a second call. Upon hearing Dennis's voice, she said, "Good news. It looks like I've secured that second computer for you."

"I'm glad about that," he replied, "because I want to let you know each computer will need a color laser printer. That's part of the package." When Glenda began to balk at this second request, Dennis became verbally aggressive. "I thought you said this research was important and that you would support it," he challenged.

"Yes," Glenda countered, "but you're asking for more resources than we have available to our department."

"Well, you can't expect me to accomplish the research you hired me to do without the equipment." Dennis was beginning to sound indignant.

"I'll look into it and call you back," Glenda replied. But when she got off the phone she said to herself, "Wait a darn minute here. Who's in charge of this department? Dennis is acting as if he calls the shots!" With her recognition of Dennis's agenda, Glenda decided to change strategy. She called him and asked him to stop by sometime after work. "I need to talk to you about the computer situation," she said.

At this meeting, Dennis once again began badgering his future boss about the equipment. "That's what I wanted to talk to you about," Glenda said. "Dennis, let me explain how things work around here. Our resources are limited. We need to make sure we use what we do have in the right places. You don't have a track record with us yet, and we're unsure what you'll need in terms of computers."

"I thought we agreed on the importance of my research."

"Listen, you prove yourself, and I'll get you what you need. Until then, you've got one computer and you can share a printer."

Dennis became conciliatory. "Okay," he said. "If that's the way it is, I'll just do my best." He had found his place in the hierarchy.

If Glenda hadn't drawn the line, Dennis wouldn't have stopped there. Most probably he would have demanded still more equipment and would have tried taking greater liberties in other areas such as hours worked, effort expended, and office space assigned. Indeed, most likely he would have had an ongoing list of demands.

Women have a hard time drawing the line, yet it's crucial to establish control and respect by asserting your limits and sticking to them. Glenda had hardly begun to develop a relationship with Dennis before he began pushing her around. By saying no so directly, she risked hurting a relationship that hadn't yet gotten off the ground, but she had to deny his escalating requests or lose power in his eyes. And in the final analysis, Dennis felt comfortable knowing his limits and his position within the hierarchy.

Warmth and Flirtatiousness

If you manage men, it's vital to master an attitude toward them that balances warmth with restraint, which will not be mistaken for flirtatiousness. Seductiveness is communicated in subtle, nonverbal cues. It comes across in how one holds one's body, the quality of eye contact, the tone of voice. Warmth may be indicated with the same markers. But flirtatiousness and warmth are distinguished by the intention beneath the behavior. Are you being friendly, or do you want to get this guy into bed?

Unfortunately, whether you're just flirting for fun and ego gratification or have serious seduction on your mind, the object of your attention may be unable to read your intent from your outward behavior. Consequently, it's wise to avoid any flirtatiousness or sexual innuendo in the business setting altogether.

Besides, when it comes to office love affairs, the woman *always* loses. Once you become involved in a flirtatious or sexual relationship with an employee, you've eliminated your one-up position in the hierarchy and lose your ability to manage him well. If, down the road a piece, you give him an undesirable work assignment or become unavailable for an evening, he can use your personal relationship to manipulate or intimidate you. It's wise to steer clear.

The Old-Boy Network

Occasionally male employees band together in a sort of "old-boy" network to intimidate or lock out their female boss. The best strategy here would be to make sure you're acting like the boss. Stick to your limits and call for meetings at which you preside over a discussion of a project's progress.

It's also wise to meet individually with male employees to discuss their work and provide negative and positive feedback. Key here: If you can tell your employee, "I want you in my office at 3:00 PM today," you're still in charge, whether or not he has joined the old-boy's club.

Jumping the Chain of Command

An individual who jumps the chain of command (by complaining to a boss's superior) may be doing so to challenge authority. Both male and female employees may attempt such a maneuver if they dislike having a female boss, or if they don't want a woman above them in the hierarchy telling them what to do.

Once an employee has approached your boss with complaints or questions about your authority, with the intent of having your superior override your decision, the critical factor is your boss's response. She should say, "Have you told Jacqueline about this?" and then send the employee back down the chain of command. If she does, your employee won't try this ploy too many more times.

If, on the other hand, your boss deals with his complaint, she will undermine your authority. In that case, your primary problem lies with your boss, not your employee. Then you should approach your boss, saying, "I know Justin was complaining about his assignment. I'd like to ask a favor of you. In the future, if any of my employees bring complaints to you, please ask them if they've spoken to me. If not, give me first shot at the problem." Bear in mind that sometimes your supervisor may help a disgruntled employee out of the goodness of her heart. You can't assume that she was colluding with the employee to undermine you.

▶ MANAGING WOMEN

When women supervise other women, they run into different, albeit no less disturbing, problems. Adrienne had been working in the accounting department of a large communications company for more than seven years when I met her at a seminar. For the previous few years she had been in a lead position, not officially a supervisor but often guiding and directing the work of her colleagues. She had done so well that a few months prior to our meeting she had been promoted to supervisor. She had looked forward to this promotion, but now that she had it, she wasn't sure management was for her.

"I like my job," Adrienne told me with a mixture of satisfaction and chagrin. "I work with some great people, mostly women. In fact my closest friend, Fran, is my colleague. But ever since I was made supervisor, work has been awful. I like the supervisory part of my position, but hate the fact that all my friends treat me differently. Whenever I walk up to the coffee pot in the morning, they all stop joking around and clam up. When I ask one of them to do something, she resists. But the worst is Fran. Our relationship seems to have become more distant. She treats me as if I've changed, but I haven't! What can I do to get things back the way they were?"

Adrienne's quandary is a common one for women. Ideally, she'd like to move up the management ladder and maintain her friendships just as they were in the past. Unfortunately, this balancing act is difficult if not impossible to pull off, because the flat relationships female friends enjoy are antithetical to the hierarchical relationships that keep most businesses going. Although I would love to say that it's possible to maintain close friendships with coworkers whom you must manage, from my experience and the testimony of hundreds of women I've worked with, it's virtually impossible over the long run to remain a bosom buddy with a friend who has become your employee. If you're playing hardball, you may have to sacrifice a friendship for the sake of a job.

May I Serve You?

Other problems can arise as well. During a workshop for the female physicians of a state medical society, I heard complaints all day long about uncooperative nurses. As one doctor put it, "The male physicians make a mess of the charts, leave their coffee cups around, give orders in a gruff manner, and they're still treated with respect. If I were to do this, it would cost me dearly." The female physicians were expected to politely ask for a nurse's help, stop to communicate appreciation, and clean up after themselves.

I was confounded by these complaints, as I frequently work with nurses and find them cooperative. I pondered this difference all the way to the airport that evening. But as I got on the plane, I saw the flight attendant and realized she was my "nurse." Suddenly I understood. How could I have forgotten that my experiences with flight attendants were parallel to those of the women physicians with their nurses?

I drink a lot of water on planes to fight dehydration, but getting water can be a tug-of-war. I once handed my empty glass to a flight attendant standing at my aisle seat with the beverage cart and asked for another glass of water. "I have better things to do than give you water," she responded. This has been such a persistent problem for me that after fighting it for twenty years I now travel with my own bottle of water; I've given up and accept the flatness of my relationship with flight attendants.

Women in workshops have often come to me confused about their relationships with female subordinates. One attorney was perplexed because she couldn't seem to keep a secretary. The male attorneys in her office could throw work on their secretaries' desks, but if she followed suit, her secretary quit.

My advice to this attorney, the women doctors, and other women who come up against these "service" issues is to accept that the rules are different for them. Yes, a male manager can make a mess and throw things on his secretary's desk, but a woman can't or she will pay. No, it's not fair; it's just the way it is. If you have direct power over an employee, you can be directive, but you still must be careful about managing the interpersonal side of the relationship. In those situations where you don't have ultimate control (for example, if you're a project manager coordinating employees from other departments or a doctor interfacing with hospital nurses), you may have to build up chips with these women in order to gain their cooperation.

Of course, sometimes you must draw the line, as most businesses are not flat organizations. A female professor told me that the department administrative assistant often returned documents to her with numerous errors. When she asked for it to be corrected, the assistant responded, "I'm very busy. You know how to use the computer." As it happened, the professor did, but her job focus was elsewhere. Besides, she didn't have direct authority over the assistant (who served many professors) to fire her. In situations like these, the flat organization is a problem that you ignore at your peril.

As I saw it, the professor had two options. She could:

1. Use a directing style. ("I'm the professor, you're the assistant. Correct the damn thing.")

2. Maintain the flat organization. ("Let's have lunch.")

Personally, I'd opt for the second approach first. It may seem strange to treat such an irritating person to lunch, but according to Paul Watzlawick, John Weakland, and Richard Fisch, authors of the classic *Change: Principles of Problem Formation and Problem Resolution,* when you act outside another's expectations, your adversary will be more open to hearing what you have to say. So if over a bite to eat the professor can talk about how she and the secretary can work "together" and "help each other," she'll be swimming downstream. If that fails, she still has the option of going to the department chair with her complaint.

Cattiness

Interesting problems arise when female managers find themselves working with other women in a hierarchical organization. Whenever I ask a workshop of female executives who's the first to attack when one of them gets a promotion, the response is always a resounding, "Women!" Most women who have been promoted into management have experienced former coworkers, now their direct reports, turning on them, often by making personal comments behind their backs. ("You know how she got the promotion, don't you? On her back.")

"What have I done to deserve this?" they ask me. They wonder whether their behavior has somehow been inappropriate, but generally their only transgression was to violate the power-dead-even rule by becoming boss. Indeed, I believe that women employees don't make a conscious decision to attack, but rather their cattiness is an unconscious attempt to reflatten the hierarchy. They learned this response decades ago and don't realize that it's inconsistent with the hierarchical structure of most organizations.

Often men observe this sabotage of women by women and just shake their heads in disbelief. I once consulted with a large corporation in the process of making significant changes, including major layoffs. The president handpicked fourteen people to make recommendations to him. One woman, an assistant vice president, was included on the committee. Within twenty-four hours, the two women senior to her had complained to the president independently of one another that they had not been chosen in her place. The president was aghast. "I don't believe this," he said to me. "I give a woman an opportunity, and the first people to complain are the most senior women."

It's important to note that the senior women didn't complain about the many junior men on the committee, but only about the one woman who, in their eyes, had been elevated above them.

Many women have complained to me during management workshops about their new female managers. "Who does she think she is, telling me what to do?" they ask indignantly. I'm amazed they fail to appreciate that their boss is doing what she's *supposed* to. And if, in fact, she's unsuccessful in having her orders stick, she won't get to stay the boss, and there will be one less woman in a leadership position as a role model. It is significant to note that hundreds of women have made the above comments to me, but a man never has.

How to counteract the tendency toward cattiness in others? First, keep in mind that an undermining woman is probably responding unconsciously to her perception of your power. Under these circumstances, you can say, "Look, dear, I'm the boss here and you'd better get used to it," and prepare yourself for the profound and eternal sabotage that's sure to follow. I suggest, however, that you choose a different tactic and establish a flatter relationship that will make your employee comfortable and put you in a more positive light. To do so, start by asking work-related questions, such as:

- What kind of work do you do?
- What do you really like to do?
- What are you good at?

Eventually work into more personal queries:

- Do you have any children?
- What does your husband do?
- Where do you like to spend your vacations?

Ideally, the more an employee feels that you're genuinely interested in her, the likelier she'll be to abandon her hostile attitude and consider you a friend.

Few of us are entirely immune from feelings of resentment toward women who are in positions of power over us. It's tough to buck a lifetime of conditioning, after all. But we must remember that we're all in this together. When one woman succeeds, we all do. We need to sing the praises of other women, and when they're promoted we need to give them a full measure of positive feedback. If you find you're having trouble managing other women, I recommend my book *In the Company of Women*. In it you will find a wealth of suggestions.

Caught Between Two Worlds

Michelle was hired right out of graduate school into her first management job as a director in an agency providing health care to the homeless and indigent in a large city. The agency was headed by a woman whom she greatly respected. Carmen had taken this community service agency from nothing to a budget of millions. As Michelle explained it, her boss had learned to play the game as men do.

But Michelle found her position far more uncomfortable than she had ever expected. She was put in charge of a department that needed a radical overhaul in short order. Either the situation would be ameliorated quickly, or the department would fold. Despite the urgency of the situation, her style was causing her all sorts of problems.

After Michelle's first month on the job, Carmen expressed dissatisfaction with her leadership abilities. "She told me I was too open, too casual with my employees, and that I needed to institute some formality, even if I was uncomfortable with it," Michelle said during a workshop. "My style didn't speak 'leader,' and I wasn't getting any respect. But I like a collaborative, win/win approach. When I use a win/lose approach, I feel guilty. I have a hard time handling conflict. When I need to take charge, I feel like I'm becoming a bully. Carmen wanted me to be a leader on her terms, which is the male way, but I must admit I didn't like it."

Michelle had learned in childhood that if people spend enough time talking things over they can all get what they need. The situation at work was made more difficult by the fact that her employees, all women, expected her to be collaborative. "My associate director, Judy, wanted to talk through everything, but we needed to make decisions faster. When I did make decisions myself, Judy got angry. She said I wasn't listening; I was unapproachable. Actually, I think I encouraged the problem by being so open in the first place. Now I'm finding myself caught in the middle." To make matters worse, Carmen told Michelle that she wasn't performing adequately after a month on the job. The required changes were not being put through quickly enough.

Michelle was trapped between the comfort of using the familiar supporting style and the need to be more directive in a leadership role. Her boss, whose style was "very male"—distant and commanding—viewed this openness as time consuming and unproductive. So Michelle had to move into an alien mode. "I want to go in and say, 'This is how I think, this is how I feel,' but I've had to take 'feel' out of my vocabulary." She was even limited in what she could express. "In my job I need to act like a man, and I hate it because I'm just acting." Her natural tendency to be authentic in interactions only added to her discomfort. And there was very little help from above.

"I told my boss I didn't know her. I didn't know if she had a husband or a family. I hadn't a clue where she lived. It was difficult to relate. She asked me, 'What do you need?' and I said, 'How about lunch?' She didn't want to do that." Clearly, Carmen needed to distance herself from her employees.

Michelle felt adrift, but I pointed out that she did have several options that she could turn to her advantage. She was presented with a great opportunity to learn how to play hardball the way her much-admired boss did. Although Carmen had signaled she didn't want to get close personally, she was willing to mentor. Michelle could then use this experience as a training ground to broaden her style and then move on to a new organization where a wider variety of styles was acceptable.

It's important to recognize that both the collaborative and directive approaches are appropriate in business, but at different times. Neither style is wrong, though one or the other may not always be effective. Unfortunately, we tend to rely on a particular style because we are most comfortable with it, not because it works the best. We need to be strategic in how we manage our conflicts. In this case, I advised Michelle of her option to use a more directive leadership approach.

As a result, Michelle switched from supporting to coaching. She solicited input but made it clear she would make final decisions herself. After some initial negative reactions, the staff began to accept this style, probably because they had no choice in the matter and also because Michelle continued to collaborate when time and the issues allowed.

With much media attention, Frances Conley, the highly respected neurosurgeon from Stanford University, made a similar move. She honed her skills at this top institution and then left because she endured harassment for being female and playing by female rules. In a *Los Angeles Times* editorial she said, "My contention was that I used power and my position as 'the surgeon' quite differently than my male counterparts. [A professor of organizational behavior who studied power relationships within the operating room environment] found that female surgeons tend to manage their operating rooms with a team approach; male surgeons remain 'captain of the ship.' Of significance, both methods can provide good patient outcome." But what didn't provide a good outcome for Conley was being expected to always do it in a directing style or be judged as incompetent.

There is no single right path for Michelle, Frances Conley, or any of us. We need to be able to strategically choose the most appropriate style at the moment. In fact, we may need to learn how to lead in a more masculine, directing way (even if it feels uncomfortable to us) because that's most appropriate at a given time. And in order to be more directive, we must take possession of our own power.

▶ POWER: THE DOUBLE BIND

When I bring up the issue of power in women's workshops, often the participants physically withdraw. Clearly, power is an uncomfortable subject for many of us. In fact, women tell me they don't want to deal with that "power stuff" because they aren't "power hungry." They act as if power were a social disease to be avoided at all costs.

Simply stated, power is the ability to get things done. If you don't have power, you're going to be ineffectual at work. Indeed, without power, you'll find it impossible to lead others. You'll also find it difficult to get raises, and ultimately you'll be sidelined, wondering why you've reached a dead end, given all of your skills and abilities. Power is essential in adult life. So why are women uncomfortable with it? The problem lies in how we define it.

When I ask workshop participants to think of someone who has wielded tremendous power, most often the names Saddam Hussein, Osama bin Laden, or Adolph Hitler—those who controlled a large government or organization with impunity—are offered. Mother Teresa never comes up. Neither does Nelson Mandela, Gandhi, or Martin Luther King Jr. And yet if power means the ability to get one's goals accomplished, these latter have been extraordinarily powerful; they've had a significant impact on human dignity and civil rights. Nevertheless, it's significant that women only think of negative examples; we find power in ourselves and others threatening.

Actually, power is like money; neither good or bad. Its negative or positive spin depends upon how we use it. Still, most of the time we don't perceive power as neutral. As girls, we worked for equality because that's how we made friends. Displaying power would have cost us our close relationships. Moreover, in our culture, "power" and "masculinity" are virtually synonymous. "Power" and "femininity" are often seen as mutually exclusive. While it's comfortable and easy for a man to be both powerful and masculine, it's much more difficult for a woman to pull off being powerful and feminine.

A former colleague, a vice president in a large company, was told by the president, "Jane, you're great. I don't even think of you as a woman." Not surprisingly, Jane was devastated (and bought a whole new wardrobe that afternoon). My guess is that the president meant his remark as a compliment. "You fit in with the guys." But wouldn't he have been insulted if Jane had responded, "Thanks, Hank. I don't think of you as a man"? Being a woman is a large part of who we are. We can't feel good about ourselves and not feel good about our femininity.

To be comfortable with her power, a woman must be both powerful and feminine. She can't be powerful in the same way as a man because she is judged on women's standards. Nevertheless, she can be clear on her goals and she can hold onto them tenaciously, without resorting to tantrums, foul language, or other male power-grabbing behavior.

In addition, she must reconcile herself to taking on authority. Finding this balance of femininity and authority is a challenge that men have never faced. But if a woman seems too masculine she will be labeled "bitch," "barracuda," or worse. Conversely, a highly feminine woman will never be heard and may be asked to take the minutes and serve the coffee. When we talk about power plays in Chapter 8, you'll find a myriad of appropriate ways to display power.

Despite the difficulties, however, be assured that a balance is possible. Take Helene. She is president of a company that provides psychological, financial, and legal assistance to individuals in large organizations; she is also the state president of her professional association. She is warm, charming, and funny, but when you have pushed her beyond her limits, you know it; her demeanor turns chillingly serious. This switch from typical feminine warmth warns those who think that she might be a pushover. Helene has been able to find that middle ground in which she can be feminine and play hardball at the same time. With practice and experimentation, you too can find a comfort zone to balance both. It may not be easy or immediately evident, but it is possible.

We Give Power to Him and Take It from Her

Our discomfort with being powerful is rooted, in part, in how the world worked when we were growing up. The person who ran the school—the principal—was usually a man. Those who did the work—the teachers—were generally women. If you went to a hospital, the doctor was a man and the nurses were women. If you went to Wal-Mart, the manager was a man; the clerks, women. The message was clear: Men give orders, women do the work.

Although times have changed, we still give power to men and take it from women. An unknown man can enter an office and tell the staff what he wants and who he must see. Likely as not, the assistants will jump. If a woman makes the same demands, she is more apt to be grilled about who sent her, whether she has an appointment, and exactly what she is after.

I used to travel with a colleague whom I'll call Jim Smith. When we boarded the plane, the first-class flight attendant would have our names on the roster as Dr. Heim and Mr. Smith. She'd look at us, refer to the roster, look back at us and say to Jim, "Dr. Heim?" If there was only one doctor between us, Jim clearly had to be it— even if that left me being Mr. Smith. We are so ready to see men in leadership positions, we become blind to obvious disparities.

Ruth was in line for a position as a vice president in a film distribution company. She lobbied for the job but was told that since she was only in her twenties she was not "seasoned" enough; certainly with age she would be ready for the position. A year later, Frank was made a vice president; he was a year younger than Ruth, and with less experience.

When Ruth asked the decision makers about Frank's age, they seemed surprised that age was an issue. It seemed natural for a man to be in the power position; it was the woman who was put through extra hurdles before she could be seen as ready for such a position.

Backing Away from Power

When women finally do achieve power and authority, they often feel so uncomfortable they sabotage themselves. Once when I offered a communication workshop at the home office of an insurance company, I spent the break talking with Inez, who, as she put it, "worked down in data processing." Several weeks later I was asked to consult with the manager of data processing. Much to my amazement, Inez showed up.

"Why didn't you tell me you're the manager of this department?" I asked.

Her answers were deferential. "Oh, well, I didn't want to make a big deal. I don't really do the work; the employees do it," she said.

More often than not, when power lands right in our laps we back away rather than embrace it. Perhaps our discomfort is related to the fear that we'll be attacked by other women if we behave as if we have more power than they. Good girls don't brag or shine the light on their own achievements. Moreover, since women are unused to being in power positions, they tend to devalue their leadership skills, or even fail to recognize them.

Miranda is president of a company that makes uniforms for a worldwide fast-food chain. When I mentioned in a workshop how women will often downplay their power, particularly with other women, Miranda shared her experience during a recent vacation spent riding horses. During her holiday, she cleaned out the stalls with a young woman who asked about her work. Miranda said she first mumbled incoherently, hoping that would be enough. The young woman pressed, "What exactly do you do?"

"I sell clothes."

The young woman probed, "Are you a salesperson?"

"Not exactly."

In the end, Miranda did divulge her position, but she had been mystified about why this had been so uncomfortable. Once she understood how difficult it is for women to display their power she said, "Probably the best thing I could have done for that young woman was to tell her I am the president of a company and talk with her about what it's like."

Hardball strategy par excellence: Don't back away from your

power. You only undermine yourself when you do. If asked, state your rank and position. Embrace reality, and others will too.

▶ MAKE IT UP

In an interview in *Modern Maturity,* CBS reporter Leslie Stahl explored some of her weaknesses in public. "I'm not a gifted writer. In the beginning, I thought I had to make my scripts perfect. I'd make three hundred phone calls and have to have every one of them returned. It drove everyone crazy. I also was too honest with the people I worked with. I was always telling them, 'I don't know if I can make my deadline. I'm so worried that my sources aren't going to call me back, I don't know how to start this story.' One day, I got a partner, Bill Plante, and noticed he never did that. He had the same anxieties but he didn't tell the office about it. In fact, he would always say, 'Everything's under control.' The office started gaining more confidence in him than me. I learned that my way was not the way to instill confidence—and I think a lot of women don't know that. I had to train myself to keep my mouth shut."

Men cover their underlying fears. They maintain an I-can-handle-the-ball; pass-it-to-me exterior, even if they worry that they can't. Women are less concerned about the I-can-handle-anything facade. Our agenda is more personal, so we have no qualms about expressing our shortcomings. For instance, if the relationship is important and your boss has asked you to perform a task you're afraid you won't do right or well, you may feel the need to confess your limitations to maintain the relationship, just like Leslie Stahl did.

Guessing at an answer and acting as if we really know is a strategy of hardball, much like bluffing. And when we act as if we're in charge, that's often exactly what happens. Of course, the reverse is also true. Blurting the painful truth or couching your statements in vagueness and insecurity can work to your detriment in the business setting.

Jan worked in a manufacturing company that was restructuring how it made its product. The organization was moving from a traditional, hierarchical command and control structure to a flatter configuration that included self-managed teams. Nobody inside the company knew how to do business this new way. The head of operations decided to pick Jan's brain, since she was a highly respected member of the quality department.

Jan's reply was as follows: "Well I'm not sure. You know I haven't had any experience in this formal approach. But I suppose we could try giving this to the work cells to solve, though I'm not sure they would resolve it. If they don't, we can have R&D, engineering, and manufacturing form a team to look at it. If those two approaches don't work, I suppose we could call in a consultant. But to be perfectly honest, I'm just not sure."

Feeling unsettled about Jan's suggestions, the head of operations asked one of Jan's peers how he would solve the problem. "I think its pretty obvious," Don replied. "We form a cross-functional team to take care of it. If they can't do it, we'll give it to one of the cells to chew on. And we can always use a consultant as a backup. No problem."

Need I mention that Don was given responsibility for this plum opportunity? Even though the suggestions were almost identical, he sounded so much more assured and knowledgeable, he was easier to bank on. The critical factor here was that Don didn't know any more than Jan did—he just acted as if he did.

In our need to be absolutely honest about our shortcomings, we women often go to extremes. Indeed, we *go into the confessional.* Our real message is, "Before I tell you any of my ideas I want you to understand the depths of my ignorance, and only when I feel sure that you understand how much I don't know will I feel comfortable telling you what I do know."

When I asked Jan why she had articulated her suggestions as she did, she explained, "I was just telling the truth." And certainly she was, but her accent was on the wrong syllable. If Jan could learn to speak with the accent of assurance, her real message— "I've got some good ideas about how to handle this"—would then be heard.

Look at it this way: When asked a question about how you'd accomplish a goal, all that's required is that you give it your best shot. Say what makes sense to you and leave it at that. Rest assured that your colleagues will find out about what you don't know on their own. You don't need to help them. So the next time someone asks you how you'd handle something, remember: Make it up and act as if you know! In the following chapter, we'll explore other power play strategies.

TAKING A LEAD ON LEADERSHIP

- There is no single appropriate leadership style.
- Choose a leadership style based on the competence and commitment level of the employee.
- Setting clear goals is key.
- Supporting and coaching may be comfortable, but directing and delegating are also effective styles.
- Don't back away from leadership positions.
- Although the flat structure may be more familiar, the hierarchy is usually where you live.
- To a man, either you're above him or below him in the hierarchy, and if you're above, you'd better call the shots.
- Women employees will often expect to be collaborative, but that isn't always the most appropriate style.
- Women resist "serving" other women.
- When another woman wins accolades, be sure to support her.
- You must be powerful to be successful.
- You can be both powerful and feminine, but it takes work and experimentation.
- Accept reality: Embrace your power.
- Don't take power away from women and hand it to men.
- Make it up and act as if you know!

7

POWER TALK:
Using Language to Your Advantage

▼
HARDBALL LESSONS BOYS LEARN

- Be aggressive; fight back and dominate your opponent.
- Act aggressively, even if you don't feel aggressive.
- Take the floor; outshout the opposition.
- Conversations should help solve problems and reach goals.
- Banter is a part of bonding and rough-and-tumble play.

▼
HOUSE AND DOLL LESSONS GIRLS LEARN

- Don't fight back, even if you're being attacked.
- Don't interrupt; wait your turn and let your friends talk.
- Conversations should enhance intimacy.
- Banter can hurt someone's feelings and should be avoided.

▼ ▼ ▼ ▼ ▼ It was a beautiful Monday morning at a mountain retreat. I was running a team-building session with the top twelve executives—all men—of a high-tech engineering firm. We were about an hour into the day when Karl spoke up. I'd been forewarned that he was going to be my biggest challenge. His boss, the president, told me that Karl was skeptical about "all this human relations stuff" and had been resisting this retreat. Besides, Karl thought a woman couldn't "handle" the group.

I was in the midst of explaining how personal perceptions impact team communication when Karl broke in with a challenging question. "Well, Pat," he asked smugly, "how do you think you're doing with this group?"

I strolled over to him, put my hands on my hips, got in his face—literally six inches away—and said slowly and deliberately, "Karl, it's always difficult to see yourself. How do *you* think I'm doing?"

Apparently this was not the meek response he had expected. "Look at Karl," exclaimed one of his colleagues. "He's blushing." Everyone turned and laughed. Most important for me, however, Karl became my biggest supporter and the strongest advocate for the team-building process.

During this incident, I wondered why this guy was beating up on me. I was just doing the job his company had hired me to do. But my logical side knew he and I were engaged in a game of aggression. How I handled Karl would determine whether these men would allow me to be the leader the rest of the day. And so I took him out. I was truly astonished at how well it worked.

Men respect tough, aggressive players. As women, however, we are brought up to be supportive of others and to avoid fighting back, even when attacked. But among men, "wimping out" can cause one to lose points—lots of them. The fact that I stood my ground against Karl forced him to perceive me as a tough player. He wanted to be on my team because I seemed powerful and assertive.

Aggression is an essential element of hardball. You will find the roots of male aggression in boys' play. Boys are concerned with dominance. They interrupt each other; they use threats, commands, and boasts of authority; they refuse to accede to domination. They heckle each other, practice one-upmanship, and call names. These verbal power plays help boys move up in the hierarchy. Conversely, if a boy is acquiescent, he will lose status.

You should note, however, that just because a male appears aggressive doesn't mean he actually is. As one man explained in a workshop, "The goal is to look mean even when you're not." Posturing belligerence is as important as being belligerent.

The pace and tenor of girls' interactions have little to do with dominance. Girls express agreement, pause to let others speak, and acknowledge what a playmate has said before chiming in. With these different orientations, problems can arise when men and women meet in the halls and around the conference table.

In this chapter we are going to focus on verbal displays of powerfulness and aggression during hardball:

- How men do it.
- What it gets them.
- How women back off and lose when others become aggressive.
- How and when it's important for women to be (or appear) powerful so that they can win at hardball too.

▶ MALE AND FEMALE TALK

Conversations between men and women are sometimes like those old transoceanic phone calls with a one-second delay. Both parties inadvertently step on each other's sentences and pause awkwardly; the discourse proceeds in fits and starts. Consequently, men and women often feel a vague discomfort when talking to each other, and neither are quite sure why. The clumsiness stems from a basic difference in our communication patterns.

When women talk, they seek to establish closeness and friendship. They validate their companions' feelings, share intimate details of their lives, and build rapport. Men, on the other hand, are goal oriented. They use conversation to convey information, make points, reach objectives, give instructions, and expound on their view of the workings of the world or how a task should be accomplished.

The characteristic ways women and men shop illustrate the differences. As I explained in Chapter 2, women frequently go to the mall with a friend, not because they need to purchase new belongings but because it gives them an opportunity to spend time with each other. For men, however, shopping is merely hunt and kill. Once they've found what they're after, they're out of there.

Phone conversations are similar. A woman told me that her father often called her simply to make contact. He missed his little girl, but he always began these conversations by asking if she had changed the oil in her car. He needed a purpose, a goal for calling. Many men see the delivery of information (the kill) as the point of conversation.

Women feel comfortable calling simply to say hello. My aunt died at the age of ninety-two. Her sister, eighty-eight, was beside herself with loneliness because they had long daily telephone conversations all their lives. Most men would be mystified about what these two would have had to say to each other after all these years.

The dissimilarity in communication styles also complicates decision-related discussions. A workshop participant told me she was facing a career crossroads: Phyllis had to decide whether to stay in her present job and advance slowly or go with an upstart organization where she might progress quickly or be out of a job if the company folded. She wanted to talk this over with her husband, Lee, but as soon as she brought it up, he simply told her which job to take. Phyllis became angry and pulled away.

"All I wanted to do was discuss my options," she complained, "but Lee started bossing me around and treating me like a child who can't make up her own mind!" Phyllis became irritated because she felt her husband was trying to control her, whereas Lee got bent out of shape because from his viewpoint, Phyllis had asked for his advice and then didn't take it.

While Phyllis and Lee's communication issues affected their relationship, the invisible linguistic devices that women use can cost far more than they realize. I was called upon as an expert witness in a case involving two female police officers in Santa Barbara, California, who sued the city because they had not won advancement to the level of sergeant. It seems that they had repeatedly scored well on the written portion of their promotion exams but their performance during the verbal part of the competition fell short. All of the examiners for the oral part of the test were men, and in 150 years, no woman had ever reached the rank of sergeant in that city's police force.

The male interviewers most likely expected the women to talk like men. When they didn't, they saw the candidates as weak and indecisive. During my testimony, I pointed out how differently men and women communicate—a fact that the police department had not taken into account in evaluating these two women, even though the women had written letters pointing out this fact. The women won their case to the tune of $3.2 million.

To resolve these communication issues, it's important to recognize that they exist. In this chapter, we will look at thirteen power talk strategies to help you communicate to men in a way that they will hear as decisive and authoritative.

▶ NOT SO CLOSE, MA'AM

Women establish closeness and intimacy by sharing hopes, concerns, wishes, and feelings. It is not uncommon for two previously unacquainted women who sit beside each other at a party or on a plane to reveal intimate details of their lives within five minutes. Indeed, women show caring and concern for others by bringing up the difficulties their friends or acquaintances face. Talking about these is a way to express solidarity.

Most men find such intimate conversation highly uncomfortable because it's often alien to childhood experiences and because it supports an openness that from the male perspective creates vulnerability. A man fears that if another is aware of his work- or home-related frustrations, he may lose his place in the hierarchy. If he were to say, for instance, "I'm so aggravated with my boss! I can't get through to him," he could be seen as weak.

The discussion of difficulties is particularly troublesome. One of my male colleagues had lost his job twice within a three-year period. His wife was eight months pregnant at the time of the most recent layoff. I phoned Jake regularly because I wanted to let him know I cared. But I was faced with a dilemma: My calling only highlighted the sad fact that Jake had lost another job. In his eyes, my concern put him in the awkward, one-down position of telling me how great the job search was going, when I suspected it wasn't. Talking about a weakness only made Jake a less desirable player in his own estimation and that of other men.

A woman is far more willing to talk about her flaws, and she'll often expose her apprehensions:

- "I hate doing presentations. I get so nervous."
- "Finance always drives me buggy. I can't make heads or tails of the numbers."
- "Mr. Carlin intimidates the hell out of me."

She establishes closeness through personal sharing. But when men hear a woman talk this way, they may determine that she isn't as strong as they thought and that she would make a poor addition to their team. It's far better to display your fortitude to men, rather than your weakness.

POWER TALK STRATEGY **1** ▼   ▼   ▼   ▼

It's a wise hardball player who is cautious about sharing her vulnerabilities with a man.

▶ WHAT'S YOUR BOTTOM LINE?

Many women are concerned about talking too much. Since childhood, we've heard jokes about the woman who goes on and on, not knowing when to stop. Yet research consistently finds that men talk more and dominate most conversations and meetings.

When a research team investigated who actually had the floor in a meeting, the men spoke from 10.66 to 17.07 seconds, while the women spoke from 3 to 10 seconds. The longest female comment was shorter than the shortest male comment. And the men spoke more frequently. Yet I've observed that women often feel hypersensitive about how much they are talking; they're afraid to dominate.

Men display dominance by controlling the conversation. But if you speak briefly and then spend the rest of the time listening, your male boss may very well see you as having nothing to contribute to his team. Therefore, getting air time is important, but you must also attend to what you talk about.

Men perceive that women talk around the point and don't get to the bottom line. But women often feel uncomfortable delivering the punchline until the interpersonal side is in place. We're afraid our listener will misunderstand us if the relationship is out of sync. Many men don't need to deal with the interpersonal component, because from their point of view, logical issues have little to do with relationships. Consequently, they see such preambles as a waste of time. The labels that result from this gap in communication are often damaging to relationships: A woman may be pegged disorganized, confused, verbose, and strange. A man is seen as uncaring, impatient, and unwilling to listen.

Deborah Tannen suggests that men believe women are loquacious because women discuss interpersonal issues that don't interest men. I saw this in action recently at a meeting between a citizens' committee and the all-male board of directors of the local airport. The committee came to present concerns about excessive airplane noise in their neighborhood. The head of the group, Leslie, began her presentation by trying to establish rapport with the board. "We really appreciate your giving us time on your agenda," she said warmly. "We know you're as concerned as we are about the noise violations. You have a tough job balancing community and pilot needs. . . ."

When Leslie sensed the board's resistance and resentment, rather than getting to the point, she stepped up her efforts in rapport building. "The community appreciates the different needs you have to balance. We know you can't do anything at this meeting and we're not expecting . . ." she went on and on.

This frustrated the board even more. Members studied their fingernails, grimaced, and shot looks at each other. They wanted the bottom line. But Leslie wasn't going to get to the bottom line until she had achieved a feeling of harmony. This led to a downward spiral: The more Leslie talked, the more irritated the board became, and so the more she felt she needed to talk. Eventually, the board psychologically dismissed her and therefore dismissed her committee and its noble objectives.

The flat culture women grew up in is another reason that they will take you through the process and share with you all the considerations they made before telling you their final recommendation. If Kari and I are working on a project and she asks me what I think we should do at this juncture, if I were to say, "Do X," that would sound too hierarchical to her. What I am more likely to do is verbally take her through the process: "I looked at A and discarded it for these reasons. I looked at B and discarded it for these other reasons. C wouldn't work either. I therefore concluded that X is the best thing to do."

That is a functional way of telling another woman what to do. But men hear this preamble as unnecessary. Even worse, it confuses and irritates them because they're looking for the bottom line. They wonder, "Why would Marla spend all that time talking about options she thinks don't work instead of just telling me what does!" This is yet another instance where goal orientation versus process gets in our way. When speaking to men, it's usually much better to simply cut to the chase: "I'm recommending X for these reasons."

This process/content conflict is analogous to what Deborah Tannen calls rapport talk vs. report talk. Imagine a couple has come home from work at night. She says, "How was your day?"

"Fine."

"What did you do today?"

"Not much."

"Well, you must have done something."

"Acme meeting."

"What happened in the Acme meeting?"

"Not much."

And on it goes. As he sees it, she poses him a question, he kills that question and she poses him another question. He wonders how many questions he has to kill before he gets to watch the news. From her perspective, she doesn't care what this guy talks about. She just wants to spend some time relating to him on a personal level.

Here's how this issue plays out in the work setting: Sarah asks her coworker Scott for his opinion on what she should do about a project problem. She's trying to build rapport with him, but he sees this as a goal he must achieve. He says, "You should do X." She then solicits opinions from Marissa, Tim, and Rob and decides to go with Rob's suggestion. Scott is outraged. "Why did she ask me in the first place if she's going to take someone else's advice?" And Sarah is miffed that Scott is upset. She doesn't understand why she has lost an ally.

POWER TALK STRATEGY **2** ▼   ▼   ▼   ▼

If you're dealing with a group of men, you'll create the perception that you're a strong player with something to offer if you limit rapport building and get to the bottom line relatively quickly. Otherwise, your colleagues may be irritated and unreceptive by the time you get to the point.

▶ MAKING YOURSELF HEARD

Are your words evaporating? If they are, you're not alone. Imagine you're in a meeting. The group is discussing the best way to deal with a problem. You throw out an excellent idea, but it seems as if no one has heard you. Five minutes later, Harry brings up the very same solution. Everybody thinks he's brilliant.

When I share this scenario in workshops, women roll their eyes and groan because it's such a common occurrence. Why? Our customary manner of speaking creates and exacerbates the problem. In meetings we tend to bring up our ideas in the form of questions, such as, "Don't you think it would be a good idea to change our marketing strategy?" rather than simple declarative sentences, such as, "We need to change our marketing strategy. Here's what I propose. . . ." We speak briefly with a high pitch and low volume, whereas men claim the floor by speaking loudly and at length in declamatory tones.

In addition, women tend to wait for their turn to speak. In most meetings, however, that turn never comes. Men, comfortable with the process of jockeying for position in the hierarchy, push into the conversation and get their ideas out. If a woman waits for others to finish before she jumps in, she may be waiting a very long time.

Moreover, men interrupt women a great deal. Research shows that when a man and woman are speaking, he is likely to do 96 percent of the interrupting. More often than not, she lets him have the floor. Why? In order to appear polite and to maintain good working relationships, women believe others deserve air time. But this can be their undoing.

Men prove the worth of their ideas by dominating the floor. If they give up easily, other men assume they're uncommitted to their own proposals. How valid can those ideas be if the originator himself is unwilling to fight for them? Unfortunately, since women have been acculturated to surrender rather than fight for their point of view, their male colleagues, applying the usual standards, believe these retreating women don't deserve to win either. As a result, women end up losing frequently.

So what can you do when you've been abruptly cut off or ignored? Most of us are polite and give over the floor when interrupted, but from my observations, powerful women deal with interruptions by ignoring them. They keep talking in the same tone, neither making eye contact with the interrupter nor changing the speed or volume of their presentation. Indeed, they simply act as if that other, extraneous voice doesn't exist.

Displaying more dominant ways of communicating makes most women very uncomfortable. But we need to remember that for men, these discussions and arguments are a game. The strong players come out on top; they're the ones with whom others want to associate in the future. At the same time, we need to be mindful that arguing forcefully can be a double-edged sword for women. Our best bet may be to target what the authors of *Breaking the Glass Ceiling* call the "narrow band of acceptable behavior"; to be strong enough to be noticed but not so strong as to be rejected and labeled overbearing.

The narrow band is hard to define, as it varies from person to person and organization to organization. But since women are all good at reading nonverbal feedback, we might try experimenting with behaviors to see how far we can go without it costing us in some way. The first step, however, is to recognize that the band exists.

How do you know if you've overstepped the bounds? Most of the signs are nonverbal: inattention, resistance (crossed arms or chest out), and anger. Bear in mind, however, that if a peer is angry, he may have just realized that he is wrong and is about to lose, so he may be going on the offensive.

POWER TALK STRATEGY **3** ▼   ▼   ▼   ▼

Make suggestions in declarative sentences, not framed as questions. Take as much time as you need and speak assertively, with low pitch. Don't wait for others to invite you to speak before you join in. If interrupted, ignore the interrupter and keep on talking, but be careful to avoid stridency.

▶ USING ANGER TO YOUR ADVANTAGE

Women often are terrified of expressing anger because they fear it will damage relationships. We have been taught that good girls are gentle, calm, and mild. An angry girl is not a nice girl, so we have learned to express our anger indirectly: We slam doors, tell others, avoid, withdraw, sabotage.

It is your right to be angry and express it, but it's important to be strategic about it. Merely looking angry isn't enough. A permanent scowl is an indirect message that's easily dismissed or ignored. Worse yet, it can irritate others who may feel you've been evasive or are playing games. Then the agenda shifts from your issues to the others' anger at your indirection.

Moreover, you need to channel your anger so you can think and say exactly what you wish. If you're out of control, you may say or do things you'll regret later. It's important not to cry, scream, or seem wild-eyed if you want to be taken seriously. If you feel as if you're going to explode, get yourself out of the situation until you've calmed down enough to direct your anger. But you don't want to wait so long that the issue becomes old business.

Mild-mannered Cheryl became angry at her boss for divulging the incomes of other employees to a manager and one of her staff, but she used her anger wisely. If Cheryl had clung to her usual approach saying, "We need to talk about the salary thing. You probably shouldn't have done that. I don't think it was such a good idea," her boss would have dismissed her concerns as unimportant.

Instead, she felt righteously indignant. She stormed into his office, shut the door, and said evenly and forcefully, "Brad, did you tell Lloyd and Shana what the others are making?"

He tried to justify himself with excuses. "Well, I was only trying to solve this other problem," he said lamely.

She thumped his chest with an outstretched finger. "You know that information is confidential and you're not supposed to divulge it to anyone!" As she backed him up against the window, eventually he apologized.

Cheryl was an outstanding, valued employee who had demonstrated her loyalty to Brad years before. She had never expressed such anger before, yet her outburst was justified. (I wouldn't try this, however, your first month on the job.)

Your anger should be a significant variance from your usual behavior for it to be attended to or taken seriously. If you use anger on a regular basis, you'll be seen as a "bitch." It's better to view this powerful emotion as a secret play that you can pull out every now and then. Indeed, sometimes it's wise to appear angry to force the resolution of a conflict.

Two of my male employees were constantly whining to me about each other. Although I wasn't angry at them, after a while I did weary of their antics. I called them both into my office. "I'm sick and tired of your uncooperative behavior," I told them. "You're going to figure out a plan to get along and you'll figure it out by this afternoon, or you'll both be sorry."

Since I had never been angry with these two before, my indignation frightened them. Soon they came up with a plan about how they were going to get their work done amenably.

POWER TALK STRATEGY **4** ▾   ▾   ▾   ▾

Be strategic about expressing your anger; never scream or appear to lose control. When appropriate, you can feign anger in order to resolve a conflict.

▶ VERBAL BANTERING

Colin Powell, secretary of state under George W. Bush, was interviewed at one time for a senior Defense Department position by John Kester, the civilian aide to President Carter's defense secretary.

"He had a very good, direct personality," said Kester in a *Los Angeles Times* article. "He gave me the sense that he was a very straight dealer. Right away he said something like, 'How did you happen to bring me here?' and I said, 'I checked you out and heard a lot of good things about you.' Powell said, 'Well, as a matter of fact, I checked you out, too, and it wasn't all good.' "

According to the report, "Powell delivered the line with a disarming grin, and Kester was impressed with his candor."

If this interchange had transpired between two women meeting for the first time, would they have responded as positively? It's hard to say. "I checked you out and it wasn't all good," might be heard as a personal attack. If Kester had been a woman, Powell might have ruined his chances for getting the job.

Men see banter as good, rough-and-tumble play. It's a way to simultaneously bond and to clarify a hierarchical relationship. Because women don't have this need to clarify relative power, they perceive such interactions as unnecessary and unwarranted attacks.

What to do if you find yourself the brunt of bantering remarks? First, realize that bantering is not true conflict but hierarchy negotiation and play for men. We often misconstrue its intent because we respond to the conflict it implies. Since conflict damages relationships (and banter slaps relationships), women often take such remarks personally.

Be aware, too, that it's important to look strong. (See Chapter 8, "Power Moves.") Indeed, you may gain the edge in these conflicts, since men don't usually expect women to fight back. Draw yourself up to your full height and square your shoulders. Then determine how to get back on top of this verbal negotiation. What can you say that will put you in a powerful position and let your colleague know "I'm not weaker than you"? For instance, if your peer says, "Why in the hell did you wear that?" you can respond, "Oh, and since when are you in charge of the dress code?" In that way, you throw the responsibility back rather than accepting it yourself and letting it make you feel small.

When you take an assertive approach to bantering, the man deflates slightly and becomes conciliatory, as in the situation with Karl, the reluctant workshop participant. In fact, this approach worked again when I flew home from a recent business trip. Seated beside a late-middle-aged airline employee in uniform, I struck up a conversation about changes in the industry. But when

I asked the man whether he was a pilot, he responded sarcastically, "No, my mother just dresses me this way."

I felt attacked and belittled but decided to play it his way. I said, "This may surprise you, but I can't differentiate among pilots, flight attendants, and gate agents. I'm sure you're wearing something important to you that indicates your job, but I haven't a clue what it might be." Sheepishly pointing to doodads on his hat and shoulders, this gentleman indicated that he was indeed a pilot.

Bantering may not only be verbal. At one company, the all-male team decided to move the desk of a highly valued new hire every morning before she arrived, much to her consternation. But they were only playing . . . welcoming her in their own way. At another company, new members of the facilities team were sent in search of a tool called a "sky hook." This was an imaginary device—it didn't exist—and was the source of glee among the veteran members of the team as the new employee went around asking for this apparatus. I have since collected a list of twenty other nonexistent objects that new team members at other companies are asked to look for, including a bucket of steam, the "long stand," and checkered paint. Women will often see this as cruel teasing and can take offense if it is directed at them, but the intent is to welcome the new member with a bit of levity.

Verbal bantering doesn't take place just at first meetings. Men use it constantly to renegotiate their position in the hierarchy. At times the tone can become quite personal. One day I was having lunch with the president and seven vice presidents, all men, of a manufacturing company with which I was consulting. One of the vice presidents said, "I saw a picture taken from a spy satellite recently. You wouldn't believe the resolution. I swear, if someone were standing on the deck of a ship holding a pack of cigarettes, you'd be able to tell the brand."

Another vice president turned to the president and said, "Hear that, Hal? You'd better be careful about going out in your Jacuzzi without any clothes on."

To that the first man replied, "Naw, the resolution wasn't that good!"

Hal laughed with the rest of the men. "Two points for you," he said. Such personal jibes might feel too close to home for many women.

Physical or scatological humor and the comparison of body parts are typical forms of male bonding. Women can find themselves in an uncomfortable situation when these interactions occur, because scatological jokes can seem offensive. My personal preference, however, is to play it cool. To display any discomfort would only emphasize that I am an alien among these men. In fact, as long as the joke isn't at my expense, I take this kind of humor as a backhanded compliment: The men have become so comfortable in my presence, they can now be themselves. As I explained in Chapter 3, however, you do need to set your own boundaries and determine what, in your value system, is your limit. If you're really uncomfortable, make light of their jokes with statements such as, "You guys are really gross. Can we change the subject?"

POWER TALK STRATEGY **5** ▼   ▼   ▼   ▼

React assertively to bantering, and most likely the man will deflate and accommodate. Within the bounds of decency and personal values, it's okay to tolerate overhearing physical humor among men.

► LET ME INTRODUCE YOU

Have you ever paid attention to the fact that men and women are introduced differently? For men, the emphasis is placed on power and control, whereas for women the accent falls on their physical attributes and their helping and social skills. Most often, old stereotypical roles are noticed and reinforced.

Introductions are an important source of information. How you're introduced influences how you're perceived, both positively and negatively. I found this to be painfully true when I overheard Lawrence, a hospital administrator, present his two second-in-command managers to a visitor from the corporate offices. "Art," he said, "I'd like you to meet John, our assistant administrator. Since he's been on board, we've gotten our computer software up and running. And this is Mary, the director of nursing. She is the glue in this hospital. We sometimes call her Mother Mary." Ouch!

Lawrence was truly trying to do his best for both parties, but he had unwittingly tarnished Mary's executive image by emphasizing her nurturing qualities. Yet if anyone were to suggest to Lawrence that he'd done Mary dirty, he would have been offended. In fact, he would probably argue that he said only "nice" things that were also true. So much damage is invisible.

Titles (or their omission) can also draw attention to those who have power—and those who don't. I once heard a woman introduce a doctoral committee as follows: "Dr. Fest, Dr. Hill, Dr. Jones, Dr. Darnell, and Joyce." Joyce, the only female, was also Dr. Hocker. Recently a woman told me she attended a roundtable of senior executives at which a panel spoke. The moderator introduced the panelists by first and last name and title, except for the lone woman, who was introduced by her first name. If I were to hazard a guess, no malice was intended. But at the same time, the message was clear: The woman wasn't equal to the rest.

What can you do when you find yourself in such a situation? You might choose to talk with the person afterward, as did Mary and Joyce. Feeling comfortable in her relationship with Lawrence, Mary approached him after the introductions: "I'm sure you don't even realize you're doing this," she said, "but with the stereotype of nurses being caretakers and the nickname 'Mother Mary,' I'm afraid you're conveying the wrong message. You know, I am responsible for 60 percent of the finances in this joint."

The woman who introduced Dr. Hocker was horrified at her gaffe, and I'm sure, never made the same mistake again. There was no point in Joyce bringing it up during the meeting, since everyone already knew she was Dr. Hocker.

In the third instance, the woman could have seized the opportunity to introduce herself during the panel discussion. This would have had to be done so as not to embarrass the moderator. To simply say in prefacing one of her comments, "In my position as vice president of planning for Megawatt Industries, I've found . . ." would allow the anonymous woman to establish her status without drawing attention to the slight.

If your position has been disregarded during an introduction, rectify the situation at the moment by injecting your rank and serial number into the conversation, or else speak to the introducer and ask for parity in the future.

▶ LET ME INTRODUCE MYSELF

It's also important to look at how we introduce ourselves. We create powerful images in the way we describe ourselves to others.

Case in point: I recently had lunch with a woman who is a magazine publisher. I asked her what publishers really do, and she proceeded to explain the process of editing, printing, managing the budget, and so on. Then she concluded with, "Anyone can do it." A man would never have suggested that someone else could easily fill his shoes. He would want to appear powerful, particularly upon meeting someone for the first time.

Take a minute to think of the moment when you made a new acquaintance who asked, "And what do you do for a living?" I've heard a few women use the deadly phrase "I'm just a _____." More often, however, we diminish our power in subtler ways. For example, we're far likelier to say, "I'm a financial analyst and I help with the budgeting and forecasting," than, "I'm a financial analyst. I'm responsible for tracking a $300 million budget and forecasting the company's five-year financial strategy." In the first instance we appear to be a stereotypical female helper; in the second, we are powerful doers.

Men often use the royal "we." Instead of describing their own position, they include everyone above them, all their peers, and everyone below them. "I work at Hercules Heating Equipment," George might say. "We are the largest producers of heating equipment in the central United States. We have $900 million in assets, and have just acquired the largest federal contract ever granted for this kind of equipment." George hasn't given a clue as to his position, but it sure sounds as if he wields tremendous power.

In introducing yourself, don't present yourself as a helper or nurturer but as a powerful go-getter. Describe your accomplishments accurately. If it feels comfortable, adopt the royal "we."

▶ LET ME EVALUATE YOU

Recommendation letters can also do women more harm than good. If you have any around the office, pull them out and take a look. I think you'll be surprised. When I was responsible for an executive trainee program, I received over three hundred such letters a year. One day, while plowing through them on the plane, I realized that the descriptions for men and women were consistently different. Males were described as dynamic, can-do go-getters. Females were charming, sweet, gentle, outgoing, and friendly. One woman was even complimented for being self-effacing. Does that sound like executive material to you?

The most common description for men was "aggressive." I never saw a woman described this way, probably because it translates into "bitch." Frequently men were hailed for their "moral character," but never a woman. To bring up morality would have touched on her sexual life. Even with the best intentions, we color the picture of men and women. Men as doers; women as nice helpers.

The performance appraisal also impacts our career. Even an outstanding evaluation can be a major stumbling block for a woman. During a workshop in a large federal agency, Alicia told me she had recently received what she thought was an excellent evaluation. During the workshop, however, it dawned on her that this appraisal would backfire.

Alicia was a manager, hoping to advance into a senior management position. Her boss had described her as caring, nurturing, dependable, helpful, and cooperative. At the time she felt great—these were all positive attributes and accurately represented her character. Yet in the workshop, Alicia realized that while she may value these traits, people looking for a senior manager would likely remain unimpressed. And she wasn't alone in this problem. A U.S. Department of Labor study found that women's evaluations often include such words as *happy, friendly,* and *gets along well with others.* Sounds like a kindergarten report card to me!

Because Alicia's boss was an ally, she was able to discuss her evaluation with him. She emphasized that she knew he had positive intentions but was concerned about the image communicated to strangers. Since this was a federal bureaucracy and the performance appraisal was already signed, sealed, and delivered, little could be done at the moment to rectify the problem. But Alicia's boss agreed to an interim appraisal at six months and to be cautious of his use of words in the future.

POWER TALK STRATEGY 8 ▼   ▼   ▼   ▼

Be on guard for terms in evaluations that emphasize your stereotypically female qualities (helping, nurturing, caring) rather than your accomplishments. Depending on your relationship with your boss, you can say, "I know you didn't mean any harm, but 'self-effacing' is not to my advantage in applying for the management trainee program."

▶ ARE YOU A GIRL, A LADY, OR A WOMAN?

The terms *girl, lady,* and *woman* are often used interchangeably to describe women well out of puberty. Yet their impact is quite different. Studies have shown that the terms *girl* and *lady* have pejorative connotations: They conjure images of someone weaker and lazier; someone more nervous, afraid, dependent, immature, and inconsiderate; someone less sexy, intelligent, and certainly less charismatic than "woman." Indeed, the term *woman* is overwhelmingly interpreted as more favorable and is most often used to describe adult females who deserve respect.

We all know that girls don't know much, can't do much, and certainly don't deserve to lead or make a lot of money. Researchers investigating the impact of these terms found nothing that would make a woman prefer being called a "girl" rather than a "woman." Yet many women refer to themselves as girls and perpetrate extraordinary damage on other women by referring to the "girls over in accounting."

Once we begin paying attention, we can easily change how we

talk about ourselves, but what if someone in your office calls a woman a girl? One good solution is to use the word *woman* in the next sentence:

"That girl you sent over to help us was super."

"Great, she's one of the most competent women I work with."

The person you're talking to may well hear the awkward juxtaposition of the two terms and change. For slow learners, I suggest the sledgehammer method. Several years ago when I was teaching part-time at a business school, I went to lunch with the dean. He looked every inch a dean—mid-forties, graying at the temples, three-piece pin-striped suit, erect posture, serious face. Four times during lunch he called me a girl—but, hey, who's counting? Each time I used the word *woman* in the next sentence.

The fifth time he said, "Pat, it must be difficult for a girl to travel as much as you do."

I paused, thought about it, and answered, "Not any more than it would be for a boy like you."

His jaw dropped, his eyes flew open. And he got it.

POWER TALK STRATEGY 9 ▼   ▼   ▼   ▼

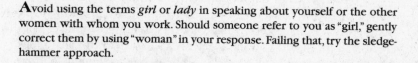

Avoid using the terms *girl* or *lady* in speaking about yourself or the other women with whom you work. Should someone refer to you as "girl," gently correct them by using "woman" in your response. Failing that, try the sledgehammer approach.

▶ VERBAL SABOTAGE

A national authority on personality types spoke at a large conference. She began her presentation with the following:

"I sort of thought what I'd cover this afternoon is some information from my book. My goal is that you learn something new and get your questions answered? And that you understand the differences in temperament and type. Okay? And that you understand the ways to integrate the two smoothly. Ooo, now that's a funny sentence."

In less than fifteen seconds this woman had sabotaged herself verbally four different ways: She used inflected sentences, tag questions, hedges, and self-derogation. These rhetorical devices function in female culture to create a sense of equality and involvement. But beware using them among men. These phrases can make it sound as if you're vulnerable, insecure, and in need of reassurance. The trick is to pay close attention to your audience and to be able to switch modes depending on the gender of the person with whom you're speaking. In mixed groups, the default mode is male. In this section, we'll talk about the extraordinary damage we women can do to ourselves when we sabotage our verbal communications.

Was That a Statement or a Question?

In an effort to avoid insisting that our way is the right way, we often ask a question when our real intent is to state our point of view: "Don't you think it would be a good idea to check everyone's calendars before making the reservations?" rather than "We need to check everyone's calendars before making the reservations." Unfortunately, a male colleague is unlikely to hear this as openness; he perceives the question as a sign of insecurity, if he hears it at all.

We often switch to question/statements when we are being verbally challenged with a query like, "Why in the hell would you say that?" At this point, keep in mind the first rule of swimming with sharks: Don't bleed. Question/statements signal to the sharks it's time to attack. You want to make crisp, assured statements ("I believe we should delay the project a month."), even if you don't feel all that crisp and assured.

Moreover, many women tag on questions to the end of their statements. These are really ways to create equality and involvement in the interaction.

"I believe this is the best way to do it, don't you?"

"Getting the budget approved was difficult, wasn't it?"

Or, as a friend wrote at the top of an article she sent me on such tag questions, "Interesting, no?"

The personality expert who punctuated her sentence with "Okay?" was signaling to the audience her uneasiness in a position of authority and her need for equity. But if she truly wanted to be the authority, she had to sound like one. If she determined it was important for her audience to understand the difference between type and temperament, she needed to tell them the difference, period. The "Okay?" asks for involvement.

You should, however, differentiate tag questions from a sincere request for information, such as, "I was thinking of starting the project next week. What do you think?" In this situation, you really do want your colleague's opinion. A tag question, on the other hand, signals to men your vulnerability and is a request for support . . . you know?

Women also craft questions from statements by way of inflection. In American English, the voice swings down at the end of a statement and up at the end of a question. Women, as did our speaker above, often unconsciously signal their vulnerability by swinging up at the end of a statement. A man told me his receptionist was driving him crazy by answering the phone, "Sebantian Construction?" To him, it sounded as if she didn't know where she worked.

POWER TALK STRATEGY **10** ▼   ▼   ▼   ▼

Don't turn statements into questions, especially if you're under fire. Avoid tag questions, and swing that voice down at the end of your statement.

Hedging Your Bet

Women often use *hedges* to flatten interactions. These include the following types of statements:

"I *sort of* thought we might start now."

"I *kind of* wanted to work on that project."

"This *could be* a better way to do it."

"I have *a little* problem with your approach."

Our expert began her presentation talking about what she "sort of thought" she'd cover. Her tentativeness was signaled loud and clear to the men in the audience.

You may wonder where we learned this verbal device. It starts early and can even be found in the Girl Scout oath.

Boy Scout oath: "On my honor I will do my duty . . ."

Girl Scout oath: "On my honor I will *try to* do my duty . . ."

We commit to nothing more than a "try." Even in our promises, we learn to hedge our bets. But hedges diminish the power of our statements. In the wrangle to get heard, these words and phrases make our point of view less valuable, since to men we sound as if we really don't believe in what we've said.

On the other hand, men make statements with conviction and assurance, even if they're uncertain. They may say "seven out of ten times" instead of "most," or "the planning department backs us all the way" instead of "the planning department thinks it will work."

One study analyzed essays written by applicants to an MBA program. The process required that applicants describe what they planned to do in the future. Men began their essays with "I will . . ." Women began with "I hope to . . ." or "I would like to . . ." Imagine you're on the selection committee. Who would you choose, the one who asserts he'll do something or the one who only hopes to?

POWER TALK STRATEGY 11 ▼   ▼   ▼   ▼

Avoid hedging in presenting your ideas; make positive assertions. Banish the verb *try* from your vocabulary.

Don't Pay Attention to This

One of the most damaging means of verbal sabotage is to discount what you're about to say in any number of ways:

"I may be wrong but . . ."

"I'm not sure about this, however."

"This is probably a stupid idea, but . . ."

"I hate to interrupt, but . . ."

These undermining declarations are another way of saying to men, "I don't want to catch you off guard. Get ready for stupidity." This is bleeding for the sharks. In using such statements, we express our vulnerability. For some men, that's all that's required to bring on an attack. Rest assured, if an idea is wrong or stupid, your colleagues will figure it out on their own.

Our expert was guilty of this faux pas when she criticized her own sentence right after she uttered it. If she didn't like what she was saying, why should we? She looked tremendously incompetent—precisely what she wanted to avoid.

Ironically, the expert is well respected professionally for her research and widely read books. As I listened to her speak, I had the feeling she unconsciously chose these words in order to say, "I want you to be comfortable with me. I'm just like you. Don't be intimidated." But the sharks in the audience got a whiff of the blood and went on the attack. I'm sure she didn't have a clue as to what went wrong.

POWER TALK STRATEGY 12 ▾   ▾   ▾   ▾

Don't discount what you're saying before you even say it. Let your listener draw his own conclusions.

▶ OH, NO! I THINK I'M GETTING MY PERIOD

I was once conducting a workshop on working in a man's world for the female managers of a company. In the next room, William was conducting a parallel workshop with the male managers on how to work with women. I nabbed this consultant for lunch and asked him what the men found most difficult about working with women. William looked me in the eye and said, "Menstruation."

I was floored. I could imagine a hundred possible issues, but that wasn't one of them. Seeing the shock on my face, he continued. "Look, it makes perfect sense from their point of view. Today's she's upset. He attributes it to being 'that time of the month.' A couple of days later she has calmed down. That only reinforces his perception."

Men may confuse our more voluable emotional responses with our menstrual cycles. When a woman expresses her disfavor or distress, she can appear out of control to a man. It's acceptable to be angry, but if you're highly volatile emotionally you can be quickly dismissed as a hysterical, menstruating female.

More important, perhaps, is how men perceive menstruation itself. Since my discussion with William, I've asked several other men what they thought about this issue. I was surprised to learn that the attitude William expressed was very common. In fact, one individual referred to executive row as "menstrual alley" because so many of his company's executives were women.

I explained to these men that a woman might become crabby before or during her period just as they would if someone cut them off on the freeway that morning. But if a woman has a client she must butter up or a sophisticated analysis to perform, she can abandon her crabbiness and become fully competent.

Many men perceive menstruation as an alien thing that invades our bodies and controls us. For instance, one fellow asked me, "Well, what if the president had a period?" as if the leader of the free world had never seen a bad day. Having never experienced it, they imbue the menstrual cycle with meaning and power it doesn't have. In fact, menstruation is a deeply mysterious process for men. And to add to its mystery, it's somehow tied to the phases of the moon.

If a woman complains to her female coworkers, "I have my period and I feel lousy," they understand the statement's significance or lack thereof. But if a woman shares this information with her male buddies, they will impute meaning to her actions and conjure inaccurate images.

The solution is to never allude to, mention, or bring up menstruation in the company of male colleagues. I have found they simply can't handle it. Neither should you draw attention to the symptoms of menopause, even if you're mopping your brow every five minutes. In fact, if you're in real physical distress, you should attribute your condition to some other illness—a cold, the flu, heartburn—or better yet, a sports injury. Unfortunately, the functioning of our female bodies evokes stereotypes that cause men to ascribe to it negative character traits such as hysteria, labile moods, and unbridled emotionality.

POWER TALK STRATEGY **13** ▾   ▾   ▾   ▾

Avoid all discussions involving the female reproductive cycle.

POWER TALK ROUNDUP

In your journal, answer the following questions:

1. How do I most effectively communicate power verbally?
2. What are some ways I sabotage myself verbally?
3. What steps am I going to take to increase my verbal communication of power?

VERBAL POWER PLAYS

- Men are goal oriented in their communication. Get to the bottom line quickly.
- Talking over interpersonal issues may be uncomfortable for a man.
- Holding the floor in a meeting can signal how important you think your idea is.
- When interrupted, just keep talking.
- Be aware of others introducing or describing you in powerless ways.
- In introducing yourself, be sure to focus on power and influence.
- Call yourself and other female colleagues *women,* not girls or ladies.
- Don't use hedges when you speak.
- Avoid ending statements with question marks or tag questions.
- Don't preface your statement with diminishing comments.
- Never bring up your period or menopause among male coworkers.

8

POWER MOVES:
Using Nonverbal Cues to Your Advantage

▼
HARDBALL LESSONS BOYS LEARN

- Demonstrate your dominance with aggressive displays.
- If you want to be a valued player, you need to look mean, rough, and tough.
- Shake hands and come out fighting.
- Don't show them when it hurts.

▼
HOUSE AND DOLL LESSONS GIRLS LEARN

- Smile and be sweet.
- Be nice and don't fight back.
- If you have power, don't show it or you'll seem too aggressive.
- Showing power breaks the power-dead-even rule.

▼ ▼ ▼ ▼ ▼ **C**ommunication always has at least two layers of meaning: the verbal (our words) and the nonverbal (what we express without words). Most often, nonverbal communication is unconscious. In this chapter, we will render it conscious, so that you can make more appropriate choices as the situation demands.

Interestingly, when verbal and nonverbal messages clash, the receiver trusts the latter. I'm sure you've experienced someone saying, "So nice to see you," when he clearly means, "Drop dead." His real intent is obvious in facial expression and posture, and you know how to read it.

Indeed, research has shown that women perceive nonverbal cues far more readily and interpret them more accurately than do men. Despite our advantage, however, we often lose ground in the tug-of-war with a man in the nonverbal arena. Boys learn myriad nonverbal displays of aggressiveness and dominance. Girls learn to avoid fighting back. In fact, we're barely concerned with aggressive nonverbal cues because we're busy building relationships. Consequently, when men display physical dominance, women often just let them have their way. So, although nonverbal communication is our strength, it can also be our downfall.

One caveat: Nonverbal cues may have a multitude of meanings. Crossed arms, a loud voice, or a sour face can send various messages. You must always evaluate a nonverbal cue in the context in which it occurs.

▶ COME ON, GIVE US A SMILE!

All humans smile when they're happy. But women often smile when they feel vulnerable. I call that the please-don't-attack-me-anymore smile. If a supervisor criticizes a woman's idea as ridiculous, the latter often smiles and unintentionally signals vulnerability.

Actually, smiling is frequently associated with subordinate status. This may be an inborn trait. Ethologist Frans de Waal explains in *Peacemaking Among the Primates* that juvenile rhesus monkeys grin when they're feeling intimidated. De Waal writes, "In social situations the grin signals submission and fear; it is the most reliable indicator of low status among rhesus monkeys. In other species, such as humans and apes, this facial expression has evolved into the smile, a sign of appeasement and affiliation, although an element of nervousness remains." If you doubt his observations, think back to your fifth-grade classroom when the teacher shouted, "And wipe that grin off your face," to a child she had just scolded.

Many women have described being deep in thought at their desks when a man comes by and says, "Come on, it can't be that bad! Give us a smile," as if she were supposed to sit there and smile all day. He wants that chirpy little powerless look.

Think of the powerful people you know. Your physician or attorney, for instance. He or she probably employs the stone face. It's a way of signaling power. In fact, as women move up the executive ladder they tend to lose their facial expression and become more inscrutable.

Now I'm not suggesting that you stop smiling or expressing other emotions. If you're happy or a situation is funny, a grin may be perfect. The problem arises, however, when you smile because you're feeling vulnerable or unhappy. Smiling under these circumstances sends a confusing mixed message.

That's what happened to one of my employees. Sandy was assigned a six-month project in information systems. After the first week, she burst into my office in tears. "I can't get any information; I don't have access to the computer. I don't even have a place to sit," she sobbed. We cooked up a strategy, but the following Friday, back she came, weeping once more. We organized a second plan, to little avail—another Friday, another tear fest.

Finally, Sandy and I met with her temporary manager. Opening the meeting, I said, "Okay, Sandy, tell us what's been going on."

In a high-pitched voice and with the biggest, sweetest smile imaginable, Sandy said, "Well, I can't get the information I need. I can't get on the computer. No one will help me . . ." No wonder Sandy's progress was stymied. She had been sending mixed messages: Her nonverbal cues communicated that her job was great;

her words said her assignment was in the pits. Predictably, the manager chose to believe the nonverbal message.

After this unproductive meeting, it was clear that Sandy needed some coaching. I talked with her about the mixed message and she agreed to try again. Several weeks later at a follow-up meeting, Sandy did a great job of controlling her smiles. She has gone on to become an extremely successful manager, and she often reports back to me how she coaches her women employees about "that smiling."

POWER MOVE STRATEGY **1** ▼　　▼　　▼　　▼

Become aware of your smiling . Learn to use a stone face, not a smile, when you're feeling vulnerable.

▶ HEAD TILTS, NODS, AND ASSENTING NOISES

Cocking your head to one side displays curiosity. Even dogs and cats do it. But, if you're speaking at the time, it also signals subordinate status. Men hold their heads upright when they speak.

Chin down is another subordinate status posture. Think of powerful people you know. Rarely will you observe them with their chins down, especially if they're talking. Sometimes I encounter the deadly triple whammy: A woman's head is down and tilted to the side while she smiles broadly. Such a move indicates extreme powerlessness.

Nodding and the assenting noises we make when we nod can confuse cross-gender communication. When women listen during a conversation, they tend to nod unconsciously as if to say, "I hear you." The gesture doesn't necessarily mean they agree. Men, on the other hand, nod in assent. When a woman listens and nods, a man may think she's a pushover, when in fact she's merely indicating she heard what he said. On the other hand, when the male listens and fails to nod, his female colleague may think he's inattentive, or that he disputes her assertions.

A top female executive at a national fast food-company told me over lunch that because of me, when she now meets with her boss, the president of the company, she keeps her finger under her chin.

"What did I do?" I wanted to know.

"I heard you talk about that nodding issue. I really pride myself on being a good listener. When I'm listening to someone, I nod as a way of letting the other person know I'm paying attention. But I had gotten feedback from my boss that I was unpredictable. When I heard you talk about how men and women nod differently, I realized that was the problem. When I would listen to him, I would nod, but then later if I differed with him, he would see me as switching positions. I realized the nods were the problem."

POWER MOVE STRATEGY 2 ▾   ▾   ▾   ▾

Watch how you hold your head: tilting and chin lowering convey vulnerability. As you communicate with male colleagues, consider limiting the noises and nods. Conversely, when you don't get those noises and nods from your colleague, he may still be listening, and even agreeable.

▶ GETTING SMALL AND BIG

Some years ago, I sat across from my boss, Diane, and next to a fellow, Raymond, at a meeting. Almost immediately, Raymond began verbally attacking Diane. "That will never work!" he shouted. "Why would you even suggest it?"

As Raymond menaced, Diane began to shrink before my very eyes. She pulled in her arms and legs, sank into the chair, and seemed to slide her head down into her shoulders. This is what I call *getting small*. Her cringing posture told Raymond his attack was effective; if he continued, she would probably surrender, even though she was dead right.

Diane was one of the world's greatest bosses, so following the meeting I told her what I had observed. She appreciated the feedback, and we agreed to signal each other in future meetings when we noticed the other giving into the shark.

Our posture communicates a great deal about our emotional response to a situation. When we're feeling particularly powerful and confident, we naturally tend to pull our bodies up and spread out. When we feel powerless, as Diane did, we instinctively pull in and get small.

This became obvious to me a while back, when I conducted

workshops on power and politics for a large newspaper. The executives were the last group to go through the training. The publisher sat right in front of me, arms slung over the backs of adjacent chairs and one leg at four o'clock, the other at eight o'clock. He must have covered about six square yards. When we came to the topic of power and posture, I turned to him and asked, "Robert, do you sit like that for purposes of power, or do you do it unconsciously?"

As soon as the words were out of my mouth, I regretted having uttered them before the assembled brass. Much to my amazement, however, he replied evenly, "Initially I sat like this for purposes of power, but now it's unconscious." Within five minutes, the men had filled that room with bodies; just like Robert, they sat with arms draped over chairs and legs splayed.

Clearly, there are limits to how much women can spread out. But it pays to notice your posture during those times you're likely to feel powerless and insecure, such as job interviews, performance appraisals, or meetings in which you must sell your ideas.

POWER STANDING AND SITTING

What are the most powerful ways to stand and sit? Try the following activity:

1. Stand in your most ladylike posture. Imagine you're wearing a pink dress and white gloves on your way to tea. When asked to assume this position, most women stand with one foot angled in front of the other and with their hands clasped over their genitals.
2. Now take a more powerful stance. Keep your feet parallel at a comfortable distance apart. Imagine a string emerging from the top of your head, pulling your spine straight. Roll your shoulders back several times, with hands to your sides.
3. Sit down daintily, assuming the society-lady carriage. Most likely your legs will be crossed at the ankles, and your hands will rest cupped in your lap. You'll probably find yourself perched at the edge of your chair.
4. Now try the power sit. Spread your body out as much as is comfortable and appropriate, shoulders back and arms to your sides. You can't spread your chest as much as men do because invariably a button will pop and spoil the whole effect, but do stay away from sitting on the edge of your chair, pulling in, and getting small.

POWER MOVE STRATEGY **3** ▼   ▼   ▼   ▼

The more confidently you sit, the more confident you will feel. In threatening situations, avoid pulling in, getting small, and perching on the edge of the chair. Instead, pull up, place your arms on the arms of the chair, and open your posture.

▶ PUT 'ER THERE, PAL

I have mixed feelings about discussing handshaking. On the one hand, it seems silly to talk so explicitly about something so mundane. On the other, both male and female executives have told me they've overpassed job candidates because of their weak handshakes. If it can cost you a promotion, a handshake is important enough to ponder.

Handshaking is a ritual form of greeting for men in our culture. It's their way of making physical contact before interaction. Many women in the United States didn't grow up shaking hands, so for them it can be awkward. A woman is often unsure about when to shake and how to shake. Let's review both.

To Shake or Not to Shake

Those are your only options. Not to shake when expected can signal you're ignorant of the team rules and therefore an outsider. Most women know to shake hands if they're in a business setting and they've never met a particular man before. But some women ask me what to do when introduced to a woman or someone from another office they encounter infrequently. Or, they wonder, what if they're about to go into a big meeting, and all the men are shaking.

My recommendation: When in doubt, stick that hand out and shake. It is possible to err on the side of undershaking ("She didn't shake my hand when she should have"). But it's quite difficult to err on the side of overshaking ("She shook my hand and shouldn't have")!

Moreover, women experience added pressure to "get it right" because many men in our culture were taught to wait for the woman to extend her hand. While she's trying to figure out if this is a shake or no-shake situation, he may stand around awkwardly. Just get your hand out there, and all will breathe a sigh of relief.

How You Shake

This may be far more important than you ever imagined. The "dead fish" handshake has lost many a job candidate her coveted position. So let's do a handshake review:

- Don't grab fingers.
- Slide your hand in all the way so the webs next to your thumbs touch.
- Shake so that your palms connect.
- Make sure your fingers are wrapped around the other person's hand.
- Squeeze firmly without making it into a macho contest.
- Look the other person in the eye.

POWER MOVE STRATEGY **4** ▼   ▼   ▼   ▼

It's difficult to err on the side of overshaking. Get that hand out there and deliver a good, firm handshake. Show everyone you know the rules.

▶ GETTING THE POINT

Several years ago I was discussing with a colleague, Neil, how I thought our project ought to be run. In midsentence, he took my finger—which was pointed at his chest—and pointed it back at me. At the time I was surprised that my finger had bothered him so much. I didn't realize that pointing is a power move. It often evokes defensiveness because it places the receiver in the one-down position.

When we feel particularly powerful in a relationship we naturally point. Parents and teachers point a great deal, because they are in the driver's seat. But pointing creates a win/lose situation. This can work well for men but generally backfires for women, who do better in win/win situations. Because pointing suggests power, a male colleague may react to it negatively. And if he points at you, don't be surprised if you feel tempted to waver and give in.

The two-finger point (using your first two fingers together) might work as an alternative. The advantage here is that while the gesture is strong, it does not send the same potentially negative message.

POWER MOVE STRATEGY **5** ▾　　▾　　▾　　▾

Avoid pointing, especially in a potential conflict.

▶ LET ME MAKE ME COMFORTABLE

Some of our most interesting and telling hand gestures are called *adaptors*. These consist of rubbing, patting, and scratching movements employed to comfort ourselves in stressful situations. You may have ignored adaptors, but once you become conscious of them, they'll be apparent everywhere. People commonly display them during job interviews, presentations, selling situations, or when they're losing or feel vulnerable.

Traffic jams are great venues for adaptor watching. Check out all the face touching, hair twirling, neck and shoulder massaging that goes on in neighboring gridlocked cars. If men have moustaches or beards, they often stroke or pull on them. Women, lacking significant facial hair, touch their cheeks or coiffures. You'll also encounter adaptors when people speak publicly: They jingle money in pockets, twist rings, or click marker caps on and off.

Why are adaptors so important? Like other nonverbal cues, we send, receive, and interpret them unconsciously. The end result, however, is that adaptors convey the impression of uneasiness. Once, for example, I found myself soliciting the business of the high-muck-a-mucks at a huge international electronics firm. As I began to talk, I also started to rub the side of my neck with my finger. Being aware of adaptors, however, I made a conscious effort to stop, because I didn't want to communicate in any way how uncomfortable I felt.

In addition, during a presentation, your voice may become warbly, your hands may shake, and your knees may knock. The normal response to these signs of nervousness is to tighten up even further, softening your voice, pulling your hands in so your listeners won't see them tremble, and standing dead still. Unfortunately, this will only cause you to shake, rattle, and roll even more. Instead, it's best to go to the opposite extreme: Speak loudly, move your arms around in broad gestures, and walk around. Even if you're quaking inside, no one will notice, and you'll release that nervous energy.

Other suggestions to alleviate nervousness: Breathe in to the count of six and exhale to the count of six. I've also found it useful to play the role of a calm person during a big presentation. I fool myself into thinking I'm at ease, and I also fool my audience!

SPOTLIGHT ON YOU

Ask a friend to videotape you in a mock job interview or confrontational situation. About ten minutes is all you need. Watching yourself on tape will dramatically expose all of your idiosyncratic adaptors, as well as head tilts, nods, and so forth. After you've watched the tape at normal speed, replay it on fast forward. You'll become instantly aware of your most frequent gestures.

POWER MOVE STRATEGY 6 ▼　　▼　　▼　　▼

Since others often interpret your ability, knowledge, and skills in light of how confident you appear, be aware that adaptors signal discomfort. Once you attend to your own fidgeting, make a conscious effort to cease. If you're nervous during a presentation, intensify your gestures.

▶ THE POWER OF TOUCH

Our culture has strong unwritten rules about touch and power: You're allowed to touch someone only of equal or lower status than yourself. While your boss might walk up to your desk and pat you on the back for a job well done, you're unlikely to do the same to her. Sociologist Erving Goffman found, in fact, that doctors touch nurses far more frequently than the reverse.

Because of these unwritten rules, touch can communicate volumes about an individual's position on the hierarchy. Therefore, touching a colleague may actually help equalize power. For instance, I've attended meetings at which a peer approached me and patted me on the back while saying, "Well, Pat, I haven't seen you in a while. How are you doing?"

I've turned around and said, "Oh, Joe, I'm just fine. And how are you?" as I patted him in return.

Or if a colleague touches me on the upper arm as he tells me how much he enjoyed my report, I touch him on the forearm in thanking him. My goal is to prevent him from feeling higher than me in the hierarchy, as he would if he had leave to touch me but I couldn't reciprocate.

Research has shown that touch can also enhance relationships and assuage interpersonal difficulties. In a study at a university library, for example, the librarian touched certain students fleetingly, as she returned their cards after checking out books. All students then took an exit survey at the library door. Questions included: "Do you like studying in the library?" "Does it have the books you need?" "Are the librarians helpful?" "Were you touched while you were in the library?" To a person, they denied being touched, but those who had been felt that the library was stocked with the books they needed, and that the librarians were great.

Similar studies have found that when doctors touch fully clothed patients during office interviews, patients' estimates of the visit's length double. When waitresses touch customers, their tips increase.

Consider testing the impact of human touch by trying an experiment a client shared when she was a student in a graduate class on human behavior. The professor asked the class to choose a coworker whom they detested. The assignment was to touch this person three times a day for a month. In her class, each of the problematic relationships significantly improved. You might want to try this experiment yourself. Think for a minute who has been giving you trouble. If he or she is not too high above you in the hierarchy, consider using the three-touch-a-day protocol and watch what happens.

Maintain your place in the hierarchy by returning colleagues' appropriate touch. Use touch to enhance relationships and assuage interpersonal difficulties. If you're in a bind, try the three-touch-a-day routine.

▶ HOW TO DEAL WITH INAPPROPRIATE TOUCHING

While touch can enhance relationships, it may also create problems for us. Women frequently ask me what to do about unwanted touches at work. Typically, in our culture, male and female casual acquaintances may touch each other briefly on the hand, arm, shoulder, or back. These are legal touches. A touch that lingers too long, turns into a caress, or lands in an erogenous zone can be considered sexual and is off limits.

Often, women confess their reluctance to make a "big deal" out of the unwanted or inappropriate touch for fear of being labeled uptight. Yet they need to draw boundaries. Some ideas:

Flinch. We flinch naturally when we're touched unexpectedly or when the touch is too cold. You might employ the flinch to clearly signal the touch was unwelcome.

Look at the touch. If the perpetrator rests his hand on your upper arm and begins rubbing, stare at his hand without moving your eyes. This so clearly draws attention to the touch that the perpetrator becomes uncomfortable and is likely to cease.

Make your needs known. You may take a more direct and assertive approach by stating your need. "I would appreciate it if you would not rub my back."

Deflect the onslaught. If the person is a kisser and/or hugger and you feel uncomfortable with so much intimacy, simply extend your hand as you approach with a wide, warm smile.

POWER MOVE STRATEGY   **8** ▼   ▼   ▼   ▼

If you feel uncomfortable with a touch, it's your right to do something about it. Draw boundaries where you feel most comfortable. Don't be intimidated by someone else's perception that he or she has a right to touch your body.

▶ DON'T LOOK UP

If you find yourself craning your neck during a conversation, particularly a difficult one, you may want to change your position. Women are frequently intimidated and back down because of disparities in eye level. Indeed, research has shown that we feel and then act more vulnerable when we look up, perhaps because in our society a man's power and height are closely related. The taller a man is, up to 6'8", the likelier he is to earn a larger salary and hold a more senior position.

We even tend to bestow important men with extra height. When given an impressive resume, individuals are more apt to guess that person is taller than someone with a mediocre vita. I've always been amused when a friend sees a heartthrob actor on the streets and exclaims, "He's so short!" While the star may not be short for the average man, he's unexpectedly so if one has "looked up" to him. Although research has found that women's height does not predicate their potential for success, from my observations and personal experience, tall women are often in positions of power.

The height/power relationship can dramatically impact you at work. It's most common for men to be taller than women, so you may find yourself looking up more than you'd like. One way of handling this is to equalize the heights if a man is lording over you. Imagine, for example, that you're working at your desk when your colleague, Andrew, walks up and starts loudly complaining about a project you've recently completed. Because you're seated and he's standing, you are on unequal eye levels. Invite Andrew to pull up a chair, or else stand up to greet his onslaught with your full authority.

On the other hand, if you're already on your feet and still find yourself looking up, you might suggest that both of you find some comfortable chairs. For example, if a colleague stops you in the hallway and you notice that you're looking up at him, manage the height relationship by saying, "I really want to hear about this, Cliff. Let's go sit in the conference room and talk about it."

Height superiority can even work if your adversary is absent. Heather, an executive woman, told me that she uses a cordless telephone. When she gets a call requiring her to be strong and confident, she stands up and paces her office as she speaks. Although the other party can't see her, Heather feels more confident and consequently projects a more powerful self-image.

You also need to be aware that height is often manipulated intentionally. This is overt in a courtroom: The judge, jury, and defendant sit at elevations that signal their relative power. Others use height as an office power tool by setting their desks on risers or furnishing low couches and chairs for visitors.

The most unusual episode of height manipulation I've ever encountered occurred several years ago when I met with a young man who had just become an executive. Joshua received me in his brand-new executive office, which was furnished with his brand-new executive furniture. Indeed, he was quite full of his brand-new executive self.

I sat in the chair indicated for me, directly across his large desk. Once seated, however, Joshua became uncomfortable with our disparate eye levels. I'm six feet tall. When he realized I was looking down at him, he sprang to his feet, turned his thronelike chair over, cranked it up, turned it back around, sat peering down at me, and said, "Now let's talk." I would have been less surprised had he adjusted the chair's height after I'd left, but that he did it in front of me was nothing short of amazing.

Since I began telling this story in workshops, dozens of people have related similar tales about chair legs being sawed off and furniture altered in creative ways. This power play may be more common than you think.

POWER MOVE STRATEGY **9** ▼   ▼   ▼   ▼

If at all possible, equalize power by equalizing heights. You may need to adjust your furniture to maximize your authority, but do so when no one is watching!

▶ HERE'S LOOKING AT YOU

When engaged in conversation, it's polite to look the other person in the eye. In real life, however, usually the most dominant person in a conversation can choose to look or not, while the subordinate is more likely to maintain eye contact. That's because the employee needs to determine her boss's frame of mind: A superior's opinion may alter the outcome of a conversation. On the other hand, the individual in the superior position has little need to maintain eye contact. What the subordinate thinks of him or her may have little to do with the outcome.

Research on eye contact is seemingly inconsistent. While it is true that the most powerful individual can choose to make eye contact or not, we also know that a common way to avoid someone when you're feeling uncomfortable is to avert the eyes. Women frequently communicate their lack of confidence by breaking eye contact. Averting the eyes is actually one of four ways people distance themselves when feeling threatened or vulnerable. (The others include literally stepping back, turning the body axis so a shoulder points at the other speaker, and blocking with crossed arms or legs.)

Because averting the eyes communicates weakness and vulnerability, it can be deadly during a job interview in which you want to exude confidence or a meeting at which you need to sell your idea. To remedy this, first notice the intensity of your eye contact when you're feeling relaxed. You can get a good sense of this during a comfortable conversation with a friend. Then, in professional situations, force yourself to look at your colleague just as frequently. By the way, you're not required to look your conversation partner in the eye—the bridge of the nose will do. No one can tell the difference.

With peers, maintain the eye contact you usually use when feeling comfortable. This can vary from person to person. In general, however, you'll want to communicate that you're secure in the position you've taken.

What to do if a male colleague looks at your body, not at your face? Resolving this situation is easier than you might imagine. Years ago, a vice president of a firm at which I worked had the disconcerting tendency to look at my belly as we spoke. I just stopped in midsentence. My colleague immediately looked at my face to discover what had happened. Once he made eye contact, I continued to speak. As his eyes drifted away again, I stopped midsentence once more and his eyes returned to my face. It took a couple of minutes of this to teach him to make eye contact.

If you're gutsier and would like to deal with this all-too-common situation in a light and humorous way, consider this strategy related by a university dean. During a formal function she found herself talking with a man who rarely took his eyes off her breasts. Finally, she asked, "Please speak up, as the left one is hard of hearing." He turned beet red and his eyes stayed riveted on her face thereafter.

POWER MOVE STRATEGY **10** ▼   ▼   ▼   ▼

Maintain appropriate eye contact, even if you're feeling threatened. If a male colleague stares at your body, subtly or overtly help him become aware of his ogling.

▶ WHAT TIME TELLS

Keeping someone waiting is one of the most significant ways to communicate power, because it indicates that your time is more important than the other person's. With a superior, of course, such a ploy would backfire miserably.

I once worked for a senior executive woman who was a master at wielding and displaying power. One afternoon, the top three attorneys in this Fortune 500 company were scheduled to meet Karen and me in her office at two o'clock. The lawyers were at an equal rung on the hierarchy as she, but they always communicated a sense of superiority.

I arrived on time and was admitted with little ado. Karen and I chatted about nothing of significance, and then her secretary buzzed at 2:10, announcing the attorneys' arrival. Still, she continued our conversation. At 2:25, when Karen's secretary came in, I caught a glimpse of the three impatient men sitting out in the waiting room, looking none too pleased—indeed, looking dangerously close to throwing a fit. I suggested that we finish our talk later—I was feeling uncomfortable with those honchos cooling their heels—but Karen waved me off and continued our conversation until 2:45.

Much to my surprise, the attorneys didn't seem angry when finally admitted. Most important, in future interactions, they seemed to understand very clearly that Karen was above them in the hierarchy.

POWER MOVE STRATEGY 11 ▾   ▾   ▾   ▾

Keeping an appointment waiting indicates your relative power. Up the hierarchy, avoid keeping your boss waiting.

▶ THE TRAPPINGS OF POWER

Women tend to look at their environment functionally. For instance, in assessing an office, we might consider if it has:

- adequate lighting
- bookshelves
- enough chairs for visitors
- a comfortable and supportive desk chair
- an aesthetically pleasing decor

Less likely to be women's top priorities are:

- the square footage
- a corner location
- the size of the window as compared with windows in other offices
- the quality of the carpeting in relation to that in other offices

We tend to look at the practicalities of working in a particular space, whereas men are more likely to evaluate how an office communicates position in the hierarchy.

I'm not suggesting that women are unaware of the trappings of power, just that when left to their own devices, they probably don't care as much. Women often feel more comfortable in the cafeteria than the executive dining room. I've heard female managers lament the expansiveness of their offices while their employees work in cramped spaces. Or they express a preference to work near their employees rather than on executive row. The trappings of power often shine a spotlight on inequality of status—a state that women find uncomfortable.

Because the relationship between environment and status is so important to men, many organizations have codified it in policy and procedure manuals. In my early years in the corporate world, I was fascinated with the policy and procedures laid out by the large engineering company where I worked. All physical accoutrements were codified by level of management:

- the height of the back of the desk chair
- the quality of carpeting
- the quality of the wall paint
- the type of lighting
- the composition of desks (metals, cheap wood, expensive wood)

In this company, managers had painted offices, whereas directors (the next level up) had paneled offices. Once, when a manager in a painted office jokingly noted that his peer's office one door down had wood paneling, the facilities people showed up and—you guessed it—painted over the wood! To women this can seem silly, but we tend to ignore hierarchical status symbols.

Indeed, sometimes our laissez-faire attitude can create problems. In a large international health care company, Helen was made a group vice president and given a suite of offices. She went to the basement where the used furniture was kept and chose to recycle some comfortable furnishings. Helen felt she was being a good corporate citizen by saving the company some money. Instead, the used look of her offices signaled to her new peers that she was clearly not in the same league. Helen made the mistake of thinking that her environment was intended to provide comfort, rather than display power.

The sum spent on office decor is a symbol of one's worth in the company. In one firm, when an executive is promoted he or she is given $150,000 to remodel the office. Men will see this as an opportunity to display power; women feel uncomfortable with the disparity between their showy offices and their employees' cubbies. As with so many issues in this chapter, however, the operative directive is that when it comes to power, one must either use it or lose it!

POWER MOVE STRATEGY **12** ▾　　▾　　▾　　▾

Recognize that your office symbolizes your place on the hierarchy and act accordingly.

▶ RESTAURANT ETIQUETTE

The restaurant you choose indicates your position in the hierarchy and impacts the impression your guest has of you. If you take a client to a hamburger stand, he may expect hamburger performance from you. Consequently, he'll want to pay only hamburger prices for your services. It's important to select an eatery with care.

What about assuring that you pick up the tab? Most men in their forties or below have little trouble with a woman paying the check at a restaurant, especially if you've asked them to lunch. Some men with old-fashioned, take-care-of-the-little-lady values may have a hard time. My favorite technique to bypass this potentially embarrassing situation is to excuse myself to go to the restroom sometime during the meal. While I'm away from the table, I give the maître d' my credit card. When the bill comes, the credit card impression has already been taken, and all I have left to do is to sign the slip.

As far as drinking is concerned, it's always best to imbibe less than more. Each organization has different norms regarding alcohol consumption. In some companies, employees never drink. For you to do so would make you appear like the local lush, even if you just have a single glass of wine when you go out to dinner with your colleagues.

Some organizations subscribe to the work-hard/play-hard ethic. In such a company, your coworkers may perceive you as prudish if you eschew alcohol (if you do drink). But even in such an organization, your safest bet is to order only one glass of wine after work. Even if the guys call for a pitcher of beer and get blasted, your joining in somehow immediately compromises you and makes you a potentially loose woman. As we've seen so many times before, standards are different for women.

POWER MOVE STRATEGY **13** ▾   ▾   ▾   ▾

When dining out with clients, choose a restaurant that will reflect well on your company. When it comes to drinking alcohol, exercise caution, no matter what the boys are doing.

POWER MOVES ROUNDUP

In your journal, answer the following questions:

1. How do I most effectively communicate power nonverbally?
2. What are some ways I sabotage myself nonverbally?
3. What steps am I going to take to increase my nonverbal communication of power?

NONVERBAL POWER PLAYS

- Avoid the please-don't-attack-me-anymore smile.
- Nods and assenting noises may tell a man you agree when you don't.
- Initiate the firm handshake.
- Be careful about pointing at others.
- Avoid rubs, pats, and scratching in uncomfortable situations.
- Maneuver your way out of having to look up.
- Maintain eye contact when you're uncomfortable.
- Remember that you may not really care about the trappings of power, but they still signal how much power you have.
- Choose restaurants wisely.
- Observe your company's ethic regarding drinking and limit your intake.

MAKING THE MOST OF CRITICISM AND PRAISE

▼
HARDBALL LESSONS BOYS LEARN

- Criticism and feedback are useful because they make you a better player.
- If a coach criticizes your behavior, it doesn't mean he doesn't like you.
- Tough coaches are good coaches.
- Big boys don't cry.

▼
HOUSE AND DOLL LESSONS GIRLS LEARN

- There's no need for an adult to evaluate your game.
- Criticism damages relationships.
- Girls should please others.
- It's all right to cry.

▼ ▼ ▼ ▼ ▼ **I** had hired JoDee into an executive trainee program in a large Fortune 500 company. She was bright, well educated, and highly motivated. After three months, it was time for her performance evaluation from Mike, her current supervisor. Mike was a what-have-you-done-for-me-lately kind of guy: high expectations and rare praise.

When we all sat down for the meeting, Mike said, "JoDee, you've been working hard, but it took longer for you to do this project than I anticipated, and I was hoping for a more in-depth financial analysis."

As the negative feedback continued, I observed JoDee's eyes dampen. I was unsure if the assessment was accurate—it was inconsistent with what I'd heard elsewhere—but that was not the point. If this was Mike's perception, JoDee had to manage it.

Suddenly Mike's tone changed. Apparently he had noticed the welling tears too, because he backed off completely. Muttering some placating inanities, he quickly ended the session. Was this a successful session? Hardly. JoDee missed the feedback she needed, and more significantly, she was banished from Mike's team forever. JoDee had taken her supervisor's comments personally and felt devastated by them. That was her downfall.

▶ CRITICISM AS FEEDBACK

Men may find it easier to deal with criticism than women because of disparate childhood lessons. Boys spend far more time practicing a sport than actually playing it. Criticism from the coach is a salient element of practice. At times the feedback is neutral: "Hold your bat higher" or "Keep your eye on the ball." Occasionally, it can be quite pointed and personal: "You run like a duck" or "You're always goofing off."

Although some coaches also incorporate praise, boys learn that the general flow of negative feedback is meant to make them stronger, more effective players. It has little to do with who they are as people or the coach's personal feelings about them. In fact, many boys learn that the only way to improve their game is through just such a negative mirror. They train themselves to get over feeling hurt and come to appreciate a "tough coach."

Eventually, boys understand that feedback is useful to their skill building and ultimately to their position in the hierarchy. Besides, there is a payoff for all that criticism: Winning the game. Success can evoke lavish praise. For boys, criticism has tangible benefits; not only will they improve their skills, but they'll eventually garner approval. Consequently, boys take negative feedback for what it's worth—instruction on what it takes to win—and move on.

While boys were learning those lessons, girls were back in the house playing with their best friends. Certainly, girls didn't have an adult around criticizing their play technique; there's no particularly right or effective way to play dolls, since one doesn't win such a game. If girls did receive admonishments, they were usually of the interpersonal or physical variety:

- "Get along with your friends."
- "Be nice."
- "Share your toys."
- "Avoid arguments."
- "Don't get dirty."
- "Look pretty."

Because of our childhood play patterns, women don't practice receiving criticism, never learn to associate it with skill building, and, more important, don't know how to separate someone's negative perceptions from who they are as people. Indeed, most often women personalize criticism and take it on face value as being true.

Many women need external approval to feel successful (see Chapter 10, "Setting Goals and Staying Focused"). It's part of their nature to associate other people's positive assessment of their work with a job well done. But since females have had little experience with negative feedback, they leave themselves wide open and vulnerable to the attacks (tackles) of others. Without the preparation that men get, women like JoDee take disapproval as total and personal.

▶ MOVIN' ON

How do you deal with criticism that comes your way? I find it best to contain it and then let it go. I learned this the hard way. Once, following one of my routine management seminars, I attacked the pile of participants' evaluations, as I always do. Most were positive, as usual, but one shot me down like a bullet from a semiautomatic. It said, "Pat Heim is a phony."

I was devastated, but I was cool. I didn't cry until I got to my car. Then I sobbed all the way home. I felt so hurt, I couldn't talk about it for two days. Finally, I asked my husband if he thought I was a phony. When he replied, "Of course not," I thought, "Oh, what does he know." For the next two weeks that feedback ran my life. I interpreted what people said to me as hinting at or reflecting my phoniness. The pain dissipated only as I became involved in new projects.

My response is not unique. According to management professor Connie Gersick, in looking at how professors dealt with negative feedback, women retained the hurt feelings for much of the course of their careers whereas men didn't mention early feedback at all.

In fact, a man might have handled this very differently: "Look at this evaluation," he might have said. "Someone thinks I'm a phony. I've conducted workshops for thousands of managers, and no one has ever said I'm a phony before. I think I'll wait for a second opinion on this." His would certainly be a far saner response than mine. I had allowed some unknown to control my life; I gave this person the power to define whether or not I was a phony.

Giving away power puts you in a vulnerable position. You can let virtually anyone determine your perception of yourself and your state of mind. Instead, I'm convinced we women must learn to repossess our power. We can do that in a number of ways:

1. Consider the source of the criticism.
2. Analyze if the attacker was motivated by a need to undermine us.
3. "Draw a box" around negative feedback.

When receiving criticism, we should say, "This is Nick's opinion about this behavior at this time." Take the reproof for what it's worth and move on. By mentally drawing a box around the criticism, we consciously contain it and limit its power over us.

For example, if your boss says, "This report is a piece of junk," you have several options. You can go home, get in bed, pull up the sheets, and never get out (for some reason this option tends to look particularly attractive to me), or you can say, "The boss didn't like these three elements of the report. I'll change the report and remember these potential problems the next time I submit one." Then *drop it.* Don't dwell on your failure feelings. Learn from your mistakes and move on.

Rather than letting go, however, we tend to stay hooked into the bad feelings the criticism engenders because we never learned how to dismiss them the way boys did. This affects us in several negative ways:

It can damage our relationships with others. When we obsess over negative feedback, we carry it around in a way that prevents us from working well with our colleague in the future. We may become saboteurs, read into the coworker's behavior a negative agenda that may not exist, or lose trust. This can also be an instance of confusing friendliness and friendship. We might think: "She must not like me anymore. A friend would never say anything like that to me."

It can damage a colleague's confidence in our abilities. A man is often surprised that a female colleague is "so sensitive" that she "can't take the heat" or learn from her mistakes. As a result, he perceives her as a weak player whom he'd rather eliminate from his team.

It puts you at risk for future attacks. Once some men recognize that a woman is vulnerable to criticism, they use that information to get to her in the future. They don't see this as vicious but just part of the game of competitive hardball.

Negative self-talk emerges. We say things to ourselves that diminish our strength, such as, "You idiot! Why did you say that? You look like you have no experience." More on that below.

YOUR CRITICISM QUOTIENT

In your journal, describe how you reacted to a recent criticism.

1. What did you say to yourself?
2. What were the consequences of your reaction?
3. Write how you would have responded had you considered the source, analyzed his motives, drawn a box, and moved on.

▶ CHANGING YOUR SELF-TALK

We talk to ourselves all day long. Sometimes our internal chatter is positive. We encourage ourselves with such statements as, "This is going to be a piece of cake." Or we give ourselves a pat on the back with, "That turned out really well." But when things go badly, the self-talk is often negative: "You looked like a fool." "He probably thinks you're an idiot." "You'll never make it." These may parrot feedback we've received in the workplace, or may elaborate on our already negative view of ourselves derived from childhood experience.

Self-talk isn't just random words rambling around in our heads. Because of our complex psychological makeup, it impacts our ability to perform. It sets up negative expectations and undermines confidence by creating self-fulfilling prophecies.

I learned the profound impact of self-talk some years ago when I became addicted to snow skiing. I quit graduate school, my job—everything—and skied full time. Unfortunately, I was a miserable skier. I would come around a corner, see a huge drop-off, and say to myself, "You're going to die!" At that moment my body would turn into rubber, and inevitably I would tumble down the mountain.

One evening, I met one of those ski gods in the lodge after a particularly bruising day. After I explained my bumps and scratches, he didn't presume to instruct me on technique. Instead, he told me to change the self-talk. Rather than negative words, he taught me to see that drop-off and say, "You can do it. You can do it. You can do it." And, much to my surprise, when I followed his good advice, I *did* do it. I made it intact to the bottom of the mountain, time and time again.

Most of us experience the impact of negative self-talk when we're trying to unlock our front door while the phone is ringing with that important call. "Oh, God," we say to ourselves, "I'll never get the door open in time." Have you noticed this is virtually the only time you drop your keys?

Returning to the work setting, if you've just received some pointed criticism from your boss, be sure to tune in to what you're saying to yourself. If your self-talk is working against you, consciously reframe your reaction. It's not easy to break decades-old patterns of thinking, but it's not impossible, either. If you've truly made a mistake, instead of saying, "You screwed up again. When will you ever learn?" try, "What can I learn from this mistake? How can I repair the damage with Gary Wilson?" or an affirmation like, "I did the best I could for now; next time I'll know how to maneuver better." And don't forget the rubber band technique, giving yourself a snap every time you hear those negative words.

It might also help to mentally take a few steps back and review the criticism in terms of the largest possible context, as in, "I have been in this position for nine months. In that time, I've made some good progress." You might like to review your successes at this juncture. Then add, "Inevitably, I will make mistakes along the way. This is only one step on my career path. From this mistake, I can learn . . ."

If, on the other hand, you believe your boss has it in for you because he just doesn't like you, instead of deprecating yourself try, "This guy hates me. His criticism has nothing to do with my performance. He's just out to get me." If you don't alter your internal monologue, self-fulfilling prophecies may rear their ugly heads again, and your future performance may suffer.

SELF-TALK TUNE-UP

In your journal, record a recent episode in which you received criticism. Now answer the following questions:

1. What words did you say to yourself? Were they negative and undermining?
2. Now change the self-talk. What could you have said instead?
3. Practice this new way of thinking in future situations.

▶ TAKING BACK THE POWER

Boys learn to shed others' negative remarks because they spend so much time bantering and have had much experience receiving it. Girls, on the other hand, have a harder time deflecting criticism because they've had little practice thwarting it.

Winning University of North Carolina women's soccer coach

Anson Dorrance drove this point home with me during my interview with him. "I've never met a male athlete in my life that's felt he has made an athletic mistake in competition. So in dealing with the male ego, videotape is critical because men just won't accept criticism unless you ram it down their throats. The irony of the women's team is that when you make any general criticism, every woman thinks you are talking about her. You make a general criticism of a men's team and every male thinks that you are talking about someone else."

Our lack of "training" can have serious consequences in the workplace. Indeed, I'm frequently amazed at how openly we embrace criticism from every Tom, Dick, and Harry. A woman may never ask a colleague for technical advice because she knows he can't find his way out of a paper bag. But if he's dishing out negative feedback, she's the first on line for a big helping. The truth is, positive strokes are often so important to us, we give power to others in order to get their blessing. We have been taught to please others, and when we don't get their approval, we feel like failures. In addition, because we have little practice taking negative feedback, we can't discriminate sources when we do get it.

That's what happened to Molly, a client in a senior executive position and a particularly caring manager. Late one afternoon, I received her distress call. Molly had finally decided to deal with Jerry, a poor performer, but the consequences of her decision had upset her enormously. Jerry became irate when she delivered the negative feedback. Sensing that she was moving to the firing line, he stomped over to her boss, the president, and accused Molly of "having a mean streak." There, the brouhaha among the three of them lasted most of the afternoon, but the upshot was that Jerry threatened to quit, and they graciously took him up on his offer.

When Molly called, however, she was near tears, mortified that Jerry had called her mean. I was astounded that she had given so much power to a man for whom she had so little regard. I reassured her, saying, "You're going to be so relieved once you have this guy out of your hair." Indeed, Molly's physical demeanor has changed since Jerry's ouster; the bags under her eyes have disappeared and her skin tone has improved. And just recently she admitted the day Jerry quit was the best day of her life, even if she wasn't able to recognize it at the time.

Consider the credibility of your source before you take his or her criticism seriously. And remember, there are always a few sharks cruising around, looking for raw meat. Don't feed them, or they're sure to come back.

▶ TAKING THE BULL BY THE HORNS: SEEKING OUT DISAPPROVAL

Because disapproval is so painful for women, we tend to avoid it at all costs. But because it is part of playing the game, men tend to seek it out—but only from appropriate parties. I first noticed this when I had employees of both genders. When performance appraisal time rolled around, the women white-knuckled the meeting and asked plaintively, "Are you going to tell me negative things?"

Interviews were quite different with men. I'd begin by saying, "I was quite pleased with your ability to quickly identify the computer software glitch and solve it."

My male employees would interrupt with statements such as, "But what am I not doing as well as I could?" They would seek disapproval (perceived as constructive criticism and guidance), particularly from the boss. One such employee is now the chief information officer in a Fortune 500 company.

Women rarely seek disapproval, probably because they know they'll get it—and they wince in anticipation. At the same time, it is critical to be aware of what those who hold our careers in their hands think of us. We can never fathom in what light others (especially our supervisors) might see us unless we ask. We must be privy to their perceptions, or we'll be unequipped to manage the negative images that might be holding us back. Like it or not, we've got to ask for the bad news.

Dana, the assistant human resources director at a company at which I frequently consult, took this bull by the horns. She told me she made one-hour appointments with each of the four vice presidents in her company. Individually, she posed essentially the following question: "What do you think of me?"

Impressed, I asked, "And did they give you nice fluffy responses or the real scoop?"

"Oh, no," Dana said. "They gave me a fair amount of negative feedback, things such as, "You're too soft in granting leaves of absence," and, "You need to hold a stronger line when you deal with Tim." I was further impressed that Dana didn't take this information as her reality but merely as the vice presidents' perceptions of her. She held the information separate from her assessment of herself and observed her own behavior. Then she went about changing her behavior as warranted. Had Dana taken the negative feedback personally, it probably would have caused her great pain—a deterrent to maintaining a powerful image and seeking out criticism in the future.

Dana was later promoted to the position of director of human resources. When she called to share the good news, I told her that I relate her story in my seminars and asked if she thought she would have gotten the promotion without those meetings. "I'm sure I would *not* have gotten the promotion," she replied. "I was perceived negatively in many more ways than I could have imagined."

Many women complain that when they ask for the feedback they get only such platitudes as, "You're doing just fine." Some supervisors are reluctant to deliver bad news. "How will she react?" they wonder. Or worse yet, "Will she cry?" If that's the case, you've got to make your superiors comfortable to say what they're afraid to. If you must, tease it out of them with statements such as: "Nobody's perfect. What could I be doing better?" or, "If I were to work on improving one thing, what would it be?"

Now comes the critical moment. After they've delivered the negative feedback, thank them. Whatever they say, express your appreciation. You may feel as if you've been hit by a truck, but don't show it. Most likely you'll need your supervisors' feedback in the future, and you want to make it ever so comfortable for them to give you this useful, albeit painful, information.

▶ NO MORE TEARS?

Men are terrified of crying. Since earliest childhood, they have been taught that big boys don't cry. At a tender age they learn that holding in their hurt feelings—particularly the tears—is all important if they're to establish their position in the hierarchy. Indeed, boys practice how not to cry and know that it will cost them dearly if they drop their guard.

As girls, we have no such rules. While we're not encouraged to cry, we are expected to be connected to our emotions. In addition, nature seems to intensify different crying patterns between males and females. An individual is more likely to cry if he or she has the chemical prolactin circulating in the bloodstream. Interestingly, after puberty, women have more of this substance than men, and so crying comes more easily to them than to their male counterparts.

Some men believe that women cry for manipulative purposes. This makes perfect sense, since men have been practicing how to turn off the tears since childhood. They may think, "If I can stop myself from crying when I want to, then she can too. So if she's crying, it must be an intentional, fraudulent act." Many men see crying as a conscious decision. Even the rare woman who can control her tears holds the same view. But for most women, including myself, choice has nothing to do with it.

Women tell me weeping isn't manipulative, it's more like the hiccups. You can feel the tears coming on—you'd do anything to prevent them—but there they come anyway. Some of us try to get cagey and tip our heads back, but then the tears run in the ears and garble everything.

So what can you do? Women have shared a number of techniques that can help you deal with your tears.

Express the anger outward. Tears are frequently preceded by repressed anger. Let out that anger at the appropriate party, and you may avoid crying altogether.

Take a break. Take a walk or go to the bathroom and have a good sob. You'll probably need some makeup to repair the damage.

Cause yourself some pain. This may sound masochistic, but several women have told me that when they feel like crying they inflict pain on themselves by digging their fingernails into their wrists. This takes their focus off the situation at hand.

Announce the cry. If you know an issue is likely to get to you, you can say to your boss: "Paul, I need to talk to you about yesterday's announcement. I want you to know I care a great deal about this and that I might cry when we talk about it. Please pay no attention." Women tell me that, ironically, once they announce the cry, the need to do it seems to fade.

Blow and go. Just bring your own tissues and make little ado of the tears. Treat them like the hiccups: an inevitable nuisance. You might even tell the other party to ignore them.

When men ask me, usually in hushed tones, "What should I do if she cries?" I suggest they offer a tissue and just keep going. The less attention we draw to this physiological reaction, the better.

Disapproval and our reaction to it is tough for women. I often think of it as our Achilles heel. It makes us vulnerable to the sharks and often undermines our effectiveness. But on the positive side, it also makes us sensitive to others: We're able to put ourselves in their place and act with empathy. I'm not suggesting that we become callous, but rather that we learn to make choices that will work for us in a variety of situations.

▶ MAKING THE MOST OF PRAISE

While criticism is our Achilles' heel, we have lots of problems taking praise as well. This became all the more evident to me during a recent conversation with a neighbor. Dolores's career was covered in our local newspaper with a feature article and a lovely picture. I was eager to congratulate her, so at the first opportunity I buttonholed her and said, "Dolores, that was a wonderful article in the paper! The picture was great too."

She cut me off in midsentence. "Would you like to have an article done on you, too?"

"That's not the point," I replied. "I want to talk to you about the article and how good it was."

I continued to compliment her, but soon she interrupted again. "I know the person who wrote the article," she volunteered. "I could have her write about you too."

"We're not talking about me. We're talking about you." And on it went. Indeed, Dolores continually diverted the conversation away from her coup back to me. I believe the power-dead-even rule was underlying her behavior.

When a woman receives praise, the praise giver bumps her up a notch in the hierarchy. Often, she will attempt to bump herself back down by underplaying the kudos in such statements as, "It was nothing," "I got it on sale," or "It didn't take all that much work." Or she may divert attention from the compliment by chang-

ing the subject or redirecting the comment back to the praiser.
"Well, you did a great job on your project too!"

This point was brought home to me during a recent workshop.
A male participant asked me why women had such poor self-
esteem.

"What makes you think that?" I asked him.

"You see it all the time," he replied. "One woman will say to another, 'Amanda, I love that outfit,' and Amanda will respond with,
'Oh this old thing? I got it on sale.' "

I explained to him that this is a linguistic device that women use
to keep the peace among them. Indeed, it may even be appropriate to play down one's successes with other women because they
live by the power-dead-even rule. But my advice to women is that
they need to be cautious in this behavior because clearly it can
look like poor self-esteem to men.

Among men, a more appropriate approach to receiving a
compliment is to accept it graciously with a "Thanks. I'm glad you
appreciate it." "Gee, it was no big deal" gets you nowhere. Moreover, depending on the situation, you may choose to extend the
compliment the way a man would.

For example, a manager may say to Ken, "Great project. Everyone in the department is talking about it."

Rather than responding, "Aw, shucks, it was nothin'," Ken is
likely to say, "Thanks. The data was much more difficult to analyze
than expected. We were pleased to come in under budget, at that.
But yes, it did come out rather well." When you extend the praise
in this way, you intensify its impact and help your coworkers remember your achievements.

In addition, accolades from the outside world should be savored
and, when possible, exploited. If a client, customer, or business associate compliments your work on a particular project, thank him
or her warmly. And if it's appropriate and you feel comfortable
doing so, jokingly hint that she tell your boss—or better yet, write
a letter.

Should you ask for praise (especially when you know you've
done a good job) if your boss is particularly withholding? Unfortunately, although you may feel better receiving solicited recognition
than no recognition at all, asking for praise may make you appear
needy and weak, so it's not an advisable hardball strategy.

If you simply can't make it without a pat on the back, however, a good approach might be to share successes with peers. Indeed, you might make a conscious effort to praise one another's work whenever it's warranted. Employees can get a good deal of satisfaction from knowing their peers appreciate their efforts, even if the head honcho refuses to acknowledge them.

▶ GETTING THE RIGHT KIND OF EVALUATION

You might have received a glowing performance review from your boss. You're thrilled with her assessment of your skills and results—especially since she felt your team did well this year. However, did you know that unless your company has a particular approach in creating evaluations, even this wonderful review may not do you as much good as you might think? According to economics professor Linda Babcock and writer Sara Laschever, authors of *Women Don't Ask: Negotiation and the Gender Divide,* "First, women fare better when an evaluation process is more structured, includes clearly understood benchmarks, and is less open to subjective judgments. . . . Second, women do better and suffer less harm from negative stereotypes about their competence when they're evaluated for their individual work products rather than their contributions to the work of a team."

One of the issues to consider when interviewing for a new job is whether their review process is individualized and structured—using a written list of goals that are measurable rather than a casual conversation. If you're able to find a position with these properties, you'll be more likely to make more money and have greater opportunities in the future.

YOUR PRAISE QUOTIENT

In your journal, record the last compliment you received.

1. How did you respond?
2. How might you respond now, extending the praise?
3. Which coworkers can you turn to for praise sharing?

KEY POINTS FOR PATS AND PANS

- Criticism can be used as a tool for self-improvement.
- Take criticism for what it's worth and move on.
- Separate criticism of an act from your feelings about yourself as a person.
- Transform negative self-talk into positive self-talk.
- Evaluate the source of the criticism.
- Seek disapproval from appropriate sources and tease it out of reluctant informants.
- Develop strategies for crying.
- Accept praise and extend it, if you're comfortable.
- Exchange praise with peers.
- Seek out a structured, individualized evaluation.

10

SETTING GOALS AND STAYING FOCUSED

▼

HARDBALL LESSONS BOYS LEARN

- All that matters is reaching the goal.
- You can knock people over on the way to the goal, but if you win, all will be forgiven.
- Align yourself with the coach's goals.
- Be available to do the coach's bidding.

▼

HOUSE AND DOLL LESSONS GIRLS LEARN

- Good girls follow the rules, don't make mistakes, and don't make a mess.
- The ultimate goal is to keep everybody happy.
- If a need exists, we should fill it.
- Be available to do everyone's bidding.

▼ ▼ ▼ ▼ ▼ **I** frequently ask the participants of my Women in Business workshops to complete the following sentence: *"I will be successful when . . ."*

Most often, the participants' initial reactions are blank stares. This is the first time many of them have considered the meaning of success. And yet if I ask these women whether they want to be successful, they will inevitably answer, "Absolutely."

Women tend to get hooked into doing their jobs and doing them well, but they can lose sight of the goal line. In our need to keep the day-to-day details under control, we forget to envision where we want the job to take us. Many of the lessons we learned in childhood, such as "Process is all there is," reinforce this behavior and thus work against us when we compete to win. Because we're blind to the goal, we're frequently unaware of strategies that will get us there. In this chapter, we'll explore the game plans I've found most helpful in defining and reaching goals.

But first let's take a brief look at how men and women differ in their definitions of success.

▶ DIFFERENT GOAL LINES

A man might see success as

- selling more parts than the New York office.
- making more money than John.
- becoming a vice president before Tony.

A woman might see success as

- pulling off the project flawlessly and keeping everyone happy in the process.
- closing all her sales in a given month.

■ providing a perfect environment for her children to grow up in.

A man knows who the competition is and what winning means. He can fantasize the moment he crosses the goal line and savors victory. He experiences exaltation when he and his colleagues realize he has won. Even if he errs along the way, if he reaches the goal all is forgiven. Note, too, that his goals are entirely business related. Traditionally, the male version of winning has little to do with a successful personal or family life.

Women, on the other hand, have an entirely different perspective. For us success means *doing* the job perfectly; the process is more important than the product. Under these circumstances, every step along the way to the completion of a task is equally important. There's little room for error. If a project or report is flawed, we feel ineffective; we focus on the 1 percent that isn't right. As a result, we rarely seem like winners in our own eyes. And if we project an unsuccessful image, our colleagues read our signals and believe we're failures too.

▶ INTERNAL AND EXTERNAL ENGINES

Your perception of success is closely linked to the source of your motivation. Think of motivation as a personal engine. It's what drives you and keeps you working at a task; it makes you want to do well, whatever the project. Predictably, this engine differs in men and women.

Men are motivated by external rewards. Specifically, money and status are often the big engines for men. When I recently had lunch with Richard, who sold training programs to large organizations, he spoke of what motivated him. "If I'm not out there selling," he said, "someone else is getting ahead." He saw himself in a footrace with his competitors, and he needed to work hard or they would gain an edge on him. The fact that he might lose to another person was his engine.

Women are motivated by internal gratification because they frequently experience no goal line outside of themselves. They may say: "I'm proud of that report," "This new product will be very helpful to our clients," or "I closed more sales this month than I ever have." Their yardstick is most often themselves and the personal standards (often perfection) they establish. Indeed, frequently women are out to beat their personal best. But as a result, they can appear uncompetitive, despite the fact that they're working themselves to death: There is no outward opponent they're aiming to beat.

This seeming lack of competitive spirit can be a detriment to women. Men in power perceive women as shying away from competition. They're not out for blood—a revered value in the male culture. In reality, a woman's standards and goals may be even higher than her male colleagues'; the energy is just not aimed at an external target.

This difference in motivations becomes apparent in the divergent strategies of male and female business owners. Twice as many women as men are starting businesses today. But women often prefer to keep their businesses small. From the female perspective, bigger is not better. We're more apt to focus on how our business lets us live our lives. We're not out to prove to our competition that we can grow faster than they.

As a result of our differing cultures and concomitant life goals, the genders look askance at one another. As a man sees it: "Eileen put in all that work and then didn't fight for the promotion. What a passive woman." As a woman sees it: "Seth killed himself to get that title, but his wife is fed up and is leaving him. What an idiot." The lens of our divergent cultures prevents us from understanding how our motivations differ.

▶ THE FAMILY FACTOR

Women may find it particularly difficult to focus on a business goal line because we frequently spread our activities over several realms. Most often we feel responsible for all the activities at work and at home. Not only must we dazzle clients with our presentations, but our children must be good students, our houses kept in good order, our meals nutritious and cooked to everyone's taste, our husbands happy and well cared for, our sick relations will attended, and on and on. We're accountable not only for our own lives but for the lives of many others whom we don't control. The subtle message to today's woman is: You'll do everything superlatively *and* you'll be a top-notch professional. This can make you terminally tired, if not endlessly crabby.

If you're parenting young children, most likely you'll find yourself putting in extra hours. How can you deal with this? First, you need to determine what's important to you and what you want to accomplish. (Later in this chapter, you'll find specific suggestions on how to do so.) Then, assess what it takes to reach your goal. If, for example, you realize that you want to become a company vice president, it may mean putting in more hours after work, networking at professional dinner meetings, or traveling more extensively than you have until now.

In making your assessment, you may realize that this extra work will kill you, if not literally then figuratively. Indeed, studies have shown that when women try to "do it all" perfectly, their careers progress and their children thrive, but they neglect their own needs in the end and can undermine their health. If you can't reach your goals from your current position, you may need to examine and redefine your relationship to household chores, child care, and your partner.

You might prioritize tasks and let go of those that drain you of energy and add little to the advancement of your goals. Or you may find it worthwhile to seek out competent full-time household help so you'll be freed of delegatable domestic duties. Why not hire a math tutor to help your son, or serve nutritious take-out food twice a week if you're too exhausted to cook? Naturally, your strategies will be somewhat dependent on your income level.

One option that usually holds great potential is simple: You can invite your spouse to share more fully in domestic responsibilities for the good of the whole family. Child care can be a major bone of contention in many marriages. Sharing parental duties will most likely improve your marriage and benefit your children as well. In *Finding Time for Fathering,* clinical psychologist Dr. Mitch Golant and Susan Golant explain that fathers' involvement in child rearing is crucial to youngsters' social, intellectual, and sex-role development. And fathering can be more than just a chore for men. Studies have shown that the more time fathers spend with their children, the closer and more mutually enriching the relationship becomes.

Of course, your spouse may turn down your invitation to participate more fully in parenting. There are myriad reasons why men balk at helping out. Some feel driven to put in long days at the office for the sake of the family's security, and count that as their contribution. Others are uncomfortable in a new role for which they have no model. Or your husband may sense your unconscious resistance to his stepping onto your turf.

How to proceed if your husband is unwilling to share parenting and other household duties equally? Once you've established your goals and priorities, you might consider the whole package in light of how much your spouse is willing to help, or failing that, how much you're willing to compensate for the lack of help. As I see it, if your mate is reluctant to take on an equal share, you have three choices: you can negotiate; you can learn to live with the arrangement as it is; or you can leave the relationship.

To negotiate, the Golants suggest that you create time-use charts delineating how many hours a week are required for child care and which tasks each of you perform. You might find it helpful to divide and shuffle the responsibilities according to shifting needs and demands each week. Formalize your agreement by writing it down, if you must.

If your husband is intractable, however, accepting the status quo is also an option. That may reduce the conflict in your relationship but increase your fatigue. You might also consider altering the timetable of your career goals. Beware, however: If you become resentful with these make-the-best-of-it arrangements, your anger or depression can have an impact on the marriage.

If you do become resentful, marriage counseling may help you and your spouse work out the kinks. Many marriages crumble over this issue. If your husband is intransigent, it may also be within the realm of possible options to realize that you have the wrong partner in life—an unhappy thought, but one that must be considered nonetheless.

▶ THE MANY COLORS OF SUCCESS

Most often in our society, success is defined in male terms, by money and status. Women must cope with an additional overlay of doing it all and doing it perfectly, although each woman varies as to how much she'll tolerate this extra burden. Still, most of us tend to adopt the male definition of success without questioning its relevance to our basic values. Accepting this standard can dramatically affect the way we balance our time and ultimately live our lives.

For men, success in life is often linear and consistent within the male culture. In the long term, this means that men tend to live more linear lives. A man is more likely to say, "I got out of school, went to work for Acme insurance, moved up through the ranks, and retired after thirty years as VP of sales." A woman, on the other hand, may juggle mutiple areas of focus during a lifetime: "I got out of school, went to work, pulled out of work after a couple of years when I had a child, went back to work part-time, pulled out of work again for my second child, went back to work, and am still involved with the school, the youth soccer league, my church, and my community. All of these activities are important to me!" Whew!

For women, success comes in an array of colors. Maggy worked for one of the largest and fastest-growing office furniture companies in the country. She was such an outstanding salesperson, her company awarded her a region to manage. Again wildly successful, she was given half of the United States as her responsibility, at which point she told me, "I was miserable. I was traveling three days a week and not doing what I loved best—sales."

Maggy set about changing her job description. She talked her boss, the president, into letting her restructure her responsibilities, and now she travels less and sells more. "At first I felt as if I was going backward," she told me, "but I'm a happier person now, and that's all that matters."

Joan was a real estate attorney in a large firm, on the track to partner. She was doing well professionally. When she became pregnant, she intended to take off three months, find a live-in nanny, and then charge right back into her career. In fact, she wasn't sure she would even take the entire furlough. But at the end of her maternity leave, the world looked entirely different. Her top priority was her baby boy, Jason. Nothing else mattered as much.

Joan began working part time but started feeling guilty about renouncing the work for which she spent so many years in training. She went through a period of gradual acceptance. First she realized she wasn't going to live out her career the way she had imagined. Then she began to embrace the value and rewards of motherhood, despite the twinges of awkwardness she experienced with "And what do you do for a living?" questions. Joan is now a full-time mother, pregnant with her second child. She told me, "If I go inside and really look at what's important to me, I know that being a mother matters most."

I strongly urge you to consciously consider what success means to you. Instead of allowing others or society to determine when you win, *you* determine it. The following exercise may help you do so:

YOU'RE A WINNER

In your journal, write the answers to these questions. These are big issues that you may be unable to answer in a single afternoon. Take time to consider your responses, and come back to them frequently. Your conception of success may change as your career evolves.

1. What does winning mean in my personal and professional life?
2. What will it cost me? Am I willing to pay the price?
3. Can I realistically meet my goals?
4. How will I know when I have won?
5. Am I defining this a win because it is important to me, or because I feel that I'm supposed to do it?

Taking back the right to decide what success means to you can be very liberating. You're now in the driver's seat, able to determine your destination and set goals that will satisfy your own criteria for winning in business and in life.

▶ EYES ON THE PRIZE

Staking out success on your own terms requires some soul searching, but that's just the first step. To achieve that success, you'll need to carefully evaluate your current situation and set specific goals, as well as specific strategies for reaching them. The following guidelines are intended to help you with this task.

1. Know where you're aiming. What do you want to accomplish? Do you want a raise? A college degree? A new position? Another assistant? Whatever it is, you must know where you're headed and on what timetable.

2. *Write down your goal or goals.* DO NOT SKIP THIS STEP. When we inscribe our goals in black and white, the subconscious begins to look for opportunities to realize them. You've probably had the experience of solving a problem when you weren't thinking about it; the answer just came to you in the shower or driving to work. Your conscious mind wasn't working on it, but your subconscious was. When you record your goals and put them in a visible place, they will become an everyday part of your subconscious processing.

3. *Pay attention to how you write down your goals.* Avoid negatives—write "I will" instead of "I will not." Make your goals as specific as possible.

- Instead of "I will go back to school," write "I will finish my MBA by 20__."
- Instead of "I will make more money," write "I will earn $150,000 by 20__."
- Instead of "I will get a better job," write "I will manage a region by 20__."
- Instead of "I will travel more," write "I will spend a month in Europe in 20__."

The more specific your goals, the clearer your subconscious will be and the more likely you'll be to achieve them.

4. *Tell a friend.* Once you've established your goals, it's helpful to share them with a few people. I do this all the time, because it keeps me honest and is particularly useful when my goals scare me. Those are the moments my inner voice says, "You can't accomplish something that big." Your goals become concrete when you tell others. Those in whom you confide will expect you and even help you to reach them. You may feel guilty if you begin to waver!

5. *Create a self-development plan.* Once you know where you're going, determine what formal education, technical skills, knowledge, abilities, and hands-on experiences you need to reach your goals. Write these down, too, as part of your list. If appropriate, talk to your boss or mentor about your professional goals and get his or her input on what self-development you need. Your boss may well have insight into what the organization—and your industry—formally or informally require for the particular goals to which you aspire.

6. *Figure out exactly what you need to do to get there.* Keep in mind that the way you eat an elephant is one bite at a time. Break your goals down into today, tomorrow, next week, next month, and next year. For instance, if your goal is to earn an MBA, your step goals might be:

- This week: Decide on three possible schools.
- Next week: Contact the schools and request catalogues and applications.
- Next month: Complete and return the applications.

Getting the MBA is a big goal. Obtaining the three catalogues and applications is a bite you can handle.

Or let's say you would like to become a regional director. Some of the steps might be:

- This week: Talk with my boss and/or mentor about preparation necessary.
- Next month: Volunteer for the cross-functional committee to get experience in operations.
- Next year: Apply for a position in operations and prepare for management.
- In two years: Apply for management position in operations.

7. *As you draw up your list of goals, decide what kinds of support you'll need along the way.* Any woman who has survived the inevitable difficulties and reached her career goals will tell you she couldn't have done it alone. At the end of this chapter I'll discuss what may be the single most important ingredient for success: a strong support system.

Keep in mind that your quest won't go as smoothly as you might like. You may not achieve every goal you target, you may get an unanticipated break, or the company may be sold, sending you in directions you had never imagined. Just keep your eyes on the goal and be tenacious yet flexible. Learn to grow from the detours life presents. They are all grist for the mill.

Staying focused on your goal will no doubt present a constant challenge. As we've seen, most women's attention and energy is demanded not only at the office but also at home. The continual tug-of-war between these two important areas of our lives can be distracting and can sap our emotional resources. Equally treacherous is our natural tendency to concentrate on process and detail rather than on the big picture. In the pages that follow, I'll point out women's most common stumbling blocks as they move toward their goals, and I'll offer some techniques for working around these obstacles.

▶ BLINDED BY THE DETAILS

Men learn early on that getting to the goal line is paramount. They may have to make a mess—or as they say, "break some china"—but winning is worth the sacrifice. Girls learn to follow the rules and keep their rooms clean and orderly. The result: Men make the big plays, while women worry about who'll sweep up the floor.

That was Ellen's experience. I met Ellen in one of my workshops for women. For four years, she had been human resources manager at a building tools manufacturer. The department ran smoothly: Deadlines were met, government regulations adhered to, policies and procedures written and implemented.

About eighteen months ago, Ellen's boss, Will, had begun talking about new payroll software used by the competition for more than a year. Enamored of its bells and whistles, he wanted to install the program by the end of the fiscal year.

"Look," Ellen patiently explained, "human resources doesn't have the staff to make the transition so quickly. Everyone is already overloaded, and if a payroll were missed, don't you agree that there would be hell to pay in the plant?"

Apparently, Will didn't agree. One Friday afternoon Will called

Ellen into his office. "I'm moving you to a staff function to work on special projects," he explained. "Carlos will take over your department as of Monday."

Ellen was devastated. But she also looked forward to being vindicated when Carlos failed. His first week on the job, Carlos made the new program his top priority, and all hell broke loose, as predicted. Soon government reports were late, vacant positions unfilled, information on benefits and vacations withheld. The place crawled with expensive consultants and temporary help. Everyone griped about how human resources had gone to the dogs since Ellen had left, and Ellen believed that any day Will would see the folly of his ways.

On the second day of the fiscal year, the paychecks arrived a day late but in shiny envelopes, fresh from the program. A couple of weeks later, Ellen heard that Carlos had been given a promotion and a substantial bonus. The department was in disarray and morale was in the pits. Ellen was mystified.

When we talked in the workshop about women's needs to do their work perfectly and how that can lead to missing the big goal, suddenly a light went on in Ellen's eyes. She understood why Carlos had been rewarded so handsomely: the game had nothing to do with running the department well and everything to do with aligning one's goals with the boss's.

I ran into Ellen a year later. Having learned the rules of hardball, she had been reinstated in a managerial position. But now she said Will had a new bee in his bonnet: an integrated financial system. It seemed the competition had one. She was not at all sure that their medium-sized company needed anything quite so elaborate, but she had learned her lesson. "This time," she explained, "I offered to head up the project. I've figured out whose team I'm on."

In her conflict with Will over the payroll software, Ellen had lost sight of the big picture: the game. When the coach called the play, she resisted and was penalized. She worried that if she implemented the new program, the rest of the department's work would fall by the wayside. Yet she failed to realize that this was irrelevant to Will. Designing and implementing the program was all that mattered. Will knew the new system would temporarily disrupt human resources, but that was a short-term loss in the service of a long-term gain. He was the coach, he called the shots. And she needed to follow.

▶ IF I DON'T DO IT, WHO WILL?

Women also lose sight of their goals by taking on extra responsibilities. We are virtual responsibility magnets. We don't make these decisions consciously or deliberately, but out of the fear that if we don't act on a need, it will never get resolved. That means the task in question will be sloppy, incomplete, less than perfect. It goes against our grain. But we fail to realize that once we become responsible for something, we may be responsible for it forever.

I've seen this in action in my own life. When Mother's Day rolled around the first year of my marriage, I woke up and called my mother. My husband, who had leapt out of bed to fiddle with a new computer, was too preoccupied to call his. As the day wore on, my guilt began to build. I imagined my mother-in-law in Cleveland, sitting by the phone just waiting for it to ring, thinking her new daughter-in-law clearly didn't care about her. But I knew that if I broke down and called her myself, I'd be calling every Mother's Day for the rest of my life.

Throughout the day, I subtly reminded my husband, still banging on his computer, that it was Mother's Day. No action. Finally, at 4:55 PM, he called. I was greatly relieved.

We women unintentionally become accountable for all kinds of distracting tasks. If something won't get done, we do it—and then everyone looks to us to do it in the future. In this way we become overwhelmed with the minutiae of life: buying all the presents and birthday cards, getting the kids new shoes, picking up the in-laws at the airport, calling the plumber. I challenge you to find a man in this country who is responsible for circulating the birthday cards at work.

We may like making life easier for those around us, but when we focus on all these details, we leave ourselves little time for activities that further our careers. It can happen to the best of us. Mary Catherine Bateson, daughter of famed anthropologist Margaret Mead and communication guru Gregory Bateson, explored this dilemma in her autobiography, *Composing a Life*. During her tenure as a dean at Amherst, Bateson became enmeshed in the doing-it-all-and-doing-it-perfectly syndrome. She writes, "I had repeatedly accepted inappropriate burdens, stepping in to do what needed to be done. In retrospect, I think I carried them well but the cost was that I was chronically overloaded, weary and short of time for politicking, smoothing ruffled feathers, and simply rest-ing." Networking becomes virtually impossible if you feel that every detail of every job must be perfect.

▶ MANAGING YOUR RESPONSIBILITIES

How do you know if you're in an unproductive cycle? Ask your-self at the end of the week or the month if you are dead tired from working like a dog, but haven't made a significant impact in your job or on the organization. If your days are consumed with trivia and it's hard to catch up and focus on the goal, it's time to play a little hardball. Here's how:

GETTING STRATEGIC

1. *Make a list.* In your journal, list all your responsibilities at work, at home, and elsewhere. Be sure to include the important items as well as all the trivial duties. The list might include the following sorts of entries:

- Send birthday cards.
- Buy holiday presents.
- Order coffee supplies.
- Read the company junk mail.
- Research that idea the boss was so hot on.
- Learn how to read a financial report.
- Return vendors' calls.
- Return Michelle's library books.
- Attend a training session on new computer program.
- Have lunch with the new consultant.
- Call Steve's Aunt Shirley to find out if she's visiting this month.
- Check the menu for the meeting.
- Bake cookies for Michelle's PTA bake sale.
- Personally return all requests for information.
- Attend company picnic.

2. *Evaluate your list.* Go back and check off what really matters. You'll probably find a lot of activities that are easily dispensed with.

3. *Identify items you can delegate to someone else.* For instance, in the above list, you might have an assistant read the company junk mail and clue you in on the hot items. Buy the cookies for your child's bake sale—sure, its wonderful if you bake them yourself, but something has to give. Why not have your husband call his aunt about her visit?

4. *Tell the troops.* After you've established your priorities, inform those whom it will affect: your children, husband, friends, coworkers. Say it once—without a hint of guilt—and don't relent. If you feel guilty, remind yourself that you've made a conscious decision to reach certain goals, and these compromises are necessary.

You can't do it all *and* have time for what can easily seem like peripheral duties—but are actually crucial for your career advancement—such as checking out what the new consultant is up to, understanding what that financial report is all about, and researching the boss's new idea.

Anita, an office manager in a data processing company, learned this lesson the hard way. Her boss, the president, started a Friday morning tradition of bagels and cream cheese in the cafeteria. All employees were invited and encouraged to stop by. Then some employees complained they didn't like bagels and would prefer Danish. Anita found a bakery that delivered the pastries. Soon, other employees griped about the cholesterol level in the food, and dutifully Anita found low-cholesterol goodies. But the people who exercised in the company gym banded together and demanded fresh fruit rather than "all this junk food."

Before long, much of Anita's work life was consumed with catering this Friday morning extravaganza, which had absolutely nothing to do with her boss's priorities or Anita's value to the company. But soon she saw the light. With her boss's permission, the cafeteria reverted to bagels and cream cheese; employees for whom this was unacceptable were invited to bring food of their choice. This change wasn't easy for Anita. Some noses got out of joint. But she just kept reminding herself that she'd been hired and rewarded for running the office smoothly. That was her goal line, not accommodating fifty divergent diets.

Often this can be easy to forget when you're confronted by an indignant, intimidating man who can't believe you won't serve him. That's what happened to me when the regional director of the national hospital company I worked for asked me to help him design a program for new chiefs-of-staff. Together we outlined the three-day seminar, and I agreed to conduct the section on leadership. This meeting was to be held at a swank resort.

Several weeks before the program, the attorney who was to present the legal responsibilities section called me. "How do I sign up for golf and tennis games with the doctors?" Marshall asked.

"Gee," I replied, "I haven't a clue."

"You mean you're not coordinating this?" he shouted.

"Of course not."

"Well, why the hell aren't you doing your job?"

"Look, Marshall," I replied firmly, "recreation has nothing to do with my job. Why don't you call the regional director?"

"Oh, your department is so ineffectual," he said disparagingly. His tirade continued for several minutes. He tried every way imaginable to bully me into becoming a social director, but I wouldn't relent.

Because verbal abuse is so uncomfortable for women, we often capitulate to it. But if I had given in, I would have become the company's social director forevermore. One small wrong decision such as this can have lasting ramifications.

▶ LETTING GO OF GUILT

Perhaps the most difficult step in freeing ourselves from distracting burdens is to stop feeling guilty about relinquishing the role of good girl. Paula fell victim to this trap. The president of a number of galleries that provide art to major hotel and restaurant chains, she confided in a workshop, "If I don't send my in-laws birthday cards, they won't get any. My husband says he'll do it, but he always forgets." As long as a superresponsible woman like Paula steps into the breach, she will always be overloaded and her husband will be robbed of the opportunity to deal with consequences of ignoring his family.

How can you let go of such unproductive guilt? I believe positive self-talk can help. Remind yourself of your primary responsibilities; card sending may not be one of them. It's also wise to back off from the immediate problem and view the larger scheme of things. You could say, for example, "In the big picture, the birthday card doesn't mean all that much. What really matters is my relationship with my in-laws." Fortify yourself with the knowledge that if you jump in, you'll become responsible for issues that don't belong to you and ultimately prevent you from accomplishing important career goals.

In the end, it's your choice as to whose responsibilities you carry. Overloading yourself with trivia out of a misguided sense of guilt hinders you from reaching the goal line, while making life easier for others.

That's not how the game is played.

▶ BEING EARTH MOTHER: THE ISSUE OF AVAILABILITY

A study investigating men and women in organizations found that women were twice as accessible as men. Those who went to see women or called them got through twice as often as they did with a man. Natasha Josefowitz studied these patterns in availability. In her findings, documented in *Paths to Power,* she reported, "Not only did [women] make themselves available to employees, colleagues and clients, but they left their offices more often to *go* and *see* if they could be 'helpful.' "

Being constantly available to meet others' needs is different from networking, during which you're open to saying hi and sharing information. Nonstop availability presupposes an inequality in the relationship, whereas networking does not.

Consequently, it's important to recognize that your availability or lack thereof can signal your importance and power. If you stop what you're doing to meet a peer's needs every time he comes to your office, you convey the message that his time is more important than yours. If, on the other hand, you say, "Can we discuss this at 3:00 PM?" you communicate that you have control in the relationship. And in the long run, being available to help others hinders your ability to meet your goals by constantly diverting your attention.

Here's a common scenario: Dave is in his office, door closed, getting things done. Julia is in her office, door open, earth mother to the world. She will stop whatever she's doing to meet the needs of others. Five o'clock comes, and Dave is ready to go home. For Julia, five o'clock means she can now get down to her own work.

Underlying this inequity is the issue of power. Men are used to having their needs met on demand; women are used to meeting the needs of others on demand. But if we let others control our time, we put them in the driver's seat. We meet their goals, not ours, and that's not hardball.

The problem is exacerbated both by our expectations and by the expectations of those around us. At a workshop Lisa told me, "If I close my door, people walk in anyway, although they don't walk in on male colleagues."

"Well, what do you do when they interrupt you?" I asked.

"Nothing really," she replied. "They're already in my office."

By allowing others to put their needs before hers, Lisa had reinforced their inconsiderate behavior. Indeed, she'd taught her colleagues that barging in was perfectly acceptable. I advised her to say, "Sorry, I can't talk to you right now," whenever her coworkers interrupted her.

In *Composing a Life,* Mary Catherine Bateson explained her difficulty in managing this expectation of availability in her personal life. "For at least twenty years, whenever I interrupted my husband when he was busy, he finished what he was doing before he responded. When he interrupted me, I would drop what I was doing to respond to him, automatically giving his concerns priority. As time passed, I learned occasionally to say please let me finish here first, but usually this made me so uncomfortable that my concentration was lost." It can be very difficult to take back the power to control our own time when we have long given this power to others.

Of course, emergencies demand that you drop what you're doing and attend to others. Moreover, if the boss says, "I want to see you, pronto," obviously you can't say, "Later, I'm busy," or you'll soon be out of a job. In fact, attentiveness is a way men learn to show allegiance to their leader. For instance, once my boss called a meeting of all thirty-five members of the department. No sooner were we assembled when his boss, the president, called. Thirty-five employees sat twiddling their thumbs for twenty minutes, wondering what the meeting was about. This cost the company thousands of dollars in wasted labor, and it wasn't the first or the last time it happened.

The practical, female side of me saw the wait as an unwarranted waste. Why couldn't Anthony tell his boss he was in a meeting with the entire staff and ask if he could call back in half an hour? But the male perspective is different. Anthony was demonstrating that he was a good soldier; this was why he is a successful executive.

▶ HOW TO MANAGE YOUR AVAILABILITY

There are a multitude of methods for managing your availability; the key is for you to do the managing, and not leave it for events or the needs of others to overtake you.

If you absolutely cannot be disturbed:

- Announce to your coworkers and employees that they're not to approach you until you've emerged from your office.
- Lock your door, if need be.
- Ask your assistant to hold all calls except those from your boss, or let your calls ring into the voice-mail system and monitor them without picking up the receiver.
- Deflect all interruptions (except from those above) with, "Sorry, I can't talk to you now. Let's set up an appointment."

You may, however, need to make yourself available for drop-by networking talk from time to time. Some women solved this problem creatively:

- Francine had a closed-door period in the morning and an open door in the afternoon.
- Wendy indicated to her assistant a limited number of people from whom she would take calls; others left messages, which Wendy returned at her convenience.
- Mallory had an open-door policy one afternoon a week—anyone could stop by. The rest of the time, meetings were arranged on an appointment-only basis.

Managing our availability for the sake of power can seem like an odd game to women. What's the point of limiting access, just to appear important? This is just another part of hardball. The bottom line: It's important to manage your time strategically. Otherwise, you will be meeting everyone else's needs, and you'll never get across your own goal line.

▶ STUBBORNNESS AS A STRENGTH

I believe that to be truly successful, you've got to be stubborn. When roadblocks are thrown before you, step back, figure the best way around them, and keep on going. When others tell you (and there will be many doubting Thomases) a pet project can't be done, just smile and do it anyway. In the end, persistence pays off.

I attended college with a woman who was monomaniacal about her goals. At the age of twenty-one, Gail decided that by the time she was twenty-seven she would tour every country in western Europe, spend six months scuba diving in Mexico, get a Ph.D., and secure a teaching appointment at a seaside Southern California university.

"People were lining up to tell me I couldn't do it," Gail told me when I ran into her recently. "They loved to point out that I had no money—in fact, I had never lived above the poverty line in my life. When I started my Ph.D. program and mentioned that I intended to be finished in three years, many were quick to inform me that that just wasn't done."

Did Gail meet her goals? Not entirely. She missed Portugal. "They were having a war each time I went to Europe," she explained. The bigger question you might ask is *how* she did it. She was persistent. Gail took an overload of classes and finished her bachelor's and master's degrees early. She worked two part-time jobs and saved half of her money. And she won stipends that helped with the tuition. Today, Gail owns a successful consulting business. I asked if her earlier experience with goal setting impacted her business life.

"Absolutely," she replied. "I know I can do anything I want if I set my mind to it."

My brother's wife, Thurza, is also an amazing woman. At the age of thirty, she decided to get her bachelor's degree. Working part-time as a nurse, she earned top grades and a scholarship that helped cover tuition at the expensive private university she had chosen. She and my brother had one young son when she started, and she gave birth to a second child during her last year of school.

At the beginning of the final semester, Thurza found a new job. To celebrate, she went on a ski trip, during which she tore all the ligaments in her knee. The first surgery caused complications that necessitated two more. Thurza spent the rest of the semester on crutches, unable to drive. She needed two to six hours of physical therapy daily, had a toddler, and worked part-time in her new profession. If anyone had reason to quit school, she did. She said it never crossed her mind.

Next Thurza set her sights on a managerial position. Once she makes a decision, nothing stands in her way. It's so easy to be swayed by others' doubts. But I believe that people who win at hardball have a mile-long stubborn streak. They hang on like pit bulls and don't let go until they've achieved what they're after. I know that once I allow my goals to slide, it's hard getting back on track. I imagine many women face the same difficulty. To win at hardball, it's crucial to stay focused on your goals, no matter what curves are thrown your way.

▶ YOUR SUPPORT SYSTEM

Recently, Thurza and I were talking about this period in her life. She was quick to point out that a supportive husband and mother-in-law were major factors in her ability to finish the semester and get her degree. Women are frequently the support givers, so when we need support, we and others often fail to notice. Indeed, it's common for us to wait for others to pitch in rather than to ask for help, because usually we're the helpers. Explicit discussions with friends and family can make a big difference.

Your support needs may be widely divergent. If you're a single parent or if you're reentering college, you may require assistance with child care or finances. You may need help from coworkers to obtain data, financial reports, or a list of salaries paid.

To assess your home and work support system, ask yourself the following questions:

- Are others aware of my need for emotional support, and are they willing to give it?

- If my goals mean that I'll be less available to my family, have I discussed the issue with them?
- Who can I rely on for emergency babysitting if my child becomes sick?
- Who's got a shoulder I can cry on, if I need to?
- Who in my organization can I count on?
- How much can I rely on my mentor?

As I've advised women in workshops across the country, I have heard many heart-warming stories such as Thurza's about support systems. But not everyone is so lucky. Nora had to face a series of obstacles that came up with unsettling frequency once she articulated her dreams and moved toward realizing them. I met Nora some years ago in one of my conflict workshops. She was a middle manager in an insurance brokerage firm, and she confided to me that she was just putting her life back together. She had married her college sweetheart, and things had been fine until her career started to take off.

"Dan seemed to turn on me and resent my success, although he denied feeling this way," she told me one evening over drinks. "He started to control more and more of my life. He insisted that he manage the money. I had to give him my paycheck. He was sullen if I had to go out of town or work late. I got blamed for all our problems from financial—although I made more money than he did—to his mother being ill. I gained thirty pounds, had headaches, and was miserable.

"Then one day I looked in the mirror and said, 'Nora, are you going to live the rest of your life like this?' That day I decided to get divorced and get on with the second part of my life."

After a messy divorce and several rocky years, Nora has come out smelling like a rose. She found a man who appreciated her talents and remarried. Then she was appointed a regional vice president. When she was promoted to the corporate offices in another state, her new husband, whom she adores, quit his job to follow her. She's happier than she ever imagined.

Aside from your family, other support systems can help you out. Many professions have associations for women such as Women in Communication, Network for Executive Women in Hospitality, Women in Medicine, Women in Business, and Roundtable for

Women in Foodservice, to name a few. When you push yourself out into new groups of people, you expand the potential of making new friends on whom you can rely when you need support. Nora was very active in her association and credits it with making a difference in the hard times. Of course, these are great places to network, too.

I have also found informal networks of colleagues to be invaluable as a support system. Sometimes we schedule lunches on a regular basis, while other times a loose telephone network connects us. Whatever your approach, you'll probably find it impossible to go it alone. Proactively identifying and building your network before you desperately need it is the best strategy.

Women live complex lives. There is no right path. We juggle personal and professional agendas, and we're expected to be available to and responsible for others. With so much activity and so many expectations, it is easy to limit ourselves to immediate needs. In the process, however, we lose sight of our long-range goals. In order to win at business, you've got to keep your eye on the ball.

GOAL POST GUIDE

- Make sure your stated goal is the goal you really want.
- Write down your goals, and put them in a visible place.
- Break down your goals into attainable steps.
- Don't demand perfection of yourself.
- Consciously decide what your responsibilities are, and delegate what's not your responsibility.
- Give up the guilt.
- Don't worry about the trivia that doesn't get done.
- Strategically limit your availability.
- Be stubborn about achieving your goals.
- Create a support system, both personal and professional.

11

WINNING IS ALL THAT MATTERS

▼

HARDBALL LESSONS BOYS LEARN

- Winning is all that matters.
- Winning means outsmarting, outrunning, or outperforming the competition.
- Boys brag about their part in the team win.

▼

HOUSE AND DOLL LESSONS GIRLS LEARN

- No one wins a game of dolls—process is all there is.
- Wining means doing a perfect job while keeping relationships intact.
- Good girls don't brag.

▼ ▼ ▼ ▼ ▼ **N**ow that you've set your goals, you're ready to play to win. In this chapter, we'll discuss winning strategies—how to feel like a winner, be perceived as one, and get treated like one. Not least, you'll learn how to negotiate for a winner's salary.

▶ SUCCESS TALK/FAILURE TALK

How we talk about ourselves shapes others' perceptions of us. Interestingly, women don't talk about their successes in a particularly flattering light, whereas men often do. A fascinating study by Stephanie Riger and Pat Galligan published in *American Psychologist* reported how men and women frame success and failure differently. Subjects in the study were assigned a task, then given pseudo results. Half were told they did particularly well and half that they did particularly poorly. Each was then asked to account for the quality of the performance.

Men in the successful group pointed to their innate skills: "Well, you asked me to do it, didn't you?" Men who were told they'd failed pointed to the intrinsic difficulty of the task: "It was so darned hard, what did you expect?"

When women were told they had succeeded, however, they attributed their achievement to effort, task ease, or luck: "Well, I tried real hard." "It wasn't very difficult to begin with." "I got lucky." Those who were told they had failed, embraced the blame: "I tried, but I just couldn't do it."

Look at these dynamics:

- When men succeed, they point to self.
- When men fail, they point outward.
- When women succeed, they point outward.
- When women fail, they point to self.

In *Composing a Life,* Mary Catherine Bateson describes this double bind as follows: "Often American men learn to project their disappointments outward, like Lee Iacocca using his rejection by Ford to fuel new achievements. Women tend to internalize their issues. When a proposal is turned down or a job not offered, women tend to say, 'I wasn't worthy.' Men often contend that the process was crooked."

The tendency to embrace failure and dismiss success causes us to feel more inadequate than we should and to experience failure more often than reality warrants. The negative fallout can become a self-fulfilling prophecy: What you expect is what you get. Moreover, our reluctance to welcome success colors the picture others have of us. Because of the way men talk about their achievements and failures, they are prone to garner promotional opportunities.

HOW DO YOU SPELL SUCCESS?

For one week, listen to how your coworkers discuss their successes and failures.

1. Can you identify differences by gender?
2. How do you talk about your successes and failures?
3. How would you like to talk about your successes and failures?

▶ THE MYTH OF HARD WORK

When a woman notices that she's not getting opportunities to advance, she often proves her mettle by digging in and working even harder. She believes this is the best way to show her superiors that she's worthy of future promotions. That's what happened to Sarah. She was the advertising director in the marketing department of a large hotel chain. She and her department were high producers and won frequent awards. Sarah was able to draw a direct link between the department's work and increased corporate revenues.

Charles was hired in to work on special projects in the marketing department. He made flashy presentations, "did lunch" with all the movers and shakers in the company, and spent a great deal of time roaming the hallways, talking to people. He also lost the com-

pany lots of money with his high-profile expensive marketing campaigns that never generated extra revenue. Sarah could see that
Charles was being favored, winning opportunities to present his
high-flying ideas to the executive committee, and even having
many of his schemes implemented.

To prove that she deserved as much, Sarah and her department
produced more than ever. When promotions were handed out in
the fall, however, Charles was made a vice president and Sarah was
not. Why this inequity? Research indicates that the road to success
may not be paved with hard work, but rather with connections.

Remember "It's not what you know, it's who you know"? Fred
Luthans, professor of management at the University of Nebraska,
and his colleagues were able to prove it scientifically. Luthan's
team investigated what causes managers to be "effective" and "successful." For the purposes of his study he defined effective managers as people whose employees were highly productive in
quantity and quality of work as well as committed to their organization and department. Successful managers were defined as those
who received frequent promotions.

His first finding was that the two groups overlapped by a mere
10 percent. That is, the managers with the highly productive, committed employees were not the managers who got promoted. Take
a minute to think about this. Have you ever found yourself mystified why some twerp like Charles made vice president while a productive, motivating manager like Sarah was passed over? It
probably wasn't a fluke, but rather part of a pattern of who is rewarded in organizations.

Luthans then investigated the behavioral differences in each
group. He found that the effective managers spent the largest part
of their time communicating with their employees, while the successful managers spent a disproportionate part of their day networking outside their departments. In fact, instead of getting their
work done, the managers who were most frequently promoted
spent an average of 41 percent of the working day in this activity.

The implications of Luthan's research for American businesses
are significant. In business, as elsewhere in life, when you reward
a behavior, you're likely to see that behavior repeated. Thus, if networkers are continually promoted, employees will spend more
time networking and less time actually producing.

The implications for women are also dramatic. Women are great at putting their noses to the grindstone. We believe that if we do top-quality work rapidly and deal effectively with others, we will be rewarded appropriately. Yet most women can confirm Luthan's findings in short order: The world isn't wired this way. And yet we do have options to make a change.

▶ WHO KNOWS YOU?

What if you're hoping for promotions in the future? First, keep in mind that it is possible to be both effective and successful. But you must get out and talk with others about your abilities and accomplishments; just working hard is not enough.

The first step is to figure out who needs to know about you and what you've accomplished. All organizations have key people who can influence one's career. But if you've been particularly good at nose-to-the-grindstone work, what you've accomplished won't matter much, because you're probably invisible. It's time to bring your talents and achievements out in the open so that others will recognize and appreciate them. If you don't, you may unwittingly throw roadblocks in front of your own progress.

That's what happened in a meeting quite early in my career at which company managers discussed whom to promote into a position with real growth potential. As they sifted through the pile of resumes, they came across one for Jill, a woman whose background paralleled the job description. Greg said, "Never heard of her." Neither had anyone else. The conversation drifted to the next resume. That candidate was known all around as a "good guy." The group enthusiastically put Justin in the to-be-interviewed pile without ever discussing his accomplishments or the fact that his background did not meet all the job requirements. Due to my own naiveté, I kept wondering, "What's going on here? What about Jill?"

If you're an unknown, all the hard work in the world won't get you where you want to go. Woody Allen said, "Eighty percent of success is showing up." Well, 80 percent of getting the opportunity is being known. Consequently, you should make yourself known to the people who can control or impact your career: managers, vice presidents, the corporation's president or CEO. Sometimes it's also useful to become acquainted with those who may not have much official power but actually wield great influence within the organization, like the president's assistant or the CEO's nephew over in marketing.

▶ NETWORKING

By connecting with others, you not only let them know about your qualifications, you also develop great channels for receiving information about your organization. Years ago, one of my employees was an amazing networker; Sam would do anything to get a scoop. At one point, he was working at a regional office in Atlanta, while I was stationed at the corporate offices in Los Angeles. Even though he was across the country, Sam knew about what was going on at corporate before I did. Fortunately, he'd be kind enough to call and pass his information on to me.

One day, he got some significant inside news from Los Angeles so fast that I could no longer contain my curiosity. "How do you do it, Sam?" I asked. "I've just got to know."

"Well, Pat," he replied, "when I came to Atlanta, I requested a particular empty desk. No one minded because the spot wasn't so great. In fact, it had a view of the men's room door on the executive floor. Now, I drink a lot of water, so when someone who's in the know goes into the men's room, I'm ready to follow right behind." You should know that when I hired this fellow he was making close to minimum wage in a small hospital in the South. Sam is now the chief information officer of a Fortune 500 company.

Obviously you can't do urinal reconnaissance, but you can build your information and support base through networking. Be aware that women tend to network with women and men with men. But research has shown that men are central to the dominant coalition in which promotion and pay decisions are made, so be sure to include them in your networking efforts.

Men show allegiance to the team by networking and helping others in the network. An extremely well endowed, highly respected hospital in an affluent area of Southern California was looking for an assistant hospital administrator. There must have been over fifty well-qualified candidates in the geographical area who would have jumped at the job. But they didn't know about it. The only ads for the position were placed in west Texas and Oklahoma newspapers! Why would a hospital that could pick and choose anyone it wanted go out of state to find candidates and then pay the relocation costs? The head of personnel was a Texan, and one of the administrators came from Oklahoma. That was their network, and they were true to the home team.

You can't wait until the opportunity arises to network with someone. You might never come across the crucial person or opportunity if you do. Sometimes you have to create the situation yourself. That point was driven home to me one day when I was at a big company meeting in Chicago making a phone call in the lobby. One of the vice presidents was making a call on the adjacent phone.

"What are you up to, Brett?" I asked.

"Oh, I'm just having my assistant change my plane tickets because I'm returning to Los Angeles this afternoon."

"Why are you leaving the meeting so early? Did a crisis come up?"

"No," Brett replied, "I just found out that Gordon [the company president] is going back this afternoon, so I'm having my assistant get me on the same flight and reserve the seat next to him." He went on to explain. "I do this all the time. It's a great way to get his undivided attention." This is a man who plays hardball in networking.

Your network needs to be wide and deep. Include those in the know, the opinion leaders, and other heavy networkers. One of my employees befriended the president's assistant. Her previous boss hadn't encouraged this relationship, but I was in heaven. I got insight into decisions and strategies that I never could have had otherwise. And so important for women, don't forget to include in your networking those whom you don't like but who have the power or the information. Your network needs a little of everything:

- people inside the department
- people outside the department
- people inside the organization
- people in other organizations
- peers
- subordinates
- superiors

- those whose opinions are valued by the higher-ups
- those who control information
- those who control budgets
- administrative assistants
- the receptionist (who probably knows more than anyone)
- industry-wide organizations
- people on boards where you may be serving

Use any pretext to get access. Ask potential members of your network to lunch—yes, you can ask "up" as long as your boss doesn't feel you're violating the chain of command or breaking company norms—send articles, or better yet, hand deliver articles, and ask others to join committees.

Business dynamo Connie is a networker par excellence. She directs a steady stream of articles and phone calls my way, constantly connecting me to other people. Yet I know I'm just peripheral in her network. I sometimes wonder how she gets the time. This reaction only points to my own inclination to think of networking as an optional activity. Connie knows it's central to her career and success.

When you build this team, you don't need to like the individuals or be their friends. Your only goal is to share and exchange information.

I also have learned that women often feel this kind of activity to be disingenuous. As one woman said to me, "I hate networking. It feels fake and phony." But I pointed out to her that's a common reaction I get from women. "Relationships are so serious in our lives," I explained. "But this is a different kind of relationship—it's one of utility. You aren't *using* people in a bad way; you're just playing the game of hardball like men do."

▶ BEING YOUR OWN PUBLIC RELATIONS DIRECTOR

As children we have been taught that good girls don't brag. They rarely talk about themselves. A girl with good social skills focuses on others, not herself. Boys, on the other hand, talk about the game. In the process, they easily brag about how they helped the team win. And as a top executive woman once told me, "Women don't have the finesse the ol' boys have."

Given their background, it's no surprise that women are uncomfortable talking up their accomplishments. Yet the only way others will know what they have done is if they bring their successes out in the open. This is part of the networking process.

But how to do it? As Deborah Tannen points out in *You Just Don't Understand,* it's not that easy. "It's tempting," she writes, "to recommend that women learn to display their accomplishments in public, to ensure they receive the respect they have earned. Unfortunately, however, women are judged by the standards of women's behavior." Personally, I find it sad and irritating that women cannot be as forthright as men in discussing their successes, but they still can make the best of a bad situation.

So what to do? First, decide which accomplishments you want to communicate. Key your discussion of achievements to the organization's stated or implied goals, such as a balanced budget or parts out the door.

Then find ways to convey your successes indirectly to the people you've determined need to hear about them. Here are some suggestions:

- One woman told me that she gives her boss a weekly report to keep him updated on her work; her real agenda is to let him know how well she's doing.
- Ask a colleague for feedback on a project in order to let him or her know how successfully it's going.
- Make sure your projects get mentioned in the company newsletter.
- Involve the power brokers in projects and committees you're working on, or at least keep them updated.
- Befriend members of the public relations department or make sure you know who to contact at the company's outside PR agency, if they use one.
- Offer to apprise other departments or project groups at their meetings on what your area is doing.
- Inform executives of strategies that have gotten the organization visibility, profit, or contacts (these, of course, are your strategies).
- Contact and perhaps befriend editors at trade magazines to increase the likelihood of your project/company getting expo-

sure. (Make sure your superiors know you've made these contacts.)

Renée, an extremely successful executive, was always talking about how excited she was for the company, what great things were occurring. These great developments always happened to be projects she had done, could claim she had done, or thought she might do. Renée once suggested to me that I toot my horn about a project that had barely gotten under way.

"I can't claim success because we haven't done much yet," I said. Her approach seemed like cheating to me.

Renée's reply: "Talk about it first; make it happen later."

▶ WHAT DO THEY KNOW?

Do you know how people really talk about you when you're out of earshot? Let's face it; when you're in the vicinity, people generally say nice things about you, but this isn't always the case in your absence. It's important to be able to manage this invisible process because it shapes how others perceive you.

Why not ask a friend or a trusted superior how you're described, and what others say or don't say about your skills, knowledge, and abilities. Then, no matter how difficult the feedback, thank your informant. You want to be able to call on this person again.

One of my friends does this on a regular basis. Robin says it keeps her "in shape." She works in the corporate offices of a large and political retail sales company. Robin has made a habit of taking peers and senior managers to lunch and asking them for "help." She tells them how much she admires them, how helpful they have been in her own development, and then she asks, "But how do other people see me?"

Robin explained that the useful part of this exercise occurs when the managers deliver bad news. Then they also feel responsible for helping her correct the problem. "If my boss tells me that the vice president sees my department as contributing insufficiently, he's now likely to point out to the VP when my department is productive in the future."

When your informant shares with you how you're perceived,

pay close attention. It might even help to take notes; our brains like to forget uncomfortable information. Tune in to factors that are the most common derailers for women. Ann Morrison's research, as reported in *Breaking the Glass Ceiling,* demonstrated these to include an inability to adapt; performance problems (from outright blunders to not being consistently excellent); or too much ambition. As with all feedback, you'll need to dig for specific examples so you'll know what behaviors to eliminate.

▶ GETTING OUT OF THE AMBITION DOUBLE BIND

Although the third most common derailment factor for women is being seen as "too ambitious," one of our most critical success factors is having a "drive to succeed." This is far more important for a woman's success than a man's. *Breaking the Glass Ceiling* reported that 44 percent of successful male executives have a strong drive to succeed, whereas 84 percent of successful female executives have the same strong drive. My guess is that this is because women who achieve a certain measure of success must work much harder than men to get there.

Can you succeed without showing just how driven you are? It's not easy, but it can be done. The trick here is to get your internal engine revving at full bore, but to refrain from expressing your desires verbally. For instance, when I was in charge of trainees for a Fortune 500 company, I found it interesting that when the president interviewed the individuals on their goals, the men answered, "I want your job," whereas the women never uttered such a thought, even if it was their fondest desire. To do so would have rendered them "pushy" and "overbearing" in others' eyes.

And yet this need not have precluded them from making a pointed statement about their professional determinations. It would be quite acceptable, for instance, to say something like, "I'm interested in marketing. I'd like to get a chance to work on a wide variety of projects. I worked on some national campaigns in my last job and found the work really challenging."

If you are a female director and hope to be promoted one day to a vice president position, let the powers-that-be know, including your boss. I was at a conference talking to the president of an international company, who said to me, "See that woman over there? She was a director in sales. But she came to me one day and told me that she hoped to be promoted to a vice president position. It never occurred to me that she might fit into that position, but once she had asked for it, I could see that it made a lot of sense. If she hadn't talked to me about it, it would never have been on my radar screen."

The issue of "pushy" comes in when a woman indicates that she wants to move into a position far away from where she is now. For instance, if she's a manager and she says, "I want to be president of this company one day," she might be seen as overly ambitious even though it's a worthy desire. Rather, it's best for her to express interest in the level directly above her. And each time she moves up into that higher level, she can express her wish to progress yet further, in a stepwise manner.

Women may also be considered "pushy" if they are direct in a male way. Here is an instance where "doing it like a man" can backfire. In *Women Don't Ask: Negotiation and the Gender Divide*, Linda Babcock and Sara Laschever cite a number of studies indicating that how you ask makes all the difference for a woman. They conclude, "All of these studies tell us that when women go into a negotiation, in addition to arming themselves with information, ideas, and resolve, they must also bring along an arsenal of 'friendly' nonthreatening social mannerisms; they must be prepared to be cooperative and interested in the needs of others; and they must avoid being confrontational."

Clearly, we can still play the game, but we can't play it in the male way—we have to be friendlier in the female mode. Yes, this makes me want to gag, but it's the reality of the workplace as it exists today.

I've had an opportunity to observe a woman who is an artist at eluding the ambition double bind. I've known and admired Connie for many years. In fact, I've seen her gradually become one of the most senior women in corporate America.

At one point in Connie's career, the promotions slowed down. She went to her boss and said, "I would like to become a vice president."

He replied, "But I thought you didn't care about those things."

She came back with, "You know it's hard to deal with these

boys [yes, she called them *boys*] when you don't have the title." She got promoted. In fact, others have said of Connie that she has the ability to tell you to go to hell in a way that makes you look forward to the trip!

Managing your image when you're a woman demands a lot of finesse.

▶ TAKING RISKS

Now that you've completed your image research, it's time to get out there and make that image work for you. You'll need to take some risks that may make you uncomfortable at first. But according to the authors of *Breaking the Glass Ceiling,* risk taking is a key success factor for women—though not necessarily a significant factor in men's success. Perhaps, again, women must gamble more to get ahead. Following are some strategies.

Volunteer for a visible position. Any project that requires you to stretch and accomplish tasks you haven't had an opportunity to do in the past will allow you to show your abilities. In one company, the offices services department needed to acquire a software network system. Tamara volunteered to head the committee. When she told me, I said, "I didn't know you were a computer person."

She replied, "I'm not, but I figure I can learn anything."

Volunteer to speak on a program or at a conference. You might try your company's annual meeting, your professional association's local or national conferences, or other public avenues that help get your name and product out.

Volunteer for cross-departmental or cross-functional committees. If your company is looking to move, you will naturally interface with directors from other departments and demonstrate your abilities by volunteering to sit on the relocation committee.

Volunteer for the United Way campaign. Many women have told me that the United Way furthered their careers by giving them access to influential people within and outside their organization.

***Go to the meetings other departments or executive decision
makers attend.*** No matter how boring the meeting, attend and
speak. Identify what's important to that group—their goal line—
and focus on it.

Go to the Christmas party and company picnic. Don't hang
out with your friends. Instead, work the room. Introduce yourself
to people you don't know, including executives. You can talk
about them ("Interesting name," "Nice tie," "I've heard you're
working on a new sales campaign"), or you can talk about the situation ("Great shrimp," "Can you believe how many turned out?"
"This is my first picnic. Have you been before?"). Remember, people love to talk about themselves.

When I mention taking part in such activities during workshops,
women often roll their eyes and groan. "Pat, you don't understand," they complain. "I'm swamped with work as it is now. And
I have two kids, one of whom is having a birthday party this weekend with fifteen friends. I just can't do more."

But the issue isn't working harder, it's working smarter. Be
strategic in what you do, because the executive to whom you
boldly introduced yourself at the Christmas party will most likely
remember your name when it comes across his or her desk for an
opportunity. Years of hard work will matter less than that brief chat
about the fact that you both went to the University of Megalopo-
lis. It's not right or fair; it's just part of the game of hardball.

▶ TOUCHDOWN: GETTING THE MONEY

Some years back, while working for a Fortune 500 company, my
boss hired a man and a woman who were to be my peers. They
had identical educational backgrounds and work experience, except that Barry had been out of school a couple of years longer,
and Melissa had been a manager for two years. I was appalled
when I heard through the grapevine that Barry was to be paid 30
percent more than Melissa for doing the same job.

I mentioned my outrage at this inequity to several people in my
network, and one fellow smuggled Barry and Melissa's "objective"
compensation analyses from human resources (chances are you
have the very same system in your organization). The analyses

showed Barry having more "points," and therefore more pay, than Melissa. I wondered how that could be. After all, their qualifications were identical.

Once I got my hands on these documents, however, I understood. The information on Barry's analysis was false. Really steamed, I used my network system again (asking a lot of "Oh, by the way . . ." questions), this time to ferret out the real story. I discovered that the vice president of HR had become Barry's drinking and carousing buddy. He wanted Barry to be paid more. He cheated.

Outraged, I showed Melissa and my boss, Tanya, the two purportedly objective evaluations. Tanya made a stink but got nowhere—the decision had been made above her. So Melissa took her complaint all the way to the Equal Employment Opportunity Commission. They were unsympathetic. Unless Melissa could prove a consistent pattern of discrimination in the company, the government wasn't interested in her case.

The moral: In case you didn't know it yet, the world is not a fair place. Don't assume that an "objective" compensation system will assure you fair compensation.

We all know that women are paid about 76 cents for every dollar that men earn. The reason often given for this unfairness is that women haven't been in the work force as long, and that men have families to support—as if women didn't. Yet studies indicate it's not that simple. In one investigation of 345 men and women who were closely matched in background, job status, motivation, and job satisfaction, the men earned an average of $8,000 to $10,000 more per year than the women.

Did the women in this study feel cheated? Not at all. They, like the men, reported being satisfied and fairly treated in all aspects of their jobs, including pay. Because Americans will talk more readily about their sex lives than their incomes, its easy for us to assume that we're being paid equitably. And since the decision-making process is invisible, women presume fairness. But do we really know for certain? I believe we become part of the problem when we stay in the dark.

Okay, so relative incomes are not posted on the bulletin board, but it's possible for you to dig them up. Indeed, you can unearth anything you want in an organization if you have enough friends in high and low places. I like to think of myself as the sleuth on a mystery case. It's not necessarily ladylike, but if I'm being cheated I want to know. I wouldn't snoop in the personnel records, but it might be helpful to befriend assistants or file clerks in HR. Higher-ups with loose lips might also come in handy. You may even ask ex-employees of the company for information; those who have been fired might be amenable to spilling all sorts of beans. Mentors can also be a great source of information regarding the going rate of salaries for those at your level.

What to do if you discover an inequity? If your organization is operating under the illusion of wanting to be fair, you could slip into a discussion with your boss a statement like, "I was hoping in my next salary review that I'd be brought up to par with my male peers." In some organizations, the fact that you know women are being paid less than men can be enough to frighten your boss into rectifying the situation. In some firms, however, it doesn't much matter. In that case, you have the option of insisting, learning to live with it, or leaving. If it were up to me, however, I would remove myself from an inflexible situation.

Often women think if they just keep moving up the organizational ladder, the inequality will eventually get straightened out. Unfortunately, usually just the opposite occurs. If a man and a woman are both offered $35,000 as their first salaries at age twenty-two, and the man negotiates a 4.3 percent increase to $36,505 while the woman can only get 2.7 percent more at $35,945 the difference between the two may seem small at only $560. But according to economist Linda Babcock, what happens over their careers becomes significant—especially if they negotiate the same kind of increase each year until they retire at age sixty-five. "By the time they retire," Babcock explains, "his salary will be $213,941, while hers will be only $110,052—about half of what he's making." The inequity compounds itself over time.

Certainly, some of this pay inequity is due to the low value placed on women's work, the extent to which the system is rigged, as I learned, and the old-boy network. Yet some of the problem is due to how women perceive money.

When I began my consulting business years ago, I found myself extremely reluctant to ask for money, particularly big chunks of it. I felt a strong urge to bill below market rate, because otherwise I'd feel "money hungry." I talked to a wise friend about my problem.

"Don't think of it as money," she said, "think of it as votes. If people like what you do, they'll be willing to give you votes." Somehow her advice made me much more comfortable, but it's no accident that the only way I could ask for what I felt I deserved was by removing the dollar signs.

In a fascinating *Working Woman* article entitled "Cookies, Dirt and Power," journalist Kathleen Fury noted that women often talk as if the desire to acquire money is somehow dirty. She took exception with an article she had read that stated that women have lowered themselves to men's standards. "Have status, money, and power become in themselves the rewards?" this outraged article posited. Fury responded that she felt "scolded in print" by a woman who seemed to feel we should be ashamed of ourselves for openly chasing after money.

"Sorry, sister," Fury wrote in response. "I'd rather chase after money than grease stains. I'd rather have a portfolio than a Dustbuster." Unfortunately, women often criticize other women's desire for money. It is the rare female who will stand up and say, like Fury, "Yes, I want the bucks."

In Chapter 10, I noted that getting money is one way men affirm to themselves that they have won. Money is related to status and success. Because men associate the dollar so closely with their worth as people, they're more willing to fight for it. Conversely, because women are more motivated by internal rewards like pride in work or a sense of accomplishment, they're less likely to push for money. They're also less apt to demand it in order to avoid appearing "too ambitious" or damaging relationships. Yet I've never heard a woman say, "I really don't care if the man who does the same work I do gets paid more." We just look the other way. The whole mess is not very "ladylike," and so we're more comfortable avoiding it.

I believe that we may need to shift our point of view regarding money. Although we may not want to go grubbing for dollars, cash is a sign of power. Consequently, if we're playing hardball, it's important for us to be appropriately remunerated in the same way that our office and other trappings of power demonstrate our position in the hierarchy. (Don't be naive and think others don't know what you're being paid. Any information is available with persistent detective work.)

▶ GETTING MORE

I have found that women often become entrapped in thought processes that prevent them from asking for more money. Many have told me that it is painful for them to ask for the salary they think they deserve in a new job or for a pay increase in their current position. It's so painful, in fact, that many would just forego making the request. This has been borne out in Linda Babcock's research. In one of her studies, women were 45 percent more likely to score low on a scale in which people rated their propensity to see possibilities for changing their circumstances. "Low scorers," Babcock explained, "are people who see little benefit to asking for what they want because they perceive their environment as unchangeable."

Part of this attitude may be linked to how we value ourselves or perceive who determines our own worth in dollars and cents. Researchers have documented that women have a lower sense of entitlement than men and even expect lower salaries upon graduation from college and at career peak. Why should this be so? Perhaps it is related to how we perceive who controls our value. Management professor Lisa Barron, in conducting post-negotiation interviews with potential job seekers, found two distinct groups: one felt that they decided how much they were worth and it was up to them to make sure that the company paid them accordingly; the second felt that the company made that determination. Perhaps not surprisingly, there were significant gender differences in these groups. The first group had 85 percent of the male participants (but only 17 percent of the females), while the second group was composed of 83 percent of the women and only 15 percent of the men.

If you permit the company to determine what you're worth and part of the game is that they want to pay you as little as possible, you allow them to get away with paying you less than men. That's why it's so important to do your research ahead of time to know your real value and to go into a negotiation expecting to be paid accordingly.

In Chapter 12, I'll lead you through the steps involved in negotiating a salary at a new organization. Meanwhile, if you decide you want a pay increase in your current job, there are several hardball strategies you can employ.

Do Your Homework

Find out what others in your position with the same number of years experience in the same geographical area are paid. You can go about this in a number of ways:

- Contact your professional organization. Most publish salary surveys every few years, and some professional newsletters may run ads for job openings around the country.
- Check ads in your local newspaper, trade journals, and the *Los Angeles Times,* the *New York Times,* or the *Wall Street Journal* websites to see what competitors are offering for comparable positions.
- Look in the business section of your local library for salary updates that the Bureau of Labor Statistics publishes for various job classifications.
- Talk to colleagues in other companies and ask what they're paid or what they pay.
- Ask headhunters what the pay range is for your type of position.
- Consult the following websites: www.salary.com, www.careerjournal.com, and monster.com.

It's essential to analyze objectively, because women frequently request less money than men. But undercharging can work to our detriment: If you want your boss to respect you, you must ask for an appropriately large sum. Asking for too little can reduce your worth in your superior's eyes. Ask for too much, and the worst that can happen is you'll begin a negotiation.

When changing companies, I once inquired of my mentor what he thought a fair salary would be in the new job. His suggestion was 20 percent more than what I had anticipated. I wasn't even sure I could utter so large a figure without blushing. Finally, I talked myself into taking the risk; at the worst, my potential new boss would turn down my request.

I'm happy to report that in the end, I got what I asked for—plus a car allowance. I was so shocked, I just sat in the new boss's office and kept my mouth shut. I also worked furiously at keeping my expression neutral, for fear that he would see my amazement and take it all back. I am sure that left to my own devices, I would have been insufficiently objective to ask for so large a salary.

Document Your Successes

Before negotiating a raise, start collecting a file of evidence showing how you've impacted the bottom line. One of the toughest salary negotiations I've ever endured as a manager was with a woman who planned the company's meetings. Over a year's time, she had kept data on how her negotiations with hotels, restaurants, and vendors had saved the company over $260,000. The pay increase she was asking for, while substantial, looked rather paltry next to the savings.

Also, keep letters commending you for your work. If you receive verbal feedback, tell those who compliment you how much you appreciate it, and ask if they'd mind putting it in writing. One of my mentor/bosses was always on my case about this. I'd come back from doing some work and Marc would ask me, "How did it go?"

"Well, Andy said he was very pleased with the retreat."

Marc would consistently reply, "Then have him tell Freddy." Freddy was the president of the company, and I never thought he'd be all that interested in my work, but that's my female perspective. His interest was of less importance than the boost a positive report would have given my career had Freddy been kept abreast of my accomplishments. Finally, after being badgered enough by my boss with this "tell Freddy" routine, I learned to say in response to a compliment on my work, "Well, would you mind letting Freddy know?" No one ever balked or even thought it unusual; generally they were glad to do the favor.

Timing Can Be Everything

Before you pop the question, aim for a time when

- your boss is in a good mood.
- the department and/or organization is turning a profit.
- you've been recognized for outstanding work.

Don't Ask for What You Need

When it's time for the negotiation, ask for only what you deserve. Many women will say, "My child-care costs just went up. I need a raise." Child-care cost has nothing to do with work and can be easily dismissed. Rather, ask for what you deserve, but at the same time leave enough room to bargain. Establish your worth by presenting your documentation.

What to Avoid

- Don't believe there's no money in the budget.
- Don't assume your boss knows how great you've been doing.
- Don't threaten to leave—you may be given the opportunity.

With enough warm-up and practice, you can be a financial winner without guilt.

WINNING POINTS

- When you succeed, attribute it to your abilities—not effort, task ease, or luck.
- Network, network, network.
- Make your accomplishments known.
- Make sure the power brokers know who you are and what you've done.
- Take calculated professional risks.
- Remember, it's okay to want to be paid well.
- Do objective research on how much money your position earns.
- Document what you have contributed financially to the organization.
- Ask for the pay you deserve, not what you need.

12

MAKING YOUR
NEXT PLAY:
What's Your Game Plan?

▼
HARDBALL LESSONS BOYS LEARN

- It's a rough-and-tumble game out there.
- You can't win if you don't have a strategy.
- Key players need to know your strategy so they can support you.
- If you get knocked down, regroup and devise a new strategy.
- Position yourself on the team so your strengths can be maximized.

▼
HOUSE AND DOLL LESSONS GIRLS LEARN

- Don't be pushy.
- Do your best and you'll get rewarded.
- Be a good person and you'll have a lot of friends.
- If you get knocked down, go to Mom and she'll make it all better.

▼ ▼ ▼ ▼ ▼ **I**n conducting workshops, I meet many women who are waiting for recognition, a promotion, a new job, more money. When I encounter these women years later, they're still patiently waiting, most likely because they've never learned to play hardball.

Business is an aggressive, pushy sport. You've got to get out on the playing field and show your stuff. You've got to weasel in where you weren't asked. You've got to be a tough player with a team to support you. And when you've honestly assessed that you can't win, you've got to cut bait and move on. You can't wait for others to graciously ask you to play in their league. If you do, like the patient Penelopes in my workshops, you'll be waiting a very long time.

▶ YOUR CURRENT FIELD POSITION

If your boss is supportive, you enjoy the work, the organization is healthy, and you have opportunities to grow, you'll probably be happiest staying right where you are. Finding such a good mix again may be difficult.

But you may be staying in a job that's wrong for you. You may feel reluctant to change, because it seems like such an effort to move to another position. Staying in the wrong job, however, can be detrimental to your career's health. It's like water-drip torture. Every day in small ways your unhappiness wears on you. You feel more insecure and take fewer risks. In the long run, staying in the wrong job is more debilitating than moving on.

If you'd like to make a change, perhaps you're mystified as to the proper move. Maybe you should go into operations. Research and development may hold the key to a brighter future. Perhaps you'd be better off in a new organization, or even going out on your own. How can you determine which path will lead to career advancement? While no one has a crystal ball, this chapter provides some strategies to help you shape the direction of your career.

▶ ASSESSING YOUR OPTIONS FOR THE NEXT PLAY

If you're unhappy in your current position, you can move to a different job or you can move out. Let's examine these options more closely.

Make an Internal Move

If you like the company but your boss is driving you buggy, or if you can see that the real opportunities lie in another function, an internal move may be your best bet. More on what to look for in a new boss and department below.

Move to Another Company

If the organization doesn't suit you, seek employment elsewhere. Research the culture, opportunities, and people in other companies in advance of making a move. You may want to look at *Fortune Magazine*'s most current list of the best companies for women. You don't need to struggle; take the time to choose carefully. More on finding the right fit below.

Change Careers

Your profession may not suit you anymore for a variety of reasons—inadequate remuneration, low growth potential, or your own evolving interests. You may want to move to another field altogether. But how do you know which one? While the subject of how to change careers is too broad to cover adequately in this book, I can offer a few tidbits as food for thought.

First, don't limit yourself by your college degree, current job title, or past experience. We often refuse to consider other options because we believe they're out of our range. Indeed, sometimes women may use their "lack of appropriate preparation" as an excuse for staying dead-ended. But unless you're transitioning into a field that requires licensure, you may not need to return to school to retool. Risk taking may be useful as well. For instance, my friend Maureen recently informed me that she was going to conduct a strategic planning seminar with international bankers in Macau.

"What do you know about strategic planning?" I asked.

"I've always been a quick study," Maureen explained. "So I figured out how to do this, too."

When changing careers, I've also found it useful to conduct information interviews with specific organizations. These help you gather information on new professions, alternative organizations, and potential opportunities, as well as the following:

- differing corporate cultures
- the broad spectrum of work that organizations do
- where you might or might not fit in (bearing in mind that other corporations may have positions that sound like yours but aren't, or that sound inappropriate but are not)
- translating language and knowledge from one field into another
- managers' most pressing needs

When going out on the interview, be ready with questions about the industry, company, or profession. Suppose, for example, you'd like to switch from computer hardware sales to software sales. You might want to discover how much technical knowledge you would need and if you'd have support—some software companies send engineers with their salespeople to explain the technical end of the program. You might also be able to ask about the risks and benefits of working for a large, established company, where advancement might be slow but steady, versus a small, start-up company with great growth potential but little security.

Whom should you contact for such an interview? It's ideal to call acquaintances or friends who are already engaged in the work you'd like to investigate. Failing that, friends of friends will also do. Put your networking skills into action: Use your professional support group; ask friends and colleagues, "Do you know someone in the software industry?" Never underestimate the value of cold calls. I've conducted dozens of information interviews with strangers and

I've been turned down only once—by industrialist Armand Hammer. There's no one you can't call!

Ask if you can have thirty minutes of the professional's time to find out about the profession, industry, or organization. You may be astonished at how many individuals will warmly accept your request—after all, it's quite flattering.

You may also find the classic books *What Color Is Your Parachute?* by Richard Nelson Bolles, and *Wishcraft,* by Barbara Sher and Annie Gottlieb, helpful as you redefine your career.

Become Your Own Boss

A final option is to peddle your skills on your own. Certainly you won't be alone. In 1973, women owned 5 percent of American small businesses, but by 1997 that number had increased to 26 percent—5.4 million in all.

You'll want to do a good deal of research before you make such a move; it's a high-risk option. As one entrepreneur who is the mother of two quipped, "To be successful, you have to be willing to let your children starve."

The stores are full of books that offer guidance for the first-time business owner, and you'll need to turn to these as well as to many other sources before taking the plunge. If you're thinking of pursuing this route:

- Learn about the business itself. Is it seasonal or cyclical?
- Look at the financial side: How well is the industry doing financially? Is it stable?
- Determine how much venture capital you will need.
- Figure out your expenses (don't forget business, disability, and health-care insurance; social security and unemployment payments; retirement funds; rent; utilities; office equipment and other overhead) and potential income.
- Determine how much money you need to live on. Will your expected profit be adequate? Be realistic about how you'll survive if times are tough.
- Research government requirements for businesses: regulations, licenses, tax I.D. numbers, and so on.
- Prepare to pay quarterly federal income tax installments.

- Ask about the percentage of failure for this type of business.
- Evaluate the competition.
- Research the importance of location and which locations can boost profits.
- Find out the appropriate skill mix of employees.
- Determine how your products or services are best marketed and sold.

Above all, however, have faith in your own abilities. While foolhardy speculation may jeopardize your future, calculated risks, careful planning, and long-range strategizing can pay off. Besides, sometimes it's wise to turn a deaf ear to the doubting Thomases.

Whatever move you make, don't do it in the heat of the moment or without thoroughly investigating your options. Jumping too fast because the grass seems greener can prove disastrous. Take the time to make your move on your own terms.

▶ MAKING AN INTERNAL MOVE

Making a move within your organization has obvious advantages: you're familiar with the playing field and the players, and you've probably developed a valuable support network. If you've taken the time to carefully evaluate your company and have decided to remain on board a while longer, you'll need to turn your attention to maneuvering your way into a more satisfying position.

The Party Line Versus the Bottom Line

To find an efficient route to the fast track, you must first ascertain what matters to the company. That is, you must determine the difference between the party line and the bottom line. The party line is what the organization says it values. The bottom line is what it actually rewards. One organization I worked in, for example, claimed that quality was its first priority. But if you analyzed who got promotions and bonuses, there was no doubt that profit was king.

You must know what your organization's core values are, but don't be misled by the mission statement; the best way to determine your company's top priorities is to check out who gets paid for what. In particular, determine where the organization spends its dollars. If the money is going into research and development, that's the key place to be. If it's going into new manufacturing equipment, there will be more opportunities for you in operations.

You need to know your organization's bottom-line values, because that's where the opportunities exist. If you dedicate your efforts to the bottom line, you'll be taking your organization's goals into consideration in all your activities and you'll be perceived as a valued player.

Corporate Culture

Next, determine your firm's corporate culture. Organizations have personalities. Some value intellectuals. If you have a scholarly bent, you'll have a greater chance of success. But if you're an intellectual and you're in a party-hearty company, you're going to be swimming upstream. To assess corporate culture, observe who fits in and why.

I once worked for a company dominated by lawyers. In that organization, I had no choice but to learn how to argue a point to be on the team. At another company, I saw a division's top producer for the year rewarded with a substantial bonus and a prostitute for the night. In an organization that demeans women, it is virtually impossible for a female executive to fit in. At that moment, I decided to spend as little time as possible in that division; no matter how hard I worked or what I accomplished, I would never be valued there.

It's also important to read the signals around you. While conducting a workshop in Silicon Valley, I met an articulate, bright African-American manager who told me she worked in an Asian organization. There were a few caucasian men above Babette's level, but no African-Americans and no women.

"I like my job, but I wonder if I have any hope for advancement there," Babette said.

I wanted to believe that she could be the first to advance, but in the end I replied, "I hate to say this, but I think you'd find it easier if you move into an organization that evaluates you for your intrinsic merits. Where you are, it looks as if you'll be fighting for a lost cause."

Take a hard look at the demographics of your organization.

- What's the age of those at the top?
- What's the ethnic background of most executives?
- What's the predominant gender of the company's leaders?

If you are unlike them, you'll always have a harder time getting into their club. But you do have a choice. You can stay and fight—giving 110 percent—to be the first woman to break down barriers, or you can opt to move to a new company that already employs women in the upper echelons of management.

▶ FINDING A NEW POSITION

According to research out of Harvard, about 75 percent of all positions are acquired through networking. Here once more, the old adage "It's not what you know, it's who you know" applies.

Before you pick up the newspaper to scan the classified ads, sit down at your computer. *Email or call everyone you know* and tell them you're considering changing jobs. To formalize your search, list your contacts and email four a day. If you have specifics in mind, like an industry or type of position, let your contacts know. Ask if there's anyone they think you should talk to who might have further leads. Even people in unrelated fields might have prospects you'd never expect. Indeed, some friends who you'd anticipate would be delighted to hear from you may be unreceptive to your call. Conversely, acquaintances whom you believe would care little about your needs may be most receptive and go out of their way to help.

Use the networking and public relations skills outlined in Chapter 11 to reach as many people as possible.

▶ LANDING A NEW POSITION

If you decide that you want to move to a new organization, you'll need to find out as much as you can before the interview. The easiest way is to go online and download the annual report, if the company is publicly held. This will provide a statement of the firm's interests, values, and future aspirations. You'll also be able to discern the company's tone: Is this a serious or creative enterprise? This information may be more difficult to obtain if the company is privately held but even privately held companies have websites. You can ask questions of your interviewers and make your own sharp-eyed observations, or you can do a computer search to see what's been written about the organization. During the interview, use the information you've gleaned earlier by pointing out how your abilities match the company's goals and values.

Be prepared to talk to the interviewer about your strengths, but be careful. The one-upmanship inherent in talking well of yourself can work against you when interviewing—the only situation where you may feel justified and comfortable extolling your many accomplishments and talents. Unfortunately, when women come across as being confident in a job interview, even if they're extremely competent, they run the risk of violating the power-dead-even rule with a female interviewer. The very information you need to convey to land a job may, in the end, prevent you from getting it!

This has been substantiated by research. In one study that relied on simulated job interviews, when a woman spoke well of herself and had the ability to enhance a male interviewer's position, he was more likely to "hire" her. But if she couldn't help him advance, no matter how competent she was, he was more likely to hire a woman who appeared modest. The situation was even more punishing when the interviewers were female. If an interviewee spoke well of herself to a female interviewer, whether or not it could enhance the interviewer's position, she was less likely to be "hired." Psychologist Laurie A. Rudman of Rutgers University concluded from these findings that "women were more punitive toward the self-promoting women than were the men." And self-effacing women won points with both genders.

You might find it helpful to rehearse a positive presentation in advance. Also be forewarned that a common question asked is "What are your weaknesses?" A good response: "Like most people, my greatest weakness is my greatest strength overdone." For instance, you might explain that you're well organized, but sometimes you become too detail oriented, to the exclusion of the overview. It would also be appropriate to review the chapters on verbal and nonverbal communication so you'll be ready to present a power image.

Be cautious in dealing with headhunters. They are rarely interested in individuals who contact them directly. Watch out, especially, for falling for the illusion that they're on your side. Remember, headhunters are paid by the corporation. If they get close to you, you may reveal perceptions or wishes that they can carry back to their client, to your detriment. Be circumspect.

▶ GO BOSS SHOPPING

Whether you're moving to a new company or a new department within your current organization, I believe you'll end up miles ahead if you *shop for a boss, not a position.* You may secure the greatest job in the world, but a miserable boss will turn gold into ashes. On the other hand, a great boss can render a mediocre position a wonderful springboard. I can't say enough about carefully choosing your coach. In many ways, your boss may be more important than the job.

As odd as it seems, not all managers are on the same side as their employees. We've all known the person who believes he has to watch employees and check on them or they won't work, or the manager who browbeats employees to perform and then takes all the credit. These are people for whom you wouldn't enjoy working.

There are ways of discerning the truth, however. In the interviewing process, you probably won't get the inside scoop from the potential boss, so request to interview with those who would be your coworkers. You'll need to do this under the guise of getting a feel for the work or a sense of the team. When you ask your potential coworkers to fill you in on nuts-and-bolts issues, you can also drop in a question or two about the boss. Be sure to listen with your logic and your gut. If the answers are vague, the news is probably bad.

Often a maverick is a good boss to target. He or she may sidestep official policy and procedure and break out on his or her own. This person is more likely to value you for what you can pull off, rather than peg you in a "woman's" slot and leave you there forever. With a maverick manager, your work is more important than your gender.

If you're interviewing with a man, try to discern if he has a working wife or daughter. If he does, he may be more willing to treat you fairly.

In an engineering firm where I worked, women had few opportunities for advancement. But one of the more senior managers was a champion for our gender. It seems Ben had gone through a metamorphosis a few years earlier. His daughter, his pride and joy, had graduated with honors from one of the country's most prestigious and expensive universities. In interviewing for jobs, however, she was offered secretarial and administrative assistant positions. Ben was outraged. But then he realized that he had been guilty of the same inequity in the past. His daughter's difficulties sensitized Ben to the roadblocks women face.

▶ THE OLD TITLE TRICK

As you evaluate your options, don't make the mistake of thinking that power goes with a title. It doesn't. Here's a scenario I've seen all too often: Six men and one woman work in a department. One of the men is promoted, and the boss hires another man to replace him. In fact, this same game of chess repeats with several new male players moving forward and others filling in. Finally, the woman begins to make some noises: "What do I need to do to get a promotion?" she asks.

To get her to stop complaining, the boss eventually promotes her to "Director of Operations." No one seems to understand what her title means, however—not even her. She occupies the same desk, performing essentially the same work, earning the same money.

The truth is, power doesn't come with a title. Your ability to make decisions and control resources such as staff and budget will give you power. If you're interviewing for a management job but sense that this may be a title-only move, ask the following question at the appropriate time in the interview: *"And what would my budget be?"* This signals that you expect to have the power that goes with the position. If you get platitudes like, "Oh, don't worry. I handle the budget," your sensors were right; you'll have the title but not much more.

Finally, in interviewing for a job, listen to your gut. If all the objective data indicate that this position was made in heaven but your gut says something's not what it appears to be, I would give more credence to gut than data. Our guts know more than we do sometimes.

▶ NEGOTIATING A SALARY IN A NEW ORGANIZATION

Corporations have numerous ways of determining pay scales. Some organizations have a salary structure already in place; when they hire, the new employee fits into a slot, also called a "salary range." At the other extreme, you may be walking into a newly created position for which your future employer has no idea what he'll have to pay. According to an article by Kirsten Schabacker in *Executive Female* magazine, employers generally use three criteria for determining salaries:

1. The job's impact on the company's bottom line.
2. The amount of technical skill or knowledge required to do the job well.
3. Accountability—how much the company's success rides on the independent judgments and decisions of the person holding the job.

Once you're in the negotiation process, don't bring up salary. Wait for your future employer to make the first move. Once he does, it's ideal to ascertain the range as soon as possible. Your conversation may proceed as follows:

Your Future Employer: "How much do you want?"

You: "Do you have a salary range?"

In large, bureaucratic organizations, your future employer might say: "Yes, it's from $50,000 to $65,000."

Usually, however, you won't get so cut-and-dried an answer. More likely, your future employer will reply: "Well, we're not really sure. How much are you paid now?"

Even with the need to be deadly honest, your answer should be considered carefully. I've learned from a former boss to look at the numbers a bit more creatively. For example, if you're close to getting a salary increase (say, within the next twelve months), you might want to factor your future raise into your current salary. Furthermore, if your former organization provided you with great benefits, you might add these to your income too. Bear in mind that there's almost no way for the new company to check on what you're really making. Also, refrain from divulging your current income to a headhunter, even if you tell her to keep the information in confidence. You can be sure that she will report your salary to her client.

If the salary range is inadequate, you need not settle for less. If a future employer really likes you, there's a good chance he'll find a way to get you what you want. For example, your new boss can redefine the position, using the slippery point system discussed in the previous chapter. A new job definition can put you in a higher category. In addition, he can offer you perks such as a car allowance for expenses and lease (or monthly cash payments in lieu of a lease if you don't want a new car), an entertainment expense account, or club memberships (health or country clubs where men maintain their old-boy system).

Before you ask for these perquisites, it would be wise to determine what's customary in the new company. That's best achieved during an interview with your future peers. If you've developed enough sympatico with them, you can naively ask, "Anything like car expenses included?" Also bear in mind that today many companies give their employees a lump sum to spend on benefits. You determine if you value vacation time over dental benefits or child care.

If you're interviewing at two organizations that both want you, be cautious about playing their offers against each other or you may anger both parties and be out two jobs, not just one. But you might say to the employer you'd really like to work for, "I've got another offer. I hate to say this but I'd really like to work for you. Here's my dilemma: They're paying $15,000 more, but you're offering more challenging work. I just can't turn away the extra money. Is there some way we can work this out?"

Such an approach helps your potential boss feel wanted and good about you. He may be willing to find a way to get you the extra money. On the other hand, ultimatums such as "Unless you can come up with more money, I'm out of here" may provoke a future employer to show you the door.

▶ HOW TO GET THE BALL

Once you've positioned yourself properly in your new job, it's time to show your superiors what you can do. Assess your ability to accomplish tasks. Typically, organizations and bosses want and reward people who can make things happen. But all the skills in the world won't do you any good if you don't get to run with the ball. The following strategies can help.

Get in Line

Opt for a line position over a staff function. The people who do the main work of the organization are in line positions. For instance, if the company makes sprinklers, then manufacturing is where the action is, and departments such as human resources, accounting, and information systems are staff functions. On the other hand, if you work in an accounting firm, then the accountants are in the line function.

In a recent article in *The Economist,* "The Trouble with Women: Why So Few of Them Are Running Big Companies," Herminia Ibarra of INSEAD made it clear that women fail to get the really stretching jobs. She cites research reinforcing that line positions are important to aim for, yet in the United States, men occupy 90 percent of these jobs. But simply having a line position may not be enough. Women also need tough, broad assignments to win experience and promotion. Perhaps that is why one study found that companies are more likely to ask men than women to turn around an ailing division or to start a new one.

It's important to target a line function, because that's where the money is made; the work is valued more. Line positions carry far more power. Companies may view staff functions as expensive and expendable. Unfortunately, many women fill staff functions, and that only reinforces the cultural stereotype of them as "helpers."

Let Your Superiors Know You Have a Brain

People are valued and paid for critical thinking. But if you perform the same function every day, no one will have the opportunity to see your problem-solving and decision-making abilities. For that reason, it's important to target nonroutine jobs, such as professional, salaried positions that require you to make discretionary decisions. Avoid repetitious jobs like administrative assistant, accounts payable clerk, or data processor in which you earn an hourly wage. These are power-poor positions.

I've seen many female administrative assistants trying to believe their jobs made them something other than what they really were. It's often difficult for employers to find smart, competent assistants. Consequently, some employers will promise that a position is challenging and provides freedom and latitude, but will neglect to mention that 80 percent of the employee's time will be spent typing and filing. If you find yourself in this situation, however, there are ways to move out and up.

Noelle was just out of college, having received a degree in business, when she made the deadly decision of taking an administrative assistant position in the mistaken belief that this was the first step into a coveted industry. In short order, she realized that since she was plastered with the secretarial label it was going to be extremely difficult to move up in the hierarchy. Men never make this mistake.

Administrative assistant work tends to be routine: typing, filing, answering the phone. To get out of her bind, Noelle volunteered to organize projects. She did this so well that her boss gave her a project to manage. Noelle had the good sense to make her success on this job highly visible. Before long, other managers approached her boss, asking for Noelle to work on their projects. Now she has the official title of project manager and a heftier salary to go with it. Only when Noelle's critical thinking skills were evident was she able to advance.

Bring in the Bucks

Target running a profit center. The more money you bring into the company, the more power you'll wield, because in the game of hardball money is equated with winning.

Courtney was the manager of training and organizational development for a large bank. Her skills and the department's contribution were widely acknowledged, but in the final analysis, training was a staff function and an expense item.

Because the department ran so smoothly and was so productive, however, Courtney was able to ask her boss for an additional challenge: managing the employee bank. This was a full-service operation (savings, loans, credit cards) for thousands of employees that brought cash into the organization. Through this strategy, Courtney was able to become "a real banker" in the eyes of her organization. Consequently, she became a full member of the team and eventually became director of a two-hundred-employee department.

▶ GETTING COACHING FROM THE COACH

Male managers often believe that a woman is happy with her station in the organization, so they mentally park her in that position forever. Since we're committed and do our jobs well, these managers often find it easiest to just leave us where we are.

If you want to move quickly in your new position, you must make your aspirations clear——without sounding too pushy. As mentioned in Chapter 10, once you know your goals, share them with your boss, if appropriate. (Be smart about it; some managers may fear you're out for their job, and this can cost you big.) I believe a larger problem is a boss who is immobilized in his job and who wants to keep everyone else frozen in theirs. Then it's probably time to move to a different department or company. A good manager, on the other hand, wants to see employees grow and will work with you.

After you've shared your goals, get the boss's input on your developmental needs: experience, education, skills, knowledge. This motivates your supervisor to buy into your growth process and helps you gain access to projects and people. For instance, if the boss says you need to have experience working with the client on a marketing project, the next time such a project comes through, ask if you can be involved. Before, the boss might not have linked you with such an opportunity, but now you can ask to be involved. It's unlikely your boss will turn you down, since it was his idea.

Once you get rolling in the new job, you'll need feedback on how you're doing. If the person you work for withholds feedback, you'll have to ask for it. And, as I explained in Chapter 9, you may have to press for bad news if your manager is reluctant to dish it out. Once you've received the evaluation, thank your boss and act on it. The more feedback you get, the better able you'll be to perform to your manager's needs and expectations.

▶ WHO BOSSES PROMOTE

Bosses promote those they like. If you're comfortable and in accord with your supervisor, he or she is more likely to see your work in a positive light. This isn't logical, it's just real. Consequently, you need to study your boss. Learn how he or she ticks. What does he find interesting and important? How does she like to get information? The more your superiors are comfortable with you, the more they'll perceive you as a kindred spirit, and the more opportunities will open up.

Of course, the reverse is also true. Brooke is a logical, analytical woman. Her boss asked her to evaluate a department restructuring. After appraising the skills necessary for the future, Brooke presented her plan to Leonard, but he rejected it out of hand. "That would upset Norma in data entry," he said. It never occurred to Brooke to take into account the feelings of those who would be affected.

"No one likes change. Besides, this is a business," Brooke protested to me. But Leonard was a "people person," and Brooke had failed to include the issues of harmony and morale in her overview. The boss saw her as a poor potential manager.

It pays to study your boss's communication style. Does he prefer dealing only with facts and data? Is she a high-risk player? Does he enjoy fiddling with ideas? Is she a people person?

In order to get ahead, talk about your ideas in your boss's language. If you don't, you may have trouble getting them actualized. The following section will help you discern your boss's communication style.

▶ LEARNING HOW YOUR BOSS THINKS

I've found it helpful to understand how people think and why they behave as they do by using an assessment tool called the *Myers-Briggs Type Instrument*. Based on the teachings of Swiss psychoanalyst Carl Jung, the Myers-Briggs organizes my understanding of individual strengths within the business setting. This inventory embraces the following classifications:

1. How we access information about the world (through our senses or our intuition).
2. How we make decisions about the information (through logic or our feelings).
3. Our lifestyle preferences and how much structure we prefer (on a continuum of highly structured to going with the flow).
4. How we become energized (from internal introspection to being with others).

It's important to understand that each of these four categories are a continuum. You can recognize yourself, for example, as being either extremely structured, extremely easy-going, or somewhere in the middle, enjoying traits from both sides. Bear in mind, too, that these strengths are neither good nor bad. There is a hitch, however: When someone's strengths are the polar opposite of yours, you may tend to see that person as misguided or wrong, rather than simply different.

Let's take a look at these classifications more carefully to help you determine how your boss thinks.

How We Access Information

Sensers know that something is true if they can weigh it, see it, or hammer it. These are concrete, down-to-earth people with practical solutions. Many accountants, machinists, builders, and nurses are sensers. *Intuitive* people are those who are happy playing in the world of ideas and possibilities. They like to create but aren't particularly concerned about the practical applications of their creations. Writers, professors, counselors, and R & D people are often intuitive.

How can you determine if your boss is a senser or an intuitive? Ask her: "Tell me about a project you really enjoyed working on." After she reveals the project, ask, "What did you like about it?" If she talks about the ideas involved, the changes it created, the new lessons she learned, she's probably an intuitive who likes to play in the world of ideas and who thinks and talks about the future.

Approach this boss with ideas, possibilities, and creative proposals. If, on the other hand, she replies with problems the project solved and its practical applications, this is most likely a senser who wants nuts-and-bolts answers to how you're going to rectify today's problems.

How We Make Decisions

Thinkers make decisions with their heads. They follow a logical train of thought. Thinkers are frequently scientists, lawyers, and engineers. *Feelers,* on the other hand, use their hearts. They're interested in how decisions impact people. Often feelers are artists, social workers, and psychologists.

To determine your boss's decision-making style, ask him, "What was the toughest work-related decision you had to make?" After he tells you, follow up with, "How did you go about making that decision?" If he focuses on a logical, analytical process, you'll want to present the logic and analysis behind your own ideas. If, on the other hand, he mentions how the people involved were affected by the decision and the personal difficulties that came of it, be sure to couch your ideas in a discussion of how individuals can benefit and grow as a result of what you're proposing.

Lifestyle Preferences

Judgers feel comfortable putting structure into their lives. They love a sense of completion. You can always tell a judger by her neat home, her to-do lists, and her frequent trips to Organizer's Paradise. Often accountants, hospital administrators, administrative assistants, and bankers are judgers. *Perceivers* find structure too confining. They prefer to take things as they come, lose their to-do lists, would rather keep projects open-ended (when the task is finished, the fun is over), and fail to see the necessity of storing belongings in their place. Artists, athletes, and construction workers are often perceivers.

To determine your boss's preference, notice how she organizes and structures the workday. Does she keep a detailed to-do list; does she live and die by the calendar? If so, have your analyses completed and conclusions reached when you approach her with new ideas. If she likes to go with the flow and take it as it comes (and writes to-do lists but always seems to misplace them), she enjoys processing ideas and wants to be involved with you as you reach decisions. Don't bring conclusions to her. Rather, involve her in the process.

Introvert or Extrovert

Extroverts get their batteries recharged by being around other people. They are often receptionists, salespeople, marketing personnel, and public relations specialists. *Introverts,* on the other hand, get their essential stimulation internally. They need to pull away from people to recharge their batteries. Frequently writers, anesthesiologists, librarians, and mechanics are introverts.

In this category, it's not so much the presentation of information but the accepting and reading of your boss's behavior that's significant. Our culture highly values extroversion. (I've never heard a parent express a desire to raise an introverted child.) Indeed, introverts are often perceived as being maladjusted because of these preferences. (In the United Kingdom, by contrast, extroversion is held in lower esteem.) As a result, introverts learn how to behave like extroverts. And so, it may be more difficult to tell which category fits your boss.

There are, however, telltale hints. If your boss declines frequent invitations to lunch, pizza parties on Friday night, or ball games; if he wants to spend lunch with book and sandwich, it may be due to introversion and not aversion. On the other hand, if you're an introvert and your boss and coworkers keep badgering you to do things with them, they may be extroverts and may assume you want to spend time with others.

▶ STAYING ON YOUR BOSS'S WAVELENGTH

There are other factors to take into account as well, such as whether your boss processes information visually or verbally. Jessica, a human resources director, shared with me the frustrations she had with her boss, Tim, in this regard. "Tim doesn't listen to my ideas," Jessica complained.

"Well, how do you present them?" I asked.

Jessica dived into an office closet and pulled out several large graphs with pie charts and histograms in glowing colors.

"Is Tim visual? Does he like to see ideas graphically?" I inquired.

"Oh, no," Jessica admitted. "He likes to talk things over."

I pointed out that the more Jessica shoved those charts in Tim's face, the more distant he would become. She reluctantly began to talk to him more, but he never really got along with her as a result of their divergent styles.

Your astute observations can make a difference. Tracy was an intelligent, thorough manager. When she had an idea for a new project, she met with her boss, Marv, and painstakingly laid out all the options, her complete analysis, and the recommended approach. Marv would usually rebuff her, saying, "Maybe later. We can't do that now."

So Tracy studied Marv. She noticed that he loved being directly involved in resolving crises. Now when Tracy has a bright idea, she says to her boss, "Marv, we've got a crisis, and I don't know what to do." She claims it works like a charm, because he loves to participate in the solution.

▶ MAKE THE BOSS LOOK GOOD

Whatever your job description says, mentally add one more item: Make the boss look good. You don't have to like her or agree with her. You just need to make her look like a winner. If the boss looks good, she's going to value you highly, and you'll be a lot more likely to advance in the future.

In one of my first jobs, I was asked to put together and deliver a class and manual entitled "Personnel: Policies and Procedures." I couldn't imagine a more boring subject and resisted at first. But I also knew my boss couldn't do it. She just didn't know how to design classes like those. So I bit the bullet and created a course and handbook. As it turned out, the class was extremely popular and the handbook most useful to the managers. As a result, my manager won many accolades; this was her idea and one of her key goals for the year.

Making the boss look good means ensuring your boss's ideas are implemented; it means being a good team member in the game of hardball. And that's one of the wisest strategies of all.

▶ YOUR EMPLOYABILITY

As companies run leaner and meaner, women must have a game plan. Virtually all of us know someone who has been laid off. With so many businesses downsizing, merging, or folding, job security is a thing of the past. Businesses of the future will need the flexibility to change and restructure quickly. This means that you may find yourself suddenly unemployed. "If security no longer comes from being employed, then it must come from being employable," suggests Harvard professor Rosabeth Moss Kanter in her book, *When Giants Learn to Dance.*

Whatever profession or position you're in today, most likely it will change dramatically throughout your lifetime. Rather than focusing solely on becoming good at your particular profession, you'll want to acquire a variety of skills that make you a valuable businessperson, no matter what situation you find yourself in.

It's important, therefore, to avoid freezing yourself into a job (by thinking, for example, "I'm the nursing director; I don't need to know about finance") and to prevent others from pigeonholing you with statements such as, "Oh, you shouldn't be doing that. Aren't you a . . . ?"

Employability means changing your mind-set from a one-career orientation toward a strategy of making yourself a good businessperson. An engineer, for example, should learn about finance so that she can read and comprehend her company's annual report. What better way to understand how her company makes or loses money as a result of her (and other) department's work? By becoming savvy in finance, she will gain an awareness of how the various parts of the corporation come together to form the big picture.

How does one move into alien territory? It's helpful to get together with a buddy who knows you well. Ask her to report to you what she sees as your strengths and abilities. Do a little reality testing. She may say, for instance, "You know about finance." If you reply, "No I don't," she may counter with, "Well, you coordinated the budget last year."

It's also helpful to volunteer for interdepartmental projects. If, for example, you work in the human resources department of a corporation that's about to restructure, it would be wise to volunteer for the restructuring task force. You won't just be there to contribute your human resources expertise, but also to understand how manufacturing works from the very first design stages all the way through to shipping, including steps along the way such as purchasing and the computerized accounting system.

Amy used these employability strategies, and they took her far. Amy found being a nurse too limiting and dead-ended. Looking for an out, she came across an opportunity to volunteer for the hospital's preaccreditation committee (the group that prepares the hospital for its accreditation review to maintain its license). The committee was required to do a lot of tedious paperwork, but Amy volunteered because she believed this was a field she could learn much in.

Amy was right. She became skilled in this area and eventually applied for a job at the corporation that owned the hospital to do the same kind of work at corporate offices. Once she reached the organization's headquarters, she realized how important complex financial systems are to hospitals, so she volunteered to sit on the finance committee. By learning about the monetary end, Amy was able to move into a job in which she assessed the financial strengths and weaknesses of hospitals being considered for acquisition. Having mastered finance, Amy then strengthened her understanding of the human side of health care by reading about organizational development. Eventually, she was hired to advise the corporation on that level.

Today, Amy is self-employed. She works as a consultant with hospitals, helping them to restructure to meet today's financial realities. She is wildly successful and in great demand. Her uniqueness in possessing so many skills contributes to her employability and her success.

Finally, employability means being strategic in your career. Using the suggestions I've offered throughout this book, you've got to take charge and chart your own course. You're the only one who will be watching out for your professional welfare.

GAME STRATEGIES

- Devise a game plan for your career.
- Assess if you're satisfied in your current position; stay if you are, plan if you're not.
- Know your company's bottom line; don't get hooked into the party line.
- Recognize your organization's corporate culture.
- Network to locate other job opportunities.
- Research the organization before you interview.
- Choose a good boss over a good job.
- Use hardball savvy in negotiating a new salary.
- Don't fall for the old title trick.
- Opt for the line position.
- Prove you have a brain.
- Bring in the bucks.
- Have a coach for your career.
- Assess your boss's style.
- Make the boss look good.
- Expand your horizons to expand your employability.

13

CREATING YOUR
OWN RULES

▼ ▼ ▼ ▼ ▼ **T**hroughout this book, I have been advising you on how to recognize male rules in the workplace and how to accept, adjust, or simply acknowledge that these rules exist. This can be exhausting work, and indeed, some women become angry when they realize there will be times they'll have to adapt to a culture that isn't their own.

I can commiserate, as I've often experienced the same feelings myself. When I was in my twenties early in my career, I was surprised the first time an incompetent man was promoted over a much sharper woman. I saw it happen repeatedly, and I thought certainly this is going to get fixed. In my thirties, I was amazed that this inequity was still going on. That's when I started to study gender differences in the work setting. In my forties, I realized how intransigent the problem really was, but I was still sure it would get resolved. Well, I'm now in my fifties, and I realize that if we don't change the situation ourselves, it's not going to happen! In this concluding chapter, rather than covering more hardball rules for you to learn, I'd like to help motivate you toward making that change.

▶ BANDING TOGETHER FOR CHANGE

The day I became a feminist was the first day I registered to vote at the age of twenty-one—the voting age at that time. I filled out the papers but balked at the question requiring me to check the "Miss" or "Mrs." box. I asked the registrar, "Do men have to indicate whether they're married?"

"No," she replied, braced for my question.

"Well, then," I continued, "I don't want to indicate whether I'm married."

"Then you can't vote!" she stated flatly, and that was the end of that.

I was infuriated. What difference did it make if I were married?

I suddenly realized what all the clamor around the Equal Rights Amendment was about. The ERA, which was never passed, simply said, "Equality of rights under the law shall not be denied or abridged by the United States or any state on account of sex." This seemed like a reasonable expectation to me, and if buying into that statement meant I was a feminist, then, by golly, I was a feminist!

But somehow the notion of being a "feminist" has become divisive over the years, and the word itself has been given various meanings ("man-hater," lesbian, radical, and "femi-Nazi," to name a few) since the early 1970s. Indeed, to many, it has become a perjorative term. Often women who attend my workshops because they are struggling to survive in the male business setting will turn to me and say, "I'm so fed up with trying to deal with this Old Boy system at my office, *but I'm not a feminist.*" Unfortunately, the concept of feminism has caused many women to pull away from each other rather than to pull together.

It's important for us to coalesce if we're really going to make some changes in the world of work. As former secretary of state Madeleine Albright exclaimed in a recent interview for *Ms.*, "We need . . . the power of sisterhood." The founding chair of a new organization, the six-hundred-member International Assembly of Women Ministers—foreign ministers, ministers of environment, finance, and others—Albright explains, "Women need more networking. We're good at making friends, but less good at networking. Men are *very* good at networking, but don't make friends. We need to turn our friendships into functional networks."

I heartily agree with Madame former Secretary, not only in the realm of world affairs but also in the world of work. Julia Stewart is a woman who understood the usefulness of what Ms. Albright calls "functional networks," and that helped her career soar. Julia began working in the food service industry as a teenager—she was sixteen when she got her first job at IHOP. Since then, she has risen through the ranks. When I first met her, she was the president of Applebee's restaurants, but she wanted to be CEO of an organization and run the whole show. Less than a year later, I read in the newspaper that Julia had been hired as president and CEO of IHOP. How did she get there?

In the mid-1980s, eleven women who worked in the food service industry decided to create an organization to help each other and also to have an impact on their industry. Julia was among the founders. "Initially," she told me, "the greatest impact we had was on each other, mentoring, coaching, and encouraging each other to 'walk' if the culture of the organization was not supportive. Eventually, we created specific mentoring programs to help woman at all levels and an annual conference attended by 2,000 to 2,500 men and women a year."

The female attendees to these conferences began bringing the CEOs and chairs of their companies, who were overwhelmingly men. These male industry leaders realized their participation wasn't just about being "noble" or "good" but that there was a whole lot of talent in the room. As a result of the Women's Food Service Forum, a few women have risen to positions of president and CEO within the industry. More importantly, there is an awareness about the glass ceiling that never existed before. Julia's experience is an example of how women pulled together to make a change in their industry.

Within many companies today, women create similar networks to help one another advance. At one Fortune 500 company, for instance, the Women's Leadership Network has provided many opportunities for men and women to learn about their respective cultures and how to work together more effectively. This organization not only provided its staff with my workshops but also created a series of cartoons (which the graphic artist, Ted Scofield, based on the concepts in this book) that were emailed weekly to employees. Soon, the cartoon characters took on a life of their own. Among others, there were:

- Herb, the nerd, a scientist who is oblivious to the gender conflicts that roil around him.
- Hurricane Nell, a force to be reckoned with who is nobody's fool.
- Marcie, who always does what she thinks is appropriate, but can't figure out why her male peers wouldn't accept her.
- Kirk, the cynic, who feels gender-related issues are a waste of his valuable time.

Eventually, employees could press a button on their email and get one of these characters' takes on a particular issue. Another button allowed employees to email me a question if they had one. The cartoons were so popular that employees would print them up and mount them on their bulletin boards. In fact, one of the senior male executives told me that a woman who reports to him came to him one day, cartoon in hand, and said, "This is what I've been trying to tell you."

"Suddenly I got it," he admitted. We would never have gotten to that "suddenly I got it" if the Women's Leadership Network had not brought the company to that point of understanding.

▶ CREATING A BUSINESS CASE FOR CHANGE

It's all well and good to provide information and agitate for change, but if there's no business case behind your push, you will have a hard time convincing others to change their behavior. In the 1980s, Procter & Gamble realized that women were their biggest customer base—think Tide and Pampers—but within the company, men reigned supreme. P&G decided that their executives needed to look like their customers. Their rationale: If you're selling to women, you must have women in positions of power because they will better know what their customers are thinking. As a result, the company has been successful in promoting and mentoring women up through the ranks.

P&G is an enlightened company that made changes over the last two decades willingly and to its advantage. Other companies, however, may be more intransigent and truly need to be hit over the head in order to understand why they must change their culture by pulling more women into top positions. In one such organization that has used my consulting services, it was the head of Human Resources who initiated the change. He came to me because he realized that the company had a major disconnect. Women comprised only 10 percent of the company's 5,000 field service employees, but the majority of sales and customer service awards were going to them. That's startling enough, but what was worse was his determination that on average, women stayed only eighteen months in the organization. Most left when they got fed up with its extremely male culture.

I was curious. "What's your culture like?" I wondered.

"We hire athletes," the vice president of HR explained. "Don't think runners; think football players." The company had been created by a group of men who had played football together in college. Parties, games on the weekends, drinking, sexually tinged jokes and stories—these were all part of this company's everyday life, and it became instantly clear to me why women might feel uncomfortable in such a macho environment.

It took a year for them to set up focus groups in order to learn from the female employees what was bothering them. My work with the organization has been to help establish why it would be financially advantageous to them to modify their culture so that it was more female-friendly . . . and so they could keep their best and most productive employees. It makes perfect business sense to do so!

If you feel that women aren't getting a fair shake in your organization, what business case can you make for the cost of the inequity to your company? How might you go about this difficult task?

Take, for instance, the issue of women, especially in a knowledge business, leaving positions in middle management. When they quit, they take with them their expertise and years of research—this has to be costly to their organization. How to stop the brain drain? First, don't attempt to do it alone. Here is one way women's networks can be quite valuable. It's likely that the HR department has statistics on the ratio of men and women quitting their jobs. It may be unlikely to give up this information easily. Therefore, when a women's network has a powerful male sponsor, that man can see to it that the information is forthcoming from HR.

Once you know the numbers about women leaving, you can also get the numbers on recruitment, training, and relocation costs for their replacements. Now all you have to do is multiply. It's clear that when a woman is unhappy in her position and takes off, it costs the company dearly. This is where you could make a strong case for change.

▶ IS QUOTAS A DIRTY WORD?

If you begin going down this road toward change, you may encounter resistance from those above you in the form of the question, "Are you talking about quotas?" This query is often conveyed with a defensive demeanor. How do I usually respond?

"You count everything in this company. You count how long it takes your product to get to market. You count your sales and profits. You count your turnaround time. And you know that people pay attention to what you count. So if you are talking about moving women into higher positions, why wouldn't you count how well you're doing and reward managers accordingly? I've got news for you. If you don't count it, it's not going to change."

I would like to see executives assess male versus female promotions, length of time in a position before promotion occurs, numbers of men versus women at various levels (do women start dropping out at higher levels), comparative salaries and other perks, and whatever they think would be barriers to female advancement.

To those companies that balk at or stigmatize the idea of "quotas," I like to point to three multinational organizations that I've worked with (an energy company, a high tech company, and one producing consumer products) that have successfully had an impact on women in their ranks by simply assessing who was where in their organization and establishing targets that managers are expected to achieve yearly. Those managers are rewarded financially for hitting those targets, just as they would be for reaching production goals.

In those three enlightened companies, I have seen measurable change—women have moved up in the ranks and have been successful. Because of their commitment to change, however, these companies do not simply support promotions but also make sure that the woman is successful once she is promoted. Rather than let her sink or swim on her own, they provide mentoring and other support.

In fact, based on research and anecdotal reports from women who have reached uppermost ranks in their companies, there is a tipping point that makes the difference in a company's culture. For some, this occurs when 15 percent of the people who report to the CEO are women. Other women have described to me "the rule of three"—that is, once there are three women at the executive management level, the culture of the organization begins to shift. People begin to feel that they can behave in ways that are natural to them rather than needing to play hardball, or for men, "Joe Jock."

The key: You've got to keep women in the game until they can get up to those levels and make a difference.

▶ ASSESSING THE BLOCKS TO CHANGE IN YOUR ORGANIZATION

Men will grouse, "But we're not doing anything to hold women back. Why are they complaining, and what do they expect us to do?" Often this is true. They are not *consciously* retarding women's success. However, you might find that what the organization is doing is often invisible.

Here are some questions you can ask to determine what those unseen roadblocks might be.

- How is the value of work measured?
- How do people accomplish work? What gets in their way?
- Who succeeds, who doesn't, and why?
- Who interacts with whom? What is the benefit? Who doesn't participate?
- What work is valued? What invisible work must be done? How is that evaluated?
- Who is selected for leadership? What characteristics must a leader have?
- How is productivity of the organization measured? How important is face time to productivity and perception?
- In promotions, what characteristics, performance, or other qualifications are considered?
- What is discussed in a performance review?
- What is looked for in a new hire?
- How and where is recruiting done?
- How are hiring decisions made?

I have found that when women begin answering these questions they gain a good deal of insight. Trends emerge and targets for change become clear. For instance, as mentioned earlier, women often do a good deal of invisible work; they serve as the connective tissue on a team, make sure that members know what the other members are discovering, smooth differences, and offer win/win solutions. Because this work is invisible they are often not rewarded for it. And, unfortunately, when leadership opportunities emerge, they are off the radar screen. But what is a leader? Is it not someone who can move a team forward?

By looking for and pointing to the answers to these questions, opportunities for organizational change will show up.

▶ WHERE CAN YOU GET STARTED?

Organizational change can seem like a monumental task, but you are not required to complete the job . . . only to start a dialogue. In fact, I have found that teaching people the language of gender differences is the first step. In our *She Said, He Said* and Gender*Speak* workshops, we make sure participants have fun, and that neither gender is made "wrong." People tend to learn information that they find fascinating and useful, often having "A-ha!" experiences. They want to go back and talk to their coworkers about what they've learned. This dialogue is the beginning of change for them personally, but also for their organization.

Using gender-savvy language in the workplace (terms like *hierarchy* and *flat culture, goal versus process orientation, talking it over* versus *getting to the bottom line*) takes what was invisible and makes it into an entity that can be actively managed. People now have a readily accessible language to work out areas where they may have found themselves in conflict before.

We also teach three strategies that participants and you can use in managing a gender-related problem. We call them levels because they increase in difficulty:

■ *Level 1: Reinterpret.* You simply see the world differently now that you understand what the other person is doing. A woman who had been promoted to the executive ranks, the first female at this level, lamented to me that her male colleagues would come in every Monday and viciously attack each other before the Monday morning meeting. She was miserable having to work with these people because they were so nasty. But when she heard me talk about verbal bantering, she realized that's what they were doing. And when they started to "attack" her, she understood that she was in actuality being included in the group. She didn't change her behavior; she simply saw their behavior in a new light, now that she understood what it was.

- **Level 2: Flex Your Style.** You change your behavior to do what would work in the other gender culture. When I had gotten a call one day about making videos based on *Hardball*, I went to lunch with the producer to discuss our joint venture. He asked me, "Do you want a series of short videos, a long one. . . ." I took this as an invitation to process and began talking about the pros and cons of the variety of options we had before us. I realized that he had mentally checked out and was waiting for the bottom line, so I asked, "What sells?" "Videos that are thirty to forty minutes long." "Let's do it." I switched to the bottom line so that he would reengage.

- **Level 3: Talk It Over (but only if you both speak gender differences).** After other coworkers have been through a workshop, read this book, watched the videos, or listened to the CDs and you all share a common language, you can use that to resolve potential problems. I was working at a high-tech company when a woman told me that both she and her male manager had attended my workshop a day before. She said, "I went to talk to him today about a problem I'm having with a project. I told him, 'I don't need you to kill this problem. I just want to process through my options with you.' He said, 'Okay, I'll be glad to process.' " And he proceeded to do so without telling her what to do.

When you find yourself in a gender dilemma, instead of seething with rage, step back, assess which of these three options is best for you, and then implement that option.

▶ CELEBRATE SMALL WINS . . . THEY CAN GROW INTO BIG ONES!

It's a long journey. One of the strategies that Debra Meyerson suggests in her book *Tempered Radicals* is to celebrate small wins, the baby steps along the way. When you're looking for a large change, it's easy to lose sight of any movement going on, and the whole process can feel frustratingly overwhelming. But by appreciating small successes, you can perceive them as steps toward a cherished goal.

In the ten years since we first wrote *Hardball for Women,* there has been monumental change in our society. Many more women are heading up Fortune 500 companies than ever before. Others have moved into the senior executive ranks and are making a difference for the women who follow. On a day-to-day basis we may miss the movement in our society, but taking the long view, each woman's individual struggle, each step along the way, begins to snowball into a greater sense of equity and justice in the workplace. Indeed, today in the business setting, the titles "Miss" and "Mrs." almost never appear in internal correspondence. We *have* come a long way, baby!

We all strive for the opportunity to do the best and most we can with our lives. As you learn hardball lessons so that you can move forward with greater ease, you are then afforded the chance to make an even bigger impact on the world. It is my deepest (if not most perverse) hope that ten years from now, we will no longer need books like *Hardball for Women* because all of our individual gains will have added up to the world we are now striving toward.

RESOURCES AND SUGGESTED READINGS

Abramson, Rudy, and John Broder. "Four-Star Power." *Los Angeles Times Magazine,* April 7, 1991.

American Association of University Women. *How Schools Shortchange Girls.* Washington, DC: American Association of University Women Education Foundation, 1992.

Angier, Natalie. *Woman: An Intimate Geography.* New York: Houghton-Mifflin, 1999.

Baron-Cohen, Simon. *The Essential Difference: The Truth About the Male and Female Brain.* New York: Basic Books, 2003.

Bateson, Mary Catherine. *Composing a Life.* New York: Penguin Books, 1990.

Bem, S. L. "Gender schema theory and its implications for child development: Raising gender-aschematic children in a gender-schematic society." *Signs* 8 (1983):598–616.

Bennis, Warren. *On Becoming a Leader.* Reading, MA: Addison-Wesley, 1989.

Best, Deborah, John Williams, Jonathan Cloud et al. "Development of Sex-Trait Stereotypes Among Young Children in the United States, England and Ireland." *Child Development* 48 (1977) 1383. Cited in Jones, Diane Carlson. "Power Structures and Perceptions of Power Holders in Same-Sex Group of Young Children." *Women and Politics* 3, no. 2/3 (summer/fall 1983).

Bjorkqvist, Kaj, Kirsti M. J. Lagerspetz, and Ari Kaukiainen. "Do Girls Manipulate and Boys Fight? Developmental Trends in Regard to Direct and Indirect Aggression." *Aggressive Behavior* 81 (1992):117–127.

Blake-Beard, Stacy. "Critical Trends and Shifts in the Mentoring Experiences of Professional Women." CGO Working Paper. Boston: The Center for Gender in Organizations, 2003.

Blum, Deborah. *Sex on the Brain: The Biological Differences Between Men and Women.* New York: Penguin Books, 1997.

Bolles, Richard Nelson. *What Color Is Your Parachute?* Berkeley, CA: Ten Speed Press, 1992.

Boyatzis, Richard E., Sott Cowen, David A Kolb, and Associates. *Innovation in Professional Education.* San Francisco: Jossey-Bass, 1995.

Bradford, Lawrence J., and Claire Raines. *Twentysomething.* New York: Master Media, 1992.

Braginsky, Dorothea. "Machiavellianism and Manipulative Interpersonal Behavior in Children." *Journal of Experimental Social Psychology* 6 (1970):77–99.

Brass, Daniel J. "Men's and Women's Networks: A Study of Interaction Patterns and Influence in an Organization." *Academy of Management Journal* 28 (1985):327–343.

Brooks, Nancy Rivera. "Women Business Owners Thriving in Southland." *Los Angeles Times,* October 24, 1988.

Brownell, Judi. "Perceptions of Effective Listeners: A Management Study." *The Journal of Business Communication* 27 (1990):401–415.

Burns, Alyson L., G. Mitchell, and Stephanie Obradovich. "Of sex roles and strollers: Male attention to toddlers at the zoo." *Sex Roles* 20 (1989):309–315.

Carter, Bill. "Wednesday Is the Prize in Networks' Latest War." *New York Times,* November 20, 1991. Living Arts Sec., p. 1.

Chamberlain, Claudia. "Future Organizations Need an 'ACE.'" *United News Journal,* May 1991.

Conley, Frances K. "Why I'm Leaving Stanford: I Want My Dignity Back." *Los Angeles Times,* June 9, 1991. Section M, p. 1.

D'Antonio, Michael. "How We Think." *Los Angeles Times Magazine,* May 2, 2004, p. 18.

Deveny, Kathleen. "Chart of Kindergarten Awards." *Wall Street Journal,* December 5, 1994, p. B1.

De Waal, Frans. *Peacemaking Among the Primates.* Cambridge, MA: Harvard University Press, 1989.

Drury, Tracey Rosenthal. "Women Business Owners Seek Equity from Lenders." *Buffalo Business First,* June 2, 1997.

Durrance, Bonnie. "Some Explicit Thoughts on Tacit Learning." *Training & Development* 52, no. 12 (1998):24–29.

Elias, Marilyn. "Marital Spats Sicken Wives, Not Husbands." *USA Today,* July 9, 1998, Section D, p. 3.

Ely, R. J. "The Effects of Organizational Demographics and Social Identity on Relationships Among Professional Women." *Administrative Science Quarterly* 39 (1994):203–238.

Erikson, Erik. *Young Man Luther.* New York: Norton, 1958.

Fisher, Murray. "One Hundred Twenty Minutes with Leslie Stahl." *Modern Maturity,* July–August 1999.

Fisher, Roger, and William Ury. *Getting to Yes.* New York: Penguin Books, 1991.

Fiske, Edward B. "Lessons: Even at a Former Women's College, Male Students Are Taken More Seriously, a Researcher Finds." *New York Times,* April 11, 1990. Living Arts Sec.

Fletcher, Joyce K. "Invisible Work: The Disappearing of Relational Practice at Work." CGO Working Paper. Boston: The Center for Gender in Organizations, 2001.

Franke, George R., Deborah F. Crown, and Deborah F. Spake. "Gender Differences in Ethical Perceptions of Business Practices: A Social Role Theory Perspective." *Journal of Applied Psychology* 82 (1997): 921–934.

Frey, William. *Crying: The Mystery of Tears.* New York: Harper & Row, 1985.

Fury, Kathleen. "Cookies, Dirt and Power." *Working Woman,* October 1988, p. 168.

Gallagher, Carol, Ph.D., with Susan Golant. *Going to the Top: A Road Map for Success from America's Leading Women Executives.* New York: Viking, 2000.

Gallup Poll. Who Men and Women Prefer to Work For. 2000.

Gersick, Connie, Jean M. Bartunek, and Jane E. Dutton. "Learning from Academia: The Importance of Relationship in Professional Life." *Academy of Management Journal* 43 (2000):1024–1044.

Gilligan, Carol. *In a Different Voice.* Cambridge, MA: Harvard University Press, 1982.

Goffman, Erving. *Interaction Ritual.* Garden City, NY: Action Books, 1967.

Golant, Mitch, and Susan Golant. *Finding Time for Fathering.* New York: Ballantine Books, 1992.

Goodwin, Marjorie Harness, and Charles Goodwin. "Children's Arguing." *Language, Gender and Sex in Comparative Perspective.* Edited by S. Philips, Susan Steele, and Christine Tanz. Cambridge, UK: Cambridge University Press, 1987, 200–248.

Gottman, John, and Nan Silver. *Why Marriages Succeed or Fail.* New York: Fireside, 1994.

Granovelter, Mark S. *Getting a Job: A Study of Contacts and Careers.* Littlejohn, MA: Harvard University Press, 1974.

Gutek, Barbara A. "Gender and Responses to Sexual Harassment." Ninth annual Claremont Symposium on Applied Psychology. The Claremont Graduate School, Claremont, CA. February 8, 1992.

Hales, Dianne. "Wired Differently." *Seattle Post-Intelligence,* June 23, 1998, p. E32.

Harragan, Betty Lehan. *Games Mother Never Taught You.* New York: Warner Books, 1977.

Hawkins, Beth. "Career Limiting Bias Found at Low Level Jobs." *Los Angeles Times,* Aug 9, 1991. Section 1, p. 1.

Heintz, Katharine E. "An Examination of Sex and Occupational Role Presentations of Female Characters in Children's Picture Books." *Women's Studies in Communication* 9 (1987):69.

Hellreigel, Don, John Slocum, and Richard Woodman. *Organizational Behavior.* 3d ed. St. Paul, MN: West Publishing Co., 1983.

Hersey, Paul, and Kenneth H. Blanchard. *Management of Organizational Behavior.* 5th ed. Englewood Cliffs, NJ: Prentice-Hall, 1988.

Hesslin, D. "A Touch of Sensitivity." A Nova Presentation, 1980.

Hochschild, Arlie, with Anne Machung. *The Second Shift: Working Parents and the Revolution at Home.* New York: Viking, 1989.

Hrdy, Sarah Blaffer. "Natural Born Mothers." *Natural History,* December 1995, pp. 30–32.

Hughes, Kathleen A. "Business Women's Broader Latitude in Dress Code Goes Just So Far." *Wall Street Journal,* Sept 1, 1987. Section 2, p. 1.

Jacklin, Carol Nagy. "Female and Male: Issues of Gender." *American Psychologist* 44 (1989):127–133.

Jacklin, Carol Nagy, and Eleanor E. Maccoby. "Social Behavior at 33 Months in Same-Sex and Mixed-Sex Dyads." *Child Development* 49 (1978):569–576.

Jardim, Anne, and Margaret Hennig. "The Last Barrier." *Working Woman,* November 1990, p. 131.

Josefowitz, Natasha. *Paths to Power.* Menlo Park, CA: Addison-Wesley, 1980.

Kanter, Rosabeth Moss. *When Giants Learn to Dance,* New York: Simon & Schuster, 1989.

Kiersey, David, and Marilyn Bates. *Please Understand Me.* Del Mar, CA: Prometheus Nemesis Book Co., 1984.

Keyes, Ralph. "The Height Report." *Esquire,* November 1979.

Kilmann, Ralph, and Kenneth Thomas. "Interpersonal Conflict-Handling Behavior as Reflections of Jungian Personality Dimensions." *Psychological Reports* 37 (1975):971–980.

Kohlberg, Lawrence. *The Philosophy of Moral Development.* San Francisco: Harper & Row, 1958.

Kuhn, Deanna, Sharon Nash, and Laura Brucken. "Sex Role Concepts of Two- and Three-Year-Olds." *Child Development* 49 (1978):445–451. Cited in Jones, Diane Carlson. "Power Structures and Perceptions of Power Holders in Same-Sex Group of Young Children." *Women and Politics* 3, no. 2/3 (summer/fall 1983).

Lakoff, Robin. *Taking Power: The Politics of Language,* New York: Basic Books, 1990.

Langer, Ellen J. *Mindfulness.* Reading, MA: Addison-Wesley, 1989.

Lever, Janet. "Sex Differences in the Games Children Play." *Social Problems* 23 (1976):478–487.

"Listen Like a Woman." *Executive Female,* Nov.–Dec., 1991, p. 9.

Loden, Marilyn. *Feminine Leadership: How to Succeed in Business Without Being One of the Boys.* New York: Times Books, 1985.

Luthans, Fred, Richard M. Hodgetts, and Stuart A. Rosenkrantz. *Real Managers.* Cambridge, MA: Bollinger Publishing Co., 1988.

Mackoff, Barbara. *What Mona Lisa Knew.* Los Angeles: Lowell House, 1990.

McCarthy, William J., Mykol Hamilton, Campbell Leaper, Ellen Pader, Sarah Rushbrook, and Nancy Henley. "Social Influences on What to Call Her: 'Woman,' 'Girl,' or 'Lady.' " Paper presented at the American Psychological Association Annual Meeting, Anaheim, CA, 1985.

Melia, Jinx. *Breaking into the Boardroom.* New York: St. Martin's Press, 1989.

Meyerson, Debra E., and Joyce Fletcher. "A Modest Manifesto for Shattering the Glass Ceiling." *Harvard Business Review,* 78 (2000):127–136.

Meyerson, Debra E. *Tempered Radicals: How People Use Difference to Inspire Change at Work.* Boston, MA: Harvard Business School Press, 2001.

Moir, Anne, and Davis Jessel. *Brain Sex: The Real Difference Between Men and Women.* New York: Delta, 1989.

Morgan, Robin. "A *Ms.* Conversation: Madeleine Albright and Robin Morgan." *Ms.* spring 2004, pp. 43–46.

Morrison, Ann M., Randall P. White, and Ellen Van Velsor. *Breaking the Glass Ceiling.* Reading, MA: Addison-Wesley, 1987.

"Newsmakers: Doing Her Part." *Los Angeles Times,* December 16, 1991. View Section, p. 1.

Olson, Cheryl B. "Social Context and Gender Effects on Success Attributions." Paper written at the University of California, Berkeley.

O'Neill, R. M., S. Horton, and F. J. Crosby. "Gender Issues in Developmental Relationships." In A. J. Murrell, F. J. Crosby, and R. J. Ely, eds. *Mentoring Dilemmas: Developmental Relationships Within Multicultural Organizations.* Mahwah, NJ: Lawrence Erlbaum Associates, 1999.

Petrosino, Maria. "Impact of Family Life on Employed Married Mothers." Ph.D. diss., California School of Professional Psychology, Los Angeles, 1992.

Pfeiffer, John. "Girl Talk—Boy Talk." *Science,* February 1985.

Pink, Daniel H. *Free Agent Nation.* New York: Warner Books, 2001.

Reza, H. G. "New Study Indicates Wide Sex Harassment in Navy." *Los Angeles Times,* Feb. 10, 1992. Section A, p. 1.

Riger, Stephanie, and Pat Galligan. "Women in Management: An Exploration of Competency Paradigms." *American Psychologist* 35 (1980):902–911.

Roggman, Lori A., and J. Craig Peery. "Parent-Infant Social Play in Brief Encounters: Early Gender Differences." *Child Study Journal* 19 (1989):65–79.

Rosener, Judy B. "Ways Women Lead." *Harvard Business Review,* Nov.–Dec. 1990, pp. 119–125.

Ruderman, Marian N., Patricia J. Ohlott, and Kathy Kram. "Promotion Decisions as a Diversity Practice." *Journal of Management Development* 14 (1995):6–23.

Rudman, Laurie A. "To Be or Not to Be (Self-Promoting): Motivational Influences on Gender Stereotyping." Paper presented at APS meeting June 30, 1995.

Sadker, Myra, and David Sadker. "Sexism in the Schoolrooms of the '80s." *Psychology Today,* March 1985, pp. 54–57.

Salyers, Eddie, and Valerie Strang. "1997 Revenues for Women-Owned Businesses Show Continued Growth, Census Bureau Reports." United States Commerce news, April 4, 2001. www.census.gov/Press Release/www/2001/cb01-61.html

Savin-Williams, Rich. "Dominance Systems Among Primate Adolescents." In *Dominance, Aggression, and War.* Edited by D. McGuinness. New York: Paragon House, 1987.

Schabacker, Kirsten. "Which Jobs Have the Biggest Pay Potential?" *Executive Female,* Nov.–Dec. 1991, pp. 24–28.

Shaywitz, B. A., S. E. Shaywitz, K. R. Pugh, R. T. Constable, P. Skudlarski, R. K. Fulbright, R. A. Bronen, D. P. Shankweiler, and L. Katz. "Sex Differences in Functional Organization of the Brain for Language." *Nature* 373 (1995):607–609.

Sher, Barbara, and Annie Gottlieb. *Wishcraft.* New York: Ballantine Books, 1986.

Skakeshaft, Charol, and Andy Perry. "The Language of Power vs. the Language of Empowerment: Gender Differences in Administrative Communication." Paper, Administration and Policy Studies, Hofstra University.

Stechert, Katherine B. "Why Aren't You Making More?" *Executive Female,* November 1990, pp. 24–27.

Stewart, R., and R. Marvin. "Sibling Relations: The Role of Conceptual Perspective-Taking in the Ontogeny of Sibling Caregiving." *Child Development* 55 (1984):1322–1332.

Tannen, Deborah. *You Just Don't Understand.* New York: William Morrow and Co., 1990.

Taylor, Shelley E., Laura Cousino-Klein, Brian P. Lewis, et al. "Biobehavioral Responses to Stress in Females: Tend-and Befriend, Not Fight or Flight." *Psychological Review* 107, no. 3 (2000):411–429.

Tharenou, Phyllis. "Going Up? Do Traits and Informal Social Processes Predict Advancing in Management?" *Academy of Management Journal* 44 (2001):1005–1017.

Thomton, Jim. "Why the Brain Is Like a Swiss Army Knife." *USA Weekend,* January 3, 1999. Health section.

"The Trouble with Women: Why So Few of Them Are Running Big Companies." *The Economist,* October 25, 2003.

Valian, Virginia. *Why So Slow?: The Advancement of Women.* Cambridge, MA: The MIT Press, 1998.

Walsh, A. M., and S. C. Borkowski. "Cross-Gender Mentoring and Career Development Within the Health Care Industry." *Health Care Management Review* 24 (1999):7–17.

Watzlawick, Paul, John Weakland, and Richard Fisch. *Change: Principles of Problem Formation and Problem Resolution.* New York: W. W. Norton, 1974.

Weiss, Robert S. *Staying the Course: The Emotional and Social Lives of Men Who Do Well at Work.* New York: Free Press, 1990.

Wojahn, Ellen. "Why There Aren't More Women in This Magazine," *Inc.,* July 1986, pp. 45–48.

Wood, Julia T., and Lisa Firing Lenze. "Gender and the Development of Self." *Women's Studies in Communication* 14 (1991):3.

Zeitz, Balla, and Lorraine Dusky. *The Best Companies for Women.* New York: Simon & Schuster, 1988.

The Heim Group is a consulting firm, specializing in strengthening an organization's competitive edge through effective communication and leadership. We specialize in gender differences, helping men and women to communicate more effectively, and assisting organizations in keeping their best and brightest. Dr. Pat Heim, who has been leading the firm since 1985, is a nationally recognized expert in the areas of gender issues in the workplace. The Heim Group delivers and coordinates a wide variety of activities to support organizational transitions, improve team effectiveness, and enhance professional and managerial skills.

Visit our website at www.heimgroup.com, email us at heimgroup @aol.com, or give us a call at (888) 917-7797.

INDEX